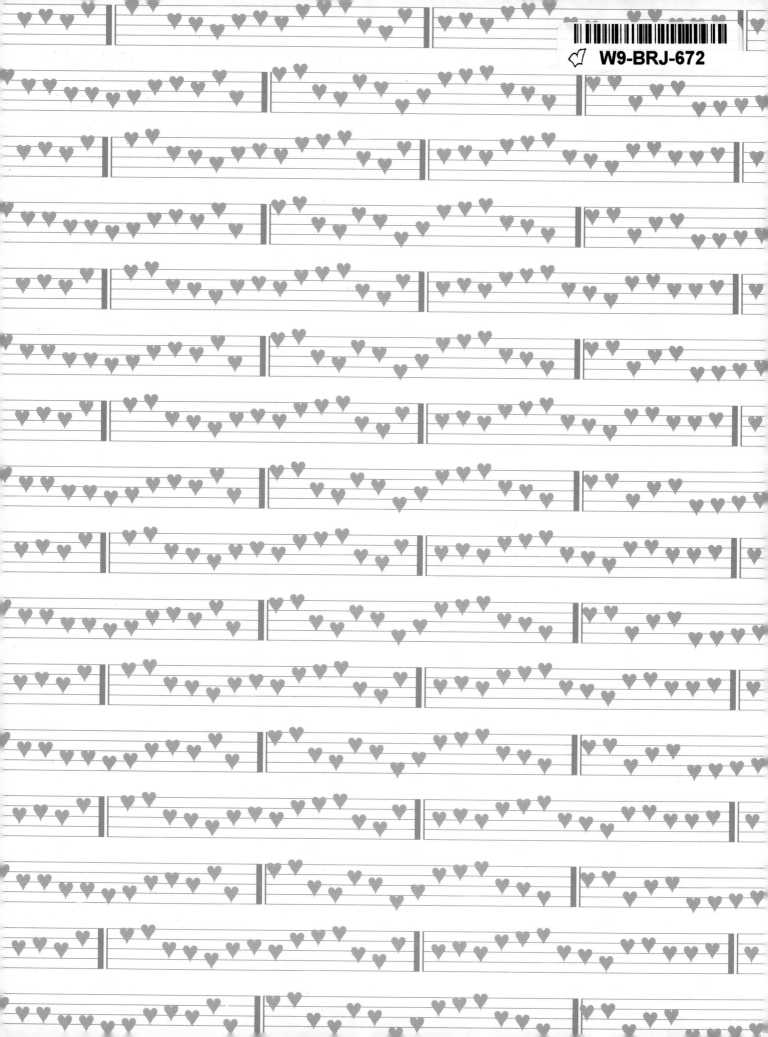

STIRRING RECIPES FROM MEMPHIS
HEART & SOUL

THE JUNIOR LEAGUE OF MEMPHIS, INC.

HEART & SOUL
   The Junior League of Memphis is an organization of women committed to promoting voluntarism and to improving the community through the effective action and leadership of trained volunteers. Its purpose is exclusively educational and charitable.
   The Junior League of Memphis reaches out to women of all races, religions, and national origins who demonstrate an interest in and commitment to voluntarism.
   Profits realized from the sale of HEART & SOUL will be used to support community projects and services of the Junior League of Memphis, Inc.

Junior League of Memphis Publications, 1992

JUNIOR LEAGUE OF MEMPHIS

For additional copies, use the order forms at the back of this book or send a check for $19.95 plus $3.50 shipping and handling (Tennessee residents add $1.65 sales tax) to:
   Junior League of Memphis
   Publications
   HEART & SOUL
   3475 Central Ave.
   Memphis, TN 38111-4401
   901-452-2151

THE JUNIOR LEAGUE OF MEMPHIS, INC.

♪ ♪ ♪

NANCY WALL HOPKINS
Creative Director/Photo Stylist

MAUCK & ASSOCIATES, INC.
GRAPHIC COMMUNICATIONS
Designer

WILLIAM HOPKINS
HOPKINS & ASSOCIATES
Photography

KIM LOUGHLIN
Food Stylist

JILL JOHNSON
Food Editor

WIMMER BROTHERS
A WIMMER COMPANY
MEMPHIS • DALLAS
Printer

ACKNOWLEDGEMENTS

SPECIAL THANK YOUS

A.S. Barboro
Babcock Gifts and (Owner) Buzzy Hussey
B.B. King's Blues Club
Buster's Liquors
Deborah Camp, Executive Director, Memphis Chapter of NARAS
Mr. Lane Carrick
Mr. Robert Crump
Goodwin's Greenhouses
Graceland
Greg's Country Market
Herb O'Mell Productions
Mary Kenner
The Meat Board Test Kitchens
Memorial Park Flower Shop
Memphis Music and Blues Museum
Mr. John Montague
Papel Fine Stationery and (Owner) Sondra Biggs
Party City
Mr. Tommy Peters
Pier 1 imports
Piggly Wiggly Memphis, Inc.
The Prop Room
Dr. Richard Ranta, Dean of the College of Communications and Fine Arts, Memphis State University
Ruetenik Gardens
Sedgwick James of Tennessee, Inc.
Mr. Irwin Sheft, World Class Jazz Productions, Jazz Foundation of Memphis
The Tobacco Bowl and (Owner) Jim Rorex
Ron Wynn and "The Memphis Star"

COMMITTEES

COORDINATING BOARD
Co-Editors
  Lisa Colcolough
  Beth Ploch
Editorial Coordinator
  Helen Patterson
Graphic Design Coordinator
  Virginia Curry
Marketing Coordinators
  Kelly Wells
  Assistant Lynn Koeneman
Recipe Collection and
Index Coordinator
  Lou Martin
Testing Coordinators
  Cynthia Cross
  Kim Pitts

CHAPTER CHAIRS
Appetizers/Beverages
  Martha Hester
Barbecue/Grilling
  Kim Blankenship
  Jeanne Hollis
  Nayla Nassar
Breads/Sauces/Vegetables
  Harriet McGeorge
Brunches/Salads/Soups
  Betsy Bell

Desserts
  Kathy Adams
Meat
  Kim Blankenship
Menu/Pasta/Seafood
  Kathy Pitts
Poultry
  Susan Huffman

COMMITTEES
Editorial Committee
  Julie Barton
  Cindy Flanzer
  Mary Harvey Gurley
  Kirk McClintock
  Scott Sellers
Graphic Design Committee
  Elisabeth Glassell
  Julia Smythe
Marketing Committee Heads
  Account Development
    Karen Kearney
  In-League Promotions
    Terry Dillard
    Sarah Walne
  Media
    Ann Leatherman
  Special Events
    Lynn Koeneman

Marketing Committee
  Sue Bartlett
  Betsy Bell
  Margaret Ann Brickey
  Antoinette Cheney
  Jennifer Goblirsch
  Lisa Guyton
  Jeannie Jones
  Jennifer Jones
  Becky Maury
  Janie Mayfield
  Susan Mays
  Emily McKinney
  Nancy Miller
  Nayla Nassar
  Debbie Patterson
  Kathy Pitts
  Jan Rochelle
  Susan Schaefer
  Allyson Stevenson
  Mary Taliaferro
  Holly Walters
  Adele Wellford

JLM PUBLICATIONS CHAIRS
  Ruthann Shelton 1990-1991
  Cindy Morrison 1991-1992
  Kim Blankenship 1992-1993
  Kathy Adams 1993-1994

*W*e would like to thank the many community members and businesses who have helped to make *Heart & Soul* what it is. Their contributions have increased the quality of our book and will serve to increase the quality of life in the Memphis community of which we are a part. ♥

◆ ◆ ◆

Heart & Soul came to be through the selfless efforts of many individuals who joined in this project. Thousands of volunteer hours brought this publication from vision to reality. We have volunteered from the heart and it is our hope that we will end up touching souls.

◆ ◆ ◆

From Our Heart and Soul...

OUR LIVES ARE FULL OF ORDINARY DAYS, BUT THERE ARE times when something magic happens to take us beyond the trivial: the loving gaze of a child, a hearty laugh shared by friends, a marriage moment when everything seems "just right." As we look back over these treasured times we realize that many of them happen as we sit together at the table.

The joy of food, in all its appeal, warmth, and satisfaction is a common bond for us right now and its special family traditions connect past, present, and future generations. Food satisfies more than one appetite. When we're hungry, we certainly long for physical and sensory contentment, but we also hunger for family base, tradition, and the "connectedness" that food provides. *Heart & Soul* celebrates this gift.

We celebrate another gift: one bestowed on us all by our city of Memphis. Many think of hardwood, cotton, and the Mississippi River when they hear our city's name, but "Ol' Man River" is first a beloved song and Memphis is first a music city. *Heart & Soul* features the special moments and memories of a golden group of Memphians who are celebrities in the wide, wonderful field of music. They travel the globe and their influence is felt the world over, but their "Hearts and Souls" are at home in Memphis, Tennessee.

Memphis music encompasses many sounds, from rockabilly to opera. It comprises a varied "buffet" from which we've chosen a tantalizing sample. There are many that we were unable to include. We hope *Heart & Soul* whets your appetite for more Memphis music.

Heart & Soul is an extraordinary cookbook, not only because it is a first-class collection of recipes, but also because it offers a heartwarming personal touch. Every chapter includes memories of the moments shared by families and friends that are as treasured as the recipes themselves. The specific names are not included but the people are very real. These experiences are universal and these times are known to all of us. We hope you find yourself in these little remembrances and smile at their familiarity. They offer a chance to pause and appreciate past traditions, and perhaps, the inspiration to begin some new ones.

Our full-page photographs tell the stories of our headliner musicians and illustrate a number of *Heart & Soul's* outstanding recipes in beautiful settings. We hope you'll enjoy finding the heart hidden in each of the food photographs.

Heart & Soul is a publication of the Junior League of Memphis, Inc. and profits from its sale will make it possible for us to continue our projects to mend, strengthen, and support the "Heart and Soul" of our community for years to come. ♥

CONTENTS

◆ ◆ ◆

PICTURED ON COVER
—
Sarah's Summer Torte
(page 249)

◆ ◆ ◆

MENUS

W.C. Handy

William Christopher Handy, born in Florence, Alabama, became one of the most famous citizens of Memphis, Tennessee. A well-trained musician, he was a singer, horn player, band leader, and composer who learned a story from the people and told it in a musical language that many others wanted to hear. The time was right for the "birth" of the blues.

W.C. Handy found himself in a pivotal Memphis moment one day in 1909. Already known locally for his soul-stirring sound, he and his band were wildly received by a downtown crowd gathered under the campaign banner of famous Mayor E.H. "Boss" Crump. The tune snatched up by the eager listeners became "The Memphis Blues" and was joined by such other Handy giants as "St. Louis Blues" and "Beale Street Blues." W.C. Handy was a genius who "felt" the times and translated them into a revolutionary sound.

Many know that he earned the title "Father of the Blues," but few know that the great George Gershwin once told Handy "Your work is the grandfather of mine."

MENUS

◆ ◆ ◆

PICTURED OVERLEAF
—
Chocolate Pound Cake
(page 257)

◆ ◆ ◆

The wines listed are
suggested complements to our
menus — but they *are* just
suggestions. Please treat them
as guidelines and enjoy the
wines of your choice.

Heart and Soul

Y OUR BEST FRIEND HAS JUST COME HOME FROM THE HOSPITAL WITH A newborn. A great-aunt is recuperating from surgery. Your next-door neighbor is flooded with out-of-town company and your tennis buddy is reeling from family troubles. The list of needs could go on and on. In gracious Southern style, you make a brief visit to offer errand services, keep a toddler for a day, or just lend an ear. When you arrive, you take something in hand: it might be the novel you read through the night, a quilted bedjacket, or one of the yummies from the list below. The sharing of self is the true gift.

NEW MOMMY ROAST CHICKEN
141

FIVE CHEESE LASAGNA
199

MAINSTREET MANICOTTI
200

BRISKET WITH ITALIAN VEGETABLES
119

SQUASH, SAUSAGE, AND SOUL
234

SOUTHERN CORN CHOWDER
61

COMFORTING CHICKEN NOODLE SOUP
58

THE FAMOUS ROLLS
108

FRENCH BREAKFAST CAKES
101

ZUCCHINI BREAD
106

CREAM CHEESE POUND CAKE WITH FRESH STRAWBERRY SAUCE
258

SPICE CAKE WITH CARAMEL ICING
260

DEATH-TO-THE-DIET BROWNIES
269

MAPLE APPLE PIE
251

Spring is Here

*L*OVE AND MARRIAGE, BREAD AND BUTTER, LAMB AND ASPARAGUS— some pairs are proven classics and don't need updating. Whether you're serving the boss, celebrating a best friend's promotion, or gathering for a graduate, this simply elegant spring menu cannot be beat. Spring evenings in Memphis are perfect for dining outside by candlelight before summertime bugs and crushing heat become uninvited guests.

"YOU-WON'T-BELIEVE-IT" CRAB DIP
33

SPINACH SALAD WITH WALNUTS AND GORGONZOLA
77

DUDLEY'S BUTTERFLIED LEG OF LAMB
174

CURRANT RICE
231

ASPARAGUS WITH CITRUS BUTTER
215

* POPOVERS

COMPANY LEMON CHEESECAKE
246

◆

RED WINE
La Crema Pinot Noir
Robert Mondavi Pinot Noir

Super Mom — A Favorite Family Dinner

*Y*OU'VE BEEN TO THREE MEETINGS, DRIVEN TWO CARPOOLS, AND lugged the dog to the veterinarian—then you realize dinner is only an hour away. Pin on your "Super Mom" medal, put these chops in the oven, and watch your family devour this wonderful dinner. (When the dishes are done, lock the bathroom door and treat yourself to a bubble bath!)

SALADE PARMESAN
77

ITALIAN BUTTERFLY PORK CHOPS
130

*STEAMED FRESH GREEN BEANS

STUTTGART RICE
232

BABY BUTTERBALL BISCUITS
103

COUNTRY FRESH APPLE BAKE
248

◆

RED WINE
J. Lohr Cabernet Sauvignon
Fetzer Barrel Select Cabernet Sauvignon

Sip and See Brunch

THAT LITTLE "BUNDLE OF JOY" IS SMILING AND COOING AND MOM IS back in her real clothes, as her life begins to get back to "normal." The "Sip and See" is an occasion where friends gather in the morning or late afternoon to sip a little something and "ooh and aah" over the new baby. It can be hosted by a grandmother, godmother, or good pal of the proud mother. The precious little one is always decked out in a beautiful day gown or like creation, well-rested, and just-fed to assure that he or she is content and full of charm!

HONEYCOMB EGG CASSEROLE
96

JALAPEÑO CHEESE GRITS
99

*FRESH FRUIT SALAD

FRENCH BREAKFAST CAKES
101

CHOCOLATE-CHIP ORANGE MUFFINS
101

HONEY BRUNCH MIMOSAS
91

Ol' Man River

GO WEST TO THE RIVER AND TAKE ALONG SOME OF THE BEST SOUTHERN tastes a basket could hold. This picnic supper, with its comfortable blend of the familiar and the novel, makes a perfect choice for one of Memphis' most celebrated events—the Sunset Symphony on the banks of the mighty Mississippi. The music, the crowd, and the scenery will entertain you as you enjoy the refreshment of gazpacho and chilled chicken, great salads, and an irresistible dessert duet. When James Hyter has finished his stirring rendition of "Ol' Man River" that always has the audience roaring its approval, you'll also be singing the praises of this memorable, movable feast.

◆

WHITE WINE
Rosemount Semillon-
Chardonnay
Georges DuBoeuf
Macon-Villages

GAZEBO GAZPACHO
64

NAYLA'S VILLA MONTANA CHICKEN (SERVED CHILLED)
181

MARINATED ASPARAGUS WITH PECANS
70

LIZZIE'S SALAD
78

GEORGIA PEACH POUND CAKE
257

MOCHA MACADAMIA CHOCOLATE CHUNK COOKIES
266

In Grandmother's Kitchen

A GRANDMOTHER'S HOUSE IS WHERE YOU NEVER HEAR THE WORD "NO." The attic is never off-limits and always full of treasures, each with a story waiting to be told. There are peppermints in the living room, feather pillows on the bed, and the cookies you love hidden in the pantry. The kitchen is a place of comforting smells that promise your favorite supper is on the way. Like grandmas everywhere, modern Southern grandmothers are often health and fitness nuts, but they're not above an old-fashioned rib-stickin' meal now and again when the family shows up. It seems that there's always enough food on the table for two families, making sure a little bit of Grandma's love goes home with everyone.

JALAPEÑO SOUTHERN FRIED CHICKEN
138

PYRAMID POTATOES
226

TOMATO PIE WITH BASIL
236

CORN FRITTERS
221

GREEN BEANS Y'ALL WON'T BELIEVE
216

FROSTY SUMMER SALAD
68

CHEWY COCONUT CHESS PIE
252

*FRENCH VANILLA ICE CREAM

*ICED TEA

*COLD MILK

Fireworks on the Fourth

ON A GREAT AMERICAN HOLIDAY, YOU SERVE A GREAT AMERICAN MEAL! THE best setting for it is the great outdoors, whether you're on your own block or in one of Memphis' beautiful green parks. From start to finish, this menu offers the finest Southern delicacies, including black-eyed peas, fresh corn, and Vidalia onions. Barbecued ribs and chicken will have everyone waiting for the dinner bell. No one *ever* turns down the desserts, even if they've already been back for seconds. Get the fireworks ready and dig into this crowd-pleaser.

◆

WHITE WINE
Kendall-Jackson Sauvignon Blanc
Kenwood Sauvignon Blanc

◆

RED WINE
Louis Jadot Beaujolais-Villages
Bolla Valpolicella

PARTY SAUSAGE
179

*ASSORTED CHEESES

DIXIE CAVIAR
46

RANDY'S YUMMY RIBS
177

WILDER'S FABULOUS BARBECUED CHICKEN
180

SCOTT STREET SLAW
74

GRILLED CORN
222

BROCCOLI WITH A TWIST
71

VIDALIA ONION CASSEROLE
225

LEMON CREAM SHERBET
263

CHOCOLATE POUND CAKE
257

*COLD BEER

A Farmers' Market Special

*I*N SUMMERTIME, WHEN SOUTHERN PRODUCE IS BOTH ABUNDANT AND at its tasty peak, it is not unusual for Memphis families to sit down to an all-vegetable dinner. This may cap off a morning visit to the Agricenter Farmers' Market and an afternoon spent helping Mom shuck corn, snap beans, and wash strawberries. Bowls of hot steaming veggies are passed, along with platters piled with ripe tomatoes and cold salads. Hot crusty corn bread and tall glasses of iced tea make it all taste just right. While it's true that there is no "main course" here, there is certainly no shortage of satisfaction.

COLMER CORN STIR-FRY
221

ONION SALAD
71

MARY JOE'S TURNIP GREENS
236

OKRA AND TOMATOES
224

SAUTÉED NEW POTATOES WITH GARLIC AND HERBS
228

ZUCCHINI AND YELLOW SQUASH
235

DEVIL IN DISGUISE CORN BREAD
104

ALMOND PEACH PIE
251

MISS BETTY'S ICED TEA
88

Meet Me By the Pool

WHEN THE TEMPERATURE ALLOWS, THERE IS NO GREATER TREAT FOR the senses than an al fresco luncheon under gorgeous blue skies. Whether on a riverside balcony or a deck in Germantown, Memphians love to gather outside to entertain. Bring out crystal wine glasses for this luscious soup, set your patio table with pastels and flowers from your garden, and wow your friends with this de*light*ful menu perfectly suited for Southern summers.

◆

WHITE WINE
Fontana Candida Frascati
Pine Ridge Chenin Blanc

COLD CUCUMBER SOUP
64

GRILLED CHICKEN AND TORTELLINI SALAD
181

*SLICED TOMATOES

*ASSORTED FRESH FRUIT

THE FAMOUS ROLLS
108

MINT ICE CREAM
262

Dog Days of Summer — Fire Up the Grill

WE ALL HAVE FRIENDS THAT WE MISS SEEING AS WE STRUGGLE WITH overplanned calendars throughout the school year. Weekdays are filled with hourly activities and the weekends that follow are spent recovering from our hectic pace. How many times have you seen a friend and thought, "We really should get together again."? This is the time! The summer schedule is slower, the grill is ready, and the menu is right here. Hand your friends a chilled white wine to complement these unbeatable flavors and spend an August evening warming up an old friendship.

◆

WHITE WINE
Trimbach Gewürztraminer
Beringer White Zinfandel

HERBED SHRIMP WITH BASIL MAYONNAISE
162

ROASTED PEPPER SALAD
70

THE KING'S GRILLED TENDERS
175

CREAMY VEGETABLE TORTELLINI
200

SAVORY CHEESE BREAD
111

KEY LIME TART
252

When I've Worked All Day...and Company's on the Way

"I NEED A FRIEND IN THE KITCHEN!" THIS ELEGANT CRABMEAT CASSEROLE certainly qualifies. If you love to entertain but you have a busy career and an active family, you can still enjoy friends at the table after a long day. With a little extra planning and the right menu, you can pull off a dinner that will be fun for you and your guests. The entrée can be ready and waiting in the refrigerator when you arrive at home to pull together the rest of this easy, delicious meal. If you've set the table the night before and the serving pieces are out, you can be a guest at your own party. Well, almost.....

HERBED HAVARTI EN CROÛTE
41

*MIXED GREENS—RED LEAF, BOSTON, AND ROMAINE LETTUCE

RINALDO'S ITALIAN SALAD DRESSING
79

ELEGANT CRABMEAT CASSEROLE
166

*STEAMED FRESH BROCCOLI

BABY BUTTERBALL BISCUITS
103

QUICK CHOCOLATE POTS DE CRÈME
242

◆

WHITE WINE
Saintsbury Chardonnay
Murphy-Goode Chardonnay

Before the Game

"FANATIC" IS THE ONLY WORD TO DESCRIBE SOUTHERN FOOTBALL fans. From cradle to grave, we share an enthusiasm for this fall sport that disregards boundaries of school loyalty, gender, and age. Whether our blood runs UT orange, Tiger blue, Rebel red, or various other shades of crimson, blue, black, and gold known around here, we love the game — and the pre-game party. This tends to be a brief, drop-by affair. If your guests are in a rush to get to the fifty-yard line, this meal can be brown-bagged to be enjoyed at the stadium. On table or tail-gate, we guarantee this menu will be a great kick-off.

*POPCORN/PRETZELS

*SALTED PECANS

COTTON ROW CHEESE SOUP
63

BAYOU BAR & GRILL MUFFULETTA SANDWICH
134

*FRESH FRUIT TRAY

WHITE CHOCOLATE BROWNIES
269

MIMOSAS
90

*BLOODY MARYS

*IMPORTED BEER

A Candlelight Dinner

*I*F YOU'RE LOOKING FOR THE MENU EQUIVALENT OF A LITTLE BLACK dress and pearls, this is it. There are times when you want the evening to be formal and elegant and you're willing to pull out all the stops. The Memphis hostess takes great care to create a special setting and looks for a menu that will be just as memorable. Most men embrace good beef and potatoes and never tire of their familiar satisfaction. Like the dress, such traditional fare can be "accessorized" to suit the occasion, and the mushroom tenderloin and boursin potatoes here will grace any table. This divine dinner begins and ends in an innovative style.

SMOKED SALMON PIZZA
29
OR
ELEGANT CAVIAR PIE
32

DINNER AT EIGHT SALAD
75

MUSHROOM-STUFFED BEEF TENDERLOIN
120

BOURSIN POTATO GRATIN
227

*STEAMED ASPARAGUS WITH LEMON BUTTER

ANGEL POCKET ROLLS
110

CHILLED ORANGE SOUFFLÉ WITH RED RASPBERRY SAUCE
244

KIR ROYALE
93

◆

RED WINE
KENDALL-JACKSON MERLOT
STERLING MERLOT

A Nutcracker Tea for the Young and the Old

ONE OF THE CLASSICS OF CHRISTMAS IN MEMPHIS IS THE NUTCRACKER BALLET. What better time could there be for a holiday hostess to open her home than for a festive Nutcracker Tea? Excited parents and children, dressed up for the late afternoon performance, gather and enjoy a table full of delights watched over by the Nutcracker himself. At the beautifully restored Orpheum theater, little ones wiggle in their seats in anticipation of the carriage ride to follow and the promise of hot chocolate in the Peabody lobby, topping off an enchanted afternoon.

CUCUMBER COCKTAIL CANAPÉS
46

DELTA QUEEN PINWHEELS
29

POPPY SEED-HAM BISCUITS
93

LULU PASTE SERVED ON COCKTAIL BREAD
81

WALDORF SALAD IN ENDIVE
44

WALNUT-GLAZED BRIE
45

TOASTED SPICE PECANS
48

CHOCOLATE RASPBERRY CAKE
261

PEANUT BUTTER FUDGE
253

YOUR HEART'S DESIRE
267

POINSETTIAS
92

POPLAR PUNCH
90

Sleigh Bells Ring — A Carolers' Buffet

*I*F YOU BELIEVE THAT CHRISTMAS IS TOO COMMERCIALIZED...IF YOU believe that love is in time shared and not in boxes...if you Believe...begin anew. Spread the true Spirit in your neighborhood with an evening of caroling. In all corners of Memphis, neighbors and friends assemble annually to spread Christmas cheer. If it's your turn to host the group, invite them in for hors d'oeuvres and a practice sing before they go out into the night. When they come back with red cheeks and frosty fingers, warm them up with steaming cups of hearty stew. This make-ahead menu will send your carolers home warmed, heart and soul.

CHUTNIED SHRIMP DIP
33

SPINACH BREAD
110

THREE O SALAD
76

ANNIVERSARY VEAL RAGOUT
128

CRUSTY ITALIAN LOAF
109

MINETRY'S MAGIC
264

DEATH-TO-THE-DIET BROWNIES
269

◆

WHITE WINE
Markham Sauvignon Blanc
Domaine Breton Sauvignon Blanc

◆

RED WINE
Columbia Crest Merlot
Stone Creek Merlot

In the Dead of Winter — A Comforting Supper

*W*INTER CAN BE LONG, COLD, AND DREARY, AND ITS WEEKENDS CAN SEEM too far apart. Having a few good friends over on Sunday night is a wonderful weekend-stretcher. For this evening, the newspapers can stay where they are and you can stay in your sweater and jeans. Winter gloom has no chance in a home filled with happy conversation, laughter, and the warming smells of this soothing supper. Monday morning will look brighter after a Sunday evening filled with friends, food, and fun.

WATERCRESS AND SPINACH SALAD WITH APPLES AND ALMONDS
76

SAUSAGE AND SWEET PEPPER PASTA
203

*FRENCH BREAD

BREAD PUDDING WITH WINTER SAUCE
255

◆

RED WINE
Rosemount Shiraz

APPETIZERS

Al Green

Al Green—a musical and spiritual soul-man—came into this world with special gifts and he has spent his life sharing them. He has a personal power and a captivating voice that have always stirred emotions. In the early '70s, he became a prince of pop, rock, and soul, forging a chain of gold and platinum hits such as "Tired of Being Alone," "Let's Stay Together," and "I'm Still in Love With You." These hits—and many others—were recorded in Memphis with performer/producer Willie Mitchell who crossed Al's fame-bound path one lucky night in Texas when they played the same stage. Since that moment, Al has come through life changes that led him through fantastic stardom, personal trials, and spiritual rebirth into a new career focused on gospel music and evangelical ministry.

"This 'new life' has been my direction all the time," Al explains, "and my mission as a singer—whether pop, rock, or gospel—has always been to try to get people to relate to God." At home in his church in Memphis, or recording and publishing in New York and Los Angeles, Al continues touching souls with both kinds of musical message: "That's the total Al Green."

APPETIZERS

◆ ◆ ◆

PICTURED OVERLEAF

—

Clockwise from bottom:
Red and Yellow Pepper Salsa
with Croûtes (page 47) and
Palace Cheesecake (page 40)

◆ ◆ ◆

*A*PPETIZERS TAKE CENTER STAGE WHEN GUESTS ARE AT THEIR hungriest. Simple or elaborate, these savory offerings are put before a very appreciative audience, primed by an afternoon's hunger and ready to relish that first bite. Appetizers can set the tone for the evening, signaling guests that time and creativity have been lavished on the preparations. Many Memphians keep the ingredients for a simple appetizer in the pantry in case friends drop in unexpectedly at the dinner hour. Part of our famous Southern hospitality is that we always offer a little something to nibble, no matter how simple.

Hostesses, however, often have a love-hate relationship with appetizers. In planning and executing a dinner party, other tasks take top priority. After shopping, table-setting, and preparing two or three courses, we often find ourselves drained of time, energy, and ideas before hors d'oeuvres are even considered. But they're fun to make, full of fascinating ingredients, and our guests love them! We know that happy hour wouldn't be the same without them, so with the clock ticking away, we pull out the cookbooks in search of something new and different.

Heart and Soul steps in here and offers this collection of starters, which should be just the inspiration needed. Whether unique flavor combinations or subtle variations on popular themes, our appetizer offerings reflect the Southern love of delicious and pretty food. Excuse us, our guests are arriving... ♥

♦ ♦ ♦

ROLLIN' ON THE
RIVER
—

Each spring Memphians spend a hectic ten days celebrating Carnival Memphis. Born as Cotton Carnival in 1931, Carnival Memphis comes complete with a king and a queen, royal court, royal pages, and Grand Krewes. The pageantry creates an aura of excitement, incorporating business with pleasure, and serves to unite the city in civic pride. Grand Krewes (Aani, Cotton-Makers Jubilee, Ennead, Memphi, Nile, Osiris, Pharoah, Ptah, Ra-Met, Shelbi, and Sphinx) select royalty each year and hold a myriad of parties in late spring, which culminate in Carnival Week in early June. Ladies and Gentlemen, call your babysitters!

♦ ♦ ♦

Carnival Crawfish Dip

Adjust the amount of red and black pepper to suit the taste buds of your guests. Always serve with plenty of cool beverages!

2	pounds fresh or frozen peeled crawfish tails, or fresh or frozen peeled and deveined shrimp
1/2	cup sliced green onion
1/2	cup butter or margarine
24	ounces cream cheese
8	cloves garlic, minced, or 2 teaspoons garlic powder
2	tablespoons ground red pepper
1 1/2	teaspoons pepper
	Salt to taste
1/4	to 1/2 cup chicken broth (if using fresh crawfish)
	Assorted crackers

Thaw crawfish, if frozen; drain, reserving liquid. In a 3-quart saucepan, cook onion in butter or margarine until tender but not brown. Add crawfish; cook over medium heat for 10 minutes or until crawfish are tender. Break up large pieces of crawfish. Stir in cheese, garlic, red pepper, pepper, and salt. Stir in enough of the reserved crawfish liquid (or chicken broth, if using fresh crawfish) until of dipping consistency. Heat through. Serve warm with assorted crackers. Makes 6 to 8 cups.

Les Carlos' Shrimp and Crawfish

This can be prepared several days in advance and refrigerated, or frozen for 2 weeks. The flavors are not as intense after freezing.

1	pound fresh or frozen peeled crawfish tails
1	pound fresh or frozen peeled shrimp
1¹/₂	cups unsalted butter, divided
2	tablespoons creole seasoning, divided
1	cup finely chopped onion
1	cup finely chopped celery
1	cup finely chopped green pepper
¹/₂	cup finely chopped sweet red pepper
6	tablespoons snipped fresh basil or 2 tablespoons dried basil, crushed
3	tablespoons snipped fresh thyme or 1 tablespoon dried thyme, crushed
3	tablespoons minced garlic
¹/₄	cup all-purpose flour
3	tablespoons tomato paste
2	tablespoons Worcestershire sauce
2	cups sliced green onion
	Hot pepper sauce
	Thin Garlic Toast (see recipe below)

Thaw crawfish and shrimp, if frozen. In a 12-inch skillet, heat ¹/₂ **cup** of the butter. Stir in **2 teaspoons** creole seasoning. Add crawfish; cook and stir over high heat for 3 to 4 minutes, scraping seasonings from bottom of pan as necessary. Remove crawfish to a large bowl. Add ¹/₂ **cup** more butter to saucepan. Stir in **2 teaspoons** more of the creole seasoning. Add shrimp; cook and stir over high heat about 4 minutes, scraping seasonings from pan as necessary. Remove shrimp and stir into crawfish in bowl. Process crawfish mixture, half at a time, until finely chopped. (Do not puree.)

In the same skillet, heat the remaining ¹/₂ cup butter; stir in the remaining 2 teaspoons creole seasoning. Add onion, celery, green pepper, and red pepper and cook for 5 minutes, stirring constantly. Reduce heat; add basil, thyme, and garlic. Cook 5 minutes more.

Stir together flour, tomato paste, and Worcestershire sauce. Stir into vegetable mixture in skillet. Stir in crawfish mixture. Cook over medium heat for 5 minutes, stirring constantly. Stir in green onion; cook and stir 5 minutes more. Season to taste with hot pepper sauce. Serve with Thin Garlic Toast. Makes about 8 cups.

Thin Garlic Toast

¹/₂	cup butter, softened
2	cloves garlic, minced
2	baguettes, sliced ¹/₂ inch thick

Preheat the oven to 300°. In a small bowl, stir together butter and garlic. Spread on baguette slices. Place on baking sheet. Bake about 20 minutes or until toasted. Makes about 30.

Seafood Buttons with Creamy Dijon Sauce

These miniature crab and shrimp cakes can be made into larger patties and served as a first course or supper entrée. Increase the cooking time to about 4 minutes per side.

8	ounces fresh or frozen peeled shrimp
8	ounces fresh or frozen lump crabmeat, cartilage removed
1/3	cup chopped onion
1/3	cup chopped celery
5	tablespoons butter, divided
2	eggs
1/4	cup heavy cream
1	tablespoon fresh lemon juice
1 1/2	teaspoons Worcestershire sauce
1/2	teaspoon salt
	Several dashes hot pepper sauce
1	cup crushed saltine crackers
	All-purpose flour
	Creamy Dijon Sauce (see recipe below)

Thaw shrimp and crabmeat, if frozen. Coarsely chop shrimp. In a 3-quart saucepan, cook onion and celery in **3 tablespoons** of the butter until tender. Stir in shrimp and cook over medium heat for 2 to 3 minutes or until shrimp turns pink. Remove from heat.

In a medium bowl, combine eggs, cream, lemon juice, Worcestershire sauce, salt, and hot pepper sauce. Stir into shrimp mixture. Stir in crushed crackers and crabmeat. Cover and chill at least one hour or until mixture is firm enough to handle.

For each cake, form one rounded teaspoonful of the mixture into a ball. Roll in flour; press slightly to flatten. In a skillet, melt remaining 2 tablespoons butter. Brown patties over medium heat about 2 minutes each side or until golden brown. Serve with Creamy Dijon Sauce. Makes 42 to 48.

Creamy Dijon Sauce

2	tablespoons water
1	tablespoon sugar
1/2	cup heavy cream
1	cup mayonnaise
2	tablespoons white wine vinegar
2	tablespoons Dijon-style mustard

In a 1-quart saucepan, combine water and sugar. Heat just until sugar dissolves. Cool to room temperature.

In a small mixer bowl, beat cream with an electric mixer until soft peaks form. In a medium bowl, combine mayonnaise, white wine vinegar, mustard, and the cooled sugar syrup. Fold in whipped cream. Makes about 2 1/2 cups.

Servin' up
BLUES

BOBBY "BLUE" BLAND

THIS SUPERSTAR HAS EARNED WELL-DESERVED PLACES IN THE ROCK AND ROLL HALL OF FAME AND THE NATIONAL RHYTHM AND BLUES HALL OF FAME. BEGINNING HIS CAREER IN THE 1950S, WHEN HE WAS KNOWN AS ONE OF THE "BEALE STREET BLUES BOYS," HE IS STILL WORLD-FAMOUS FOR SUCH HITS AS "BLUES IN THE NIGHT" AND "AIN'T THAT LOVIN' YOU."

Smoked Salmon Pizza

1	package active dry yeast
1/4	cup warm water (110° to 115°)
3/4	cup cool water
2	tablespoons olive oil
1	tablespoon honey
1	teaspoon salt
3	cups all-purpose flour
	Olive oil
	Flour (semolina preferred)
1	cup very thinly sliced red onion
1	cup dairy sour cream
1/2	cup snipped fresh dill, divided
1	teaspoon lemon juice
1	teaspoon Worcestershire sauce
	Salt and white pepper to taste
6	ounces sliced smoked salmon
	Caviar or capers

In a small bowl, soften yeast in warm water. Let stand about 5 minutes or until foamy. In a large bowl, combine cool water, olive oil, honey, and salt; mix well. Stir in the yeast mixture. Add **1/2 cup** of the all-purpose flour and stir to mix well. Add remaining all-purpose flour. Turn out onto a lightly floured surface and knead until smooth. Divide into 4 equal parts. Cover and let rise until doubled in size. (At this point, dough can be covered and refrigerated.)

Preheat the oven to 425°. Press or roll out each portion of dough into an 8-inch circle. Pinch edges to give a raised crust. Prick with a fork and brush with additional olive oil. Spread a thin layer of semolina flour over baking sheets. Place dough circles on flour-coated baking sheets. Bake for 2 minutes. (At this point, crusts can be cooled, wrapped, and refrigerated for several days.)

Arrange red onion slices evenly over crusts and brush again with olive oil. Return to oven and bake directly on oven rack about 8 minutes or until lightly golden. Cool.

For dill sour cream, in a small bowl, stir together sour cream, **1/4 cup** of the fresh dill, lemon juice, Worcestershire sauce, salt, and white pepper until well combined. Spread a thin layer of the dill sour cream over the red onion. Layer smoked salmon over dill sour cream. Cut into wedges. Garnish with remaining 1/4 cup fresh dill and caviar or capers. Makes 24 servings.

Hemmings Restaurant, Paul Westphal and Don Heidel

Delta Queen Pinwheels

1/2	medium red onion
8	ounces cream cheese, softened
2	tablespoons snipped chives
1/2	cup packed watercress leaves
	Pepper
10	slices soft-textured wheat bread
6	ounces smoked salmon, thinly sliced

In a food processor bowl, process onion until finely chopped. Add cream cheese and chives; process until blended. Add watercress; process until smooth. Add pepper to taste.

Trim crusts from bread. Spread about **2 tablespoons** of the cream cheese mixture on each bread slice. Place a slice of salmon on top of each. Roll up and wrap individually in clear plastic wrap, twisting at each end to seal rolls. Freeze overnight.

About 30 minutes before serving, remove plastic wrap from rolls. Cut each frozen roll into 6 to 8 slices. Makes 60 to 80.

Seafood en Coquilles

For an unforgettable first course, serve this in coquille shells atop glass plates sprinkled with rock salt. Garnish with lemon wedges and parsley. White wine is its perfect partner: try a good California Chardonnay.

8	ounces fresh or frozen bay scallops
8	ounces fresh or frozen peeled medium shrimp, halved crosswise
1/4	cup butter or margarine
1 1/2	cups chopped fresh mushrooms (4 ounces)
1/4	cup sliced green onion
1	clove garlic, minced
2	tablespoons all-purpose flour
1/2	to 2/3 cup light cream
2	tablespoons dry white wine
	Dash white pepper
1/4	cup chicken broth
1	teaspoon snipped parsley
	Salt to taste
1/4	cup finely shredded Swiss cheese (1 ounce)
	Paprika
	Rock salt
	Lemon wedges
	Parsley sprigs

Thaw scallops and shrimp, if frozen. Preheat the broiler. In a 10-inch skillet, melt butter or margarine. Add mushrooms, green onion, and garlic; cook until tender. Stir in flour. Add 1/2 cup cream; cook and stir until thickened and bubbly. Stir in wine and pepper. If necessary, thin with additional cream. Cover and remove from heat.

In another 10-inch skillet, heat broth over medium-high heat. Stir in scallops and shrimp. Cook, uncovered, for 2 to 4 minutes or just until scallops are opaque and shrimp turn pink. Drain.

Stir scallops, shrimp, and parsley into cream mixture. Season to taste with salt. Spoon into 4 coquille shells, au gratin dishes, or ramekins. Sprinkle with cheese, then paprika. Place shells in a shallow baking pan. Broil about 4 minutes or until brown and bubbly.

To serve, spread a thin layer of rock salt on small serving plates and top with coquille shells. Serve with lemon wedges and parsley sprigs. Makes 4 servings.

Smoked Catfish Pâté

1	pound catfish fillets
3/4	cup water
2	tablespoons vermouth
16	ounces cream cheese, softened
2	tablespoons fresh lemon juice
1	teaspoon paprika
1/2	teaspoon liquid smoke
1	clove garlic, minced
	Salt and pepper to taste
	Assorted crackers or garlic toast rounds

In a 12-inch deep skillet, cook catfish in the water and the vermouth until fish flakes with a fork. Drain. In a food processor bowl, combine catfish, cream cheese, lemon juice, paprika, liquid smoke, garlic, and salt and pepper. Process until smooth. Transfer to a bowl; cover and chill for 2 to 48 hours. Serve with assorted crackers or garlic toast rounds. Makes about 4 cups.

♪♪♪

NICE TO NOTE
—

When shopping for scallops, remember that they vary in size. Small varieties, including the highly-prized bay scallop, are bite-size (approximately one-half inch across). Medium and large scallops, just as sweet and delicious, can be two to three inches across and are usually sliced in half horizontally for serving. The "sea" and "rock" scallops from Atlantic Waters and the "giant rock" scallop from the Pacific Coast are examples of larger types.

Crabmeat Beignets with Unlikely Sauce

Not to be confused with beignets of New Orleans French Quarter fame, these savory puffs are made with crabmeat and Swiss cheese and artfully seasoned with ginger.

1	cup water
1/2	cup butter or margarine
1	teaspoon salt
1	teaspoon sugar
1	cup all-purpose flour
4	eggs
2	teaspoons grated gingerroot or 1/2 teaspoon ground ginger
1	teaspoon paprika
1/2	cup shredded Swiss cheese (2 ounces)
8	ounces lump crabmeat, cartilage removed
	Shortening or cooking oil for deep-fat frying
	Unlikely Sauce (see recipe below)

In a medium saucepan combine water, butter, salt, and sugar. Bring to boiling. Add flour all at once and cook over low heat, beating vigorously until mixture rolls away from sides of saucepan. Remove from heat; cool 10 minutes.

Add eggs, one at a time, beating well after each addition until smooth. Stir in gingerroot and paprika. Stir in cheese. Gently fold crabmeat into mixture.

Drop by tablespoons, four or five at a time, into deep hot fat (375°). Cook until puffed and golden brown. Remove and drain on paper towels. Serve warm with Unlikely Sauce. Makes 24 to 30.

Unlikely Sauce

8	ounces cream cheese, softened
1/3	cup lemon juice
1/4	cup pure maple syrup
1/2	teaspoon salt
1/2	teaspoon paprika
2	or 3 dashes hot pepper sauce

In a 1-quart saucepan, melt cream cheese over low heat. Stir in lemon juice, maple syrup, salt, paprika, and hot pepper sauce until blended. Makes about 1 1/2 cups.

Hot Onion Soufflé

This hot appetizer is not really a soufflé, but a delectable dip for corn chips and crackers. It is also one of the best-kept secrets of Memphis cooks. We want to share it with you.

12	to 16 ounces frozen chopped onions (3 to 4 cups)
24	ounces cream cheese, softened
2	cups grated Parmesan cheese
1/2	cup mayonnaise
	Corn chips or assorted crackers

Thaw onions. Roll them in paper towels, squeezing to remove excess moisture. Preheat the oven to 425°. Stir together onions, cream cheese, Parmesan cheese, and mayonnaise until well combined. Transfer to a shallow 2-quart soufflé dish. Bake about 15 minutes or until golden brown. Serve with corn chips or assorted crackers. Makes about 6 cups.

Layered Shrimp Dip

1¹/₂ pounds fresh or frozen shrimp, cooked and peeled
8 ounces cream cheese, softened
2 tablespoons dairy sour cream
2 teaspoons Worcestershire sauce
1 teaspoon lemon juice
¹/₂ teaspoon ground red pepper
1 clove garlic, minced
1 12-ounce bottle chili sauce
¹/₂ cup chopped onion
³/₄ cup sliced ripe olives
1 small green pepper, seeded and finely chopped
2 cups shredded mozzarella cheese (8 ounces)
    Corn chips, tortilla chips, or assorted crackers

Thaw shrimp, if frozen. Reserve 6 whole shrimp for garnish. Chop remaining shrimp; set aside. In a medium bowl, stir together cream cheese and sour cream. Stir in Worcestershire sauce, lemon juice, red pepper, and garlic. Spread mixture in the bottom of an 8-inch round baking dish. Layer chili sauce, onion, shrimp, olives, green pepper, and cheese on top. Garnish with reserved whole shrimp. Serve with corn chips, tortilla chips, or assorted crackers. Makes 10 to 12 servings.

Elegant Caviar Pie

For your elegant dinner party, make up the base of this appetizer pie in advance. Just before your guests arrive, spoon on the caviar. This is very pretty for Christmas when made with red caviar and garnished with a bit of greenery.

6 hard-cooked eggs, chopped
1 cup butter, softened
4 green onions, sliced
1 cup dairy sour cream
¹/₂ teaspoon finely shredded lemon peel
1 teaspoon fresh lemon juice
    Several dashes hot pepper sauce
    Fresh chives or thin green onions, cut into 4¹/₂-inch lengths
1 4-ounce jar black caviar
1 4-ounce jar red caviar
    Buttered toast points
    Toasted pita wedges
    Assorted crackers

In a medium bowl, stir together hard-cooked eggs and softened butter. Press egg mixture into a 9-inch quiche pan or pie plate. Sprinkle with sliced green onion. Combine sour cream, lemon peel, lemon juice, and hot pepper sauce; spread over onion.

Just before serving, place the 4¹/₂-inch lengths of chives or green onions on sour cream in spoke design, dividing the pie into wedges. Rinse and drain caviar. Spoon caviar onto each wedge, alternating colors and spreading evenly and completely over sour cream. Serve with buttered toast points, toasted pita wedges, or crackers. Makes 10 to 12 servings.

"You-Won't-Believe-It" Crab Dip

You won't believe it because it's so good!

8	ounces cream cheese
1/2	cup butter
2	tablespoons sliced green onions
1	tablespoon fresh lemon juice
1	clove garlic, minced
	Dash vermouth
8	ounces lump crabmeat, cartilage removed
	Salt to taste
	Bagel chips, Croûtes (see recipe, page 47), or assorted crackers

In a 1-quart saucepan, cook and stir cream cheese and butter over low heat until melted. Stir in green onions, lemon juice, garlic, and vermouth. Gently fold in crabmeat. Heat through. Season to taste with salt. To serve, transfer to chafing dish. Serve with bagel chips, Croûtes, or assorted crackers. Makes about 2 1/2 cups.

Chutnied Shrimp Dip

"Chopping" raisins with kitchen shears makes the job less sticky.

6	ounces small fresh or frozen shrimp, cooked and peeled
3	tablespoons sliced almonds
3	tablespoons coarsely shredded coconut
8	ounces cream cheese, softened
3	tablespoons dairy sour cream
1 1/2	teaspoons curry powder
1/2	cup sliced green onion
1/2	cup golden raisins, coarsely chopped
1	8 1/2-ounce jar prepared chutney

Thaw shrimp, if frozen. Preheat the oven to 350°. Spread almonds and coconut in a shallow baking pan. Bake for 5 to 10 minutes or until light golden brown, stirring once.

In a medium bowl, stir together cream cheese, sour cream, and curry powder until smooth. Stir in onions and raisins. Gently fold in shrimp. Shape into a ball and place on a serving plate. Pour chutney over top and sprinkle with almonds and coconut. Makes about 4 cups.

♪ ♪ ♪

NICE TO NOTE

—

To serve this dip warm, place the shrimp mixture in a shallow 1-quart baking dish instead of on a serving plate. Cover the mixture with the chutney and bake in a preheated 350° oven for 10 to 15 minutes. Top with the almonds and coconut and serve.

Sunday Pâté in Puff Pastry

8	ounces boneless pork shoulder, cut into 1-inch cubes
8	ounces boneless veal, cut into 1-inch cubes
1/3	cup Madeira
1/4	cup dry white wine
1/4	cup sliced celery
1/4	cup sliced carrot
1	tablespoon finely chopped shallots
1	tablespoon finely chopped onion
2	teaspoons salt
2	cloves garlic, minced
1/2	teaspoon dried rosemary leaves, crushed
1/4	teaspoon pepper
1	bay leaf
2	beaten eggs
1	teaspoon Cognac
1/2	of a 17¼-ounce package frozen puff pastry (1 sheet), thawed
1	beaten egg
1	teaspoon water

Place pork and veal in a plastic bag set into a shallow dish. For marinade, in a small bowl, stir together Madeira, white wine, celery, carrot, shallots, onion, salt, garlic, rosemary, pepper, and bay leaf. Pour marinade over meat; close bag. Marinate in the refrigerator for 8 to 24 hours, turning bag occasionally.

Remove bay leaf from marinade. Place meat and marinade mixture in a food processor bowl. Cover and process until ground and well combined. Stir in the 2 beaten eggs and cognac.

Preheat the oven to 350°. On a lightly floured surface, roll the sheet of puff pastry into a 12x11-inch rectangle. Cut pastry crosswise in half to form two 12x5½-inch strips. In a custard cup, stir together the beaten egg and water.

Place **one** of the pastry strips on an ungreased baking sheet. Brush the egg-water mixture in a 1-inch band around the outer edges of the pastry strip. Mound the meat mixture down the center of the strip. Place the remaining pastry strip on top. Press edges together to seal.

To let the steam escape from pastry during baking, make a "chimney" by folding a 2-inch piece of foil around a pencil. Remove pencil from foil. Cut a small hole in the center of the pastry and insert the foil chimney. Brush the entire surface of the pastry with the remaining egg-water mixture. Bake about 40 minutes or until a meat thermometer inserted through the foil chimney registers 160°. (If necessary, cover with foil the last 15 minutes of baking to prevent overbrowning.) Cut into slices to serve. Makes 6 servings.

◆ ◆ ◆

ONLY ON SUNDAY
—

"While in college, I spent a semester in Aix-en-Provence, France. I lived in a garage apartment with another American and a French girl whose parents lived in Algiers. Sunday was a very special day for us, because Monsieur and Madame Rouger, our landlords, would invite us into their home for an elaborate mid-day meal, which lasted about four hours. Each course was served separately and unhurriedly, with much conversation. I remember Madame's pâté, which was always my favorite. She would make a delicious mixture of meats, vegetables, and seasonings, and encase it all in the most wonderful crust. After the meal was over, Monsieur would turn on the hot water to our apartment. This was the only time during the week that we had that luxury. Sunday was truly heaven for us."

◆ ◆ ◆

Spicy Chicken on Pita Wedges

The chicken mixture freezes well, making this a great fix-ahead hors d'oeuvre. Thaw in the refrigerator before party time and just spread it on the pitas and bake.

1	whole medium chicken breast
1/2	cup water
	Lemon-pepper seasoning
12	ounces cream cheese, softened
1 1/2	cups shredded cheddar or Monterey Jack cheese (6 ounces)
1/4	cup dairy sour cream
1/4	cup chopped red onion
3	green onions, sliced
1	to 3 tablespoons chopped pickled jalapeño peppers
1	teaspoon ground cumin
1	teaspoon chili powder
1/2	teaspoon ground coriander
2	cloves garlic, minced
	Salt and pepper to taste
4	pita bread rounds, split lengthwise into rounds
	Sliced ripe olives
	Sliced green onion
	Shredded cheddar or Monterey Jack cheese

Place chicken in a 2-quart saucepan. Pour water over chicken; sprinkle with lemon-pepper seasoning. Bring to boiling; reduce heat. Cover and cook until chicken is tender. Remove chicken. If desired, save broth for another use. When chicken is cool, remove meat from bones and finely chop chicken.

Preheat the oven to 375°. In a large bowl, combine chicken, cream cheese, cheddar or Monterey Jack cheese, sour cream, red onion, green onion, jalapeño peppers, cumin, chili powder, coriander, garlic, salt, and pepper. Spread **one-eighth** of the chicken mixture on each pita bread round. With a sharp knife or pizza cutter, cut each round into 8 wedges. Place on a baking sheet. Bake for 5 to 7 minutes or until bubbly.

Garnish with sliced ripe olives, additional sliced green onion, and additional shredded cheese. Serve immediately. Makes 64 wedges.

Hot Sausage and Mushroom Dip

1	pound bulk hot pork or Italian sausage
1	tablespoon cooking oil
8	ounces sliced fresh mushrooms (3 cups)
1/2	cup chopped onion
1/2	cup chopped sweet red pepper
8	ounces cream cheese, softened
1/2	teaspoon Worcestershire sauce
	Assorted crackers or corn chips

In a 12-inch skillet, brown sausage. Remove sausage and drain well. Set aside. Remove drippings from skillet. In the same skillet, heat oil; cook mushrooms, onion, and pepper until tender. Stir together cream cheese and Worcestershire sauce; stir into vegetable mixture. Add cooked sausage. Heat and stir until cheese is melted. Transfer to chafing dish. Serve with assorted crackers or corn chips. Makes about 4 cups.

Chicken Puffs on Toast Rounds

¼ cup butter or margarine
½ cup finely chopped fresh mushrooms
¼ cup finely chopped onion
¼ cup finely chopped sweet red pepper
1 clove garlic, minced
5 tablespoons all-purpose flour
2 cups chicken broth
2 cups finely chopped cooked chicken
½ cup almonds, toasted and finely chopped
   Several dashes ground red pepper
   Salt and pepper to taste
2 baguettes, sliced ¼ inch thick
   Freshly grated Parmesan cheese

In a 2-quart saucepan, melt butter or margarine. Add mushrooms, onion, and red pepper; cook for 4 minutes. Add garlic and cook 2 minutes more. Stir in flour. Stir in broth. Cook and stir until thickened and bubbly. Cook and stir 1 to 2 minutes more. Stir in chicken, almonds, ground red pepper, salt, and pepper. If desired, cool; cover and chill until serving time.

Preheat the oven to 450°. Spread a tablespoon of the chicken mixture on each bread slice. Sprinkle with Parmesan cheese. Bake for 5 minutes, then broil until bubbly. Makes 5 to 6 dozen.

Chicken-Pecan Bites

These unique puffs are studded with chicken, pecans, and savory seasonings, then baked or deep-fried.

1 whole medium chicken breast
½ cup butter or margarine
1 cup all-purpose flour
4 eggs
½ cup pecans, toasted and chopped
3 tablespoons snipped parsley or 1 tablespoon dried parsley flakes
2 teaspoons Worcestershire sauce
1 teaspoon seasoned salt
½ teaspoon celery salt
1 cup mayonnaise
¼ cup honey
¼ teaspoon curry powder

Cook chicken in enough water to cover until tender. Remove chicken, reserving **1 cup** broth. Remove meat from bones; finely chop chicken and set aside.

In a medium saucepan, combine reserved broth and the butter. Cook over medium heat until butter melts. Add flour and stir vigorously. Cook and stir until mixture rolls away from sides of pan. Remove from heat and allow to cool slightly. Add eggs, one at a time, beating after each addition for 1 to 2 minutes or until smooth.

Preheat the oven to 400°. Stir reserved chicken, pecans, parsley, Worcestershire sauce, seasoned salt, and celery salt into egg mixture in saucepan. Drop by heaping teaspoons onto a greased baking sheet. Bake about 20 minutes or until golden brown. (Or, drop by heaping teaspoons into deep, hot fat at 375° about 1 minute per side or until golden, turning once with a slotted spoon.)

For dipping sauce, stir together mayonnaise, honey, and curry powder. Serve with chicken-pecan bites. Makes about 4 dozen.

NICE TO NOTE

This recipe can be prepared in advance up to the point of cooking. Spoon the dough onto waxed paper-lined baking sheets and freeze. When firm to the touch, transfer with a spatula to freezer bags or containers and return them to the freezer. Before baking or frying, thaw in the refrigerator.

Chicken Liver Pâté

The garnishes are an important part of the enjoyment of a pâté. The tiny cornichon pickles, briny capers, and red onion give just the right crunch and flavor to accent the mellow pâté.

8   ounces sliced fresh mushrooms (3 cups)
1/3 cup finely sliced shallots or green onions
1   clove garlic, minced
2/3 cup butter or margarine, divided
1   pound chicken livers
1/4 cup dry white wine
2   tablespoons brandy
2   teaspoons Dijon-style mustard
1/4 teaspoon salt
1/4 teaspoon dried thyme, crushed
1/8 teaspoon pepper
6   drops hot pepper sauce
    Cornichons, capers, finely chopped red onion, finely chopped hard-cooked egg
    Assorted crackers and toast points

In a 10-inch skillet, cook mushrooms, shallots, and garlic in 1/3 **cup** of the butter or margarine until almost tender. Add chicken livers, wine, brandy, mustard, salt, thyme, pepper, and hot pepper sauce. Simmer about 10 minutes or until livers are no longer pink. Remove from heat; cut up remaining butter and stir into mixture. Cool 5 minutes. Process liver mixture in a food processor or blender until smooth.

Line a 8x4x2-inch loaf pan with plastic wrap. Transfer liver mixture to lined loaf pan. Cover and chill for 6 hours or overnight. Unmold onto serving platter and garnish with cornichons, capers, red onion, and hard-cooked egg. Serve with crackers or toast points. Makes about 2 1/2 cups.

Pinwheel Olé with Black Bean Filling

Watching your fat intake? Substitute Neufchâtel cheese for the cream cheese and use low-fat cheddar cheese.

3/4 cup cooked black beans
3   ounces cream cheese, softened
2   teaspoons finely chopped jalapeño peppers
1   cup shredded cheddar cheese (4 ounces)
1/2 medium sweet red pepper, finely chopped
4   green onions, sliced
8   6-inch flour tortillas
    Salsa or guacamole

In a medium bowl, mash 1/2 **cup** of the beans. Stir in remaining 1/4 cup beans, cream cheese, and jalapeño peppers. Spread on tortillas. Sprinkle with cheese, red pepper, and onions. Roll up tightly. Wrap in plastic wrap and chill 2 to 8 hours. To serve, remove plastic wrap. Slice 1/2 to 3/4 inch thick. Place cut side up on serving platter. Serve with salsa or guacamole. Makes about 60.

NICE TO NOTE

The line of distinction between pâtés and terrines has become very fuzzy. You will find the words used interchangeably and with much license in cooking circles. They are both pureed mixtures of meat or fish with vegetables, spices, and seasonings. However, terrines (from the French word "terre" meaning "earth") traditionally are cooked in earthenware molds.

Chicken Empanada Appetizers

The chicken mixture also makes a great "sandwich" filling for flour tortillas or taco shells. Try it over lettuce for a Mexican salad.

♪ ♪ ♪

NICE TO NOTE
—

These small turnovers can be frozen after baking. To reheat, bake the frozen empanadas, uncovered, in a preheated 400° oven for 8 minutes.

*To turn these appetizers into a main course, quarter each pastry sheet and mound **one eighth** of the meat mixture in the center of each square. Fold in the four corners and seal at the top. Serve with Spanish rice, green salad, and fruit. Makes 8 servings.*

∾

1   17¼-ounce package frozen puff pastry
5   chicken breast halves, skinned and boned
1   1¼-ounce envelope taco seasoning mix, divided
2   tablespoons cooking oil, divided
¼   cup water
½   cup finely chopped onion
2   cups shredded cheddar or Monterey Jack cheese (8 ounces)
¾   cup finely chopped ripe olives
1   4-ounce can diced green chili peppers, drained
     Guacamole, salsa, or dairy sour cream

Thaw pastry sheets according to package directions. Sprinkle chicken breasts with **one-fourth** of the taco seasoning. In a 12-inch skillet, heat **1 tablespoon** of the oil. Brown chicken on both sides. Add remaining taco seasoning and the water. Bring to boiling; reduce heat. Cover and simmer over medium heat for 15 minutes or until chicken is tender. Remove chicken, reserving cooking liquid.

In the same skillet, heat remaining oil and cook onion until tender. In a food processor bowl, coarsely chop cooked chicken. Stir together chicken, onion, cheese, olives, chili peppers, and just enough of the reserved cooking liquid to moisten.

Preheat the oven to 400°. On a lightly floured surface, roll out pastry to ¹⁄₁₆-inch thickness. Cut into 3-inch rounds using a cookie cutter. Place 1 to 2 tablespoons of filling in center of each dough circle, being careful not to get the filling on the pastry edges. Moisten edges with water and fold over to form a semi-circle. Press edges firmly with a fork. Place on an ungreased baking sheet. Prick tops with a fork. Bake about 20 minutes or until golden. Serve hot with guacamole, salsa, or sour cream. Makes about 40.

◆ ◆ ◆

CARNIVAL CAPERS
—

The Secret Order of Carnival Boll-Weevils, also dubbed the "Mutants of Mirth," began in 1966. Named for the legendary enemy of cotton, they accompany the king and queen of Carnival on goodwill trips to schools and hospitals and Carnival events, and serve as mischievous ambassadors of Carnival. They go rumbling around town, sirens blaring, throwing candy and beads from the back of a wildly decorated, ancient green truck. Their presence is never a secret, but their identity is kept hidden behind outrageous boll-weevil headpieces. Only one Boll-weevil is unmasked each year in order to serve as coordinator of their activities.

◆ ◆ ◆

Boll-Weevil Bacon Snacks

Served hot or cold, this treat appeals to mature snackers as well as little tykes.

2   cups shredded cheddar cheese (8 ounces)
½   cup mayonnaise or salad dressing
6   slices bacon, cooked crisp and crumbled
¼   cup finely chopped onion
¼   cup slivered almonds, divided
     Dash Worcestershire sauce

For a cold spread, combine cheese, mayonnaise, bacon, onion, **3 tablespoons** of the almonds, and the Worcestershire sauce. Shape into a mound or place in a serving bowl. Cover and chill several hours or overnight. To serve, top with remaining almonds. Serve with assorted crackers.

For a toasted snack, preheat the oven to 350°. Combine the ingredients for the cold spread as above. Spread some of the mixture on English muffin halves or French bread slices. Sprinkle each with some of the remaining almonds. Bake about 15 minutes or just until bubbly. Halve or quarter and serve immediately. Makes 3 cups spread.

Herbed Mushroom Pâté

Here's a pâté for those who don't appreciate one made with liver. It has a mellow, wonderful flavor that will be even better if the pâté is made a day or so before serving.

- 1 pound sliced fresh mushrooms (6 cups)
- 1 clove garlic, minced
- 2 tablespoons butter or margarine
- 8 ounces cream cheese, softened
- 3 tablespoons dry sherry
- 1 tablespoon snipped fresh tarragon or 1 teaspoon dried tarragon, crushed
- 1 tablespoon snipped fresh marjoram or 1 teaspoon dried marjoram, crushed
- 1 tablespoon snipped fresh thyme or 1 teaspoon dried thyme, crushed
- 1/2 teaspoon snipped fresh rosemary or 1/8 teaspoon dried rosemary, crushed
- 1 teaspoon pepper
- 1 teaspoon lemon-pepper seasoning
- 1/2 teaspoon salt
  Assorted fresh herb sprigs
  Bagel chips or assorted crackers

In a 12-inch skillet, cook mushrooms and garlic in butter about 5 minutes or until liquid is absorbed. Cool to room temperature. In a food processor bowl, combine mushroom mixture, cream cheese, sherry, tarragon, marjoram, thyme, rosemary, pepper, lemon-pepper seasoning, and salt. Process until smooth.

Generously brush a 2 1/2- to 3-cup mold with cooking oil. Transfer mushroom mixture to mold. Cover and chill at least 8 hours. Unmold onto a serving plate. Garnish with fresh herbs and additional fresh mushroom slices. Serve with bagel chips or assorted crackers. Makes 2 1/2 cups.

Mushrooms Stuffed with Spinach

Smart hostesses have learned to save a few for themselves in the kitchen—these mushrooms vanish as soon as the tray is set down! They make an excellent appetizer, first course, or side dish.

- 12 large mushrooms (1 pound)
- 1 or 2 cloves garlic, minced
- 3 tablespoons butter or margarine
- 1 10-ounce package frozen chopped spinach
- 5 tablespoons freshly grated Parmesan cheese, divided
- 3 tablespoons mayonnaise
- 1/2 teaspoon seasoned salt
- 1/2 teaspoon Worcestershire sauce

Remove mushroom stems and save for another use. Clean mushroom caps with a moist paper towel. In a small saucepan, cook garlic in butter. Dip mushroom caps in the garlic-flavored butter. Arrange mushroom caps, smooth side down, in a 13x9x2-inch baking dish.

Preheat the oven to 350°. Cook spinach according to package directions; drain well in colander, pressing the back of a spoon against spinach to force out excess moisture. Stir in **3 tablespoons** of the Parmesan cheese, the mayonnaise, seasoned salt, and Worcestershire sauce. Spoon mixture into mushroom caps. Bake for 20 minutes. Sprinkle with remaining Parmesan cheese. Serve immediately. Makes 12.

Mamma-Mia Crostini

    1   medium eggplant, peeled and diced
    1   teaspoon salt
    3   tablespoons snipped fresh basil or 1 tablespoon dried basil, crushed
    1   tablespoon minced garlic
  1/4   cup olive oil
         Pepper to taste
    1   baguette, sliced 1/4 inch thick
  1/2   cup prepared pesto
    1   7-ounce jar roasted red bell pepper, thinly sliced
    1   cup shredded Provolone cheese (4 ounces)
  1/2   cup crumbled feta cheese (2 ounces)

Spread eggplant on paper towels and sprinkle with the salt. Let stand 30 to 45 minutes. Pat dry firmly to remove excess water. In a 10-inch skillet, cook eggplant, basil, and garlic in olive oil over medium heat about 10 minutes or until eggplant is soft and beginning to brown. Season with pepper.

Preheat the broiler. On each slice of bread, spread **1 teaspoon** of the pesto, then **2 teaspoons** of the eggplant mixture. Top each with 2 slivers of the roasted pepper arranged in an X fashion. Sprinkle each with **2 teaspoons** of the Provolone and **1 teaspoon** feta cheese. (If necessary, adjust proportions of toppings according to bread size.)

Place on baking sheet. Broil about 4 minutes or until cheese melts. Serve immediately. Makes about 30.

Palace Cheesecake

Photograph on page 22.

    6   stone-ground wheat crackers, crushed
   16   ounces cream cheese
    1   egg
         Dash salt
   10   sun-dried tomatoes packed in oil, drained
    1   cup prepared pesto
  3/4   cup dairy sour cream
    1   teaspoon all-purpose flour
         Assorted baby lettuce leaves
         Edible flower petals
         Chives

Preheat the oven to 325°. Butter a 7-inch springform pan. Sprinkle crushed crackers into bottom of pan. In a large bowl, beat cream cheese with an electric mixer until softened. Add egg and salt, beating on low speed just until combined; set aside. In a food processor bowl, process sun-dried tomatoes. Add pesto and process to mix.

Spread **half** of the cream cheese mixture into prepared pan, spreading evenly. Top with tomato mixture, spreading evenly to the edge. Spread remaining cheese mixture over tomato mixture. Bake about 35 minutes.

Stir together sour cream and flour; carefully spread over cheesecake. Bake 5 minutes more. Cool; cover and chill 4 to 24 hours. Remove side of pan. Serve on a bed of baby lettuce leaves. Garnish with desired edible flower petals and chives. Serve chilled or at room temperature for spreading on stone-ground wheat crackers. Makes 24 servings.

◆ ◆ ◆

PIGGLY WIGGLY PLAYGROUND

—

In the heart of Memphis is a little jewel called Chickasaw Gardens. Once the estate of Clarence Saunders, grocery magnate, it was the backyard of his "Pink Palace," now a fine museum. Today, handsome residences surround the picturesque lake in the center of the Gardens and many Memphians gather there to spend happy hours chatting on the bank, playing with frisky dogs, people-watching, and picnicking. Many a family photograph has been posed in front of the beautiful old magnolias and it is certain that countless family stories began here with a marriage proposal offered in this perfectly romantic setting.

◆ ◆ ◆

Burgundy Mushrooms

The mushrooms will shrink a bit, but will keep a firm texture. If need be, the cooking process can be stopped and restarted at any point. (If you have any of these mushrooms left after cocktail hour, you'll love what they do for a grilled steak!)

2	pounds fresh medium mushrooms
1²/₃	cups burgundy
1	cup beef broth
¼	cup butter or margarine
2	teaspoons Worcestershire sauce
¾	teaspoon salt
½	teaspoon dillseed
½	teaspoon pepper
3	or 4 cloves garlic, minced

In a 4-quart Dutch oven, combine all ingredients. Bring to boiling; reduce heat. Simmer, covered, for 1 hour. Uncover and simmer 2 hours more or until only a small amount of liquid remains. Transfer to a 1½- or 2-quart chafing dish. Serve hot. Makes about 4 cups.

Herbed Havarti en Croûte

½	of a 17¼-ounce package (1 sheet) frozen puff pastry
1	teaspoon Dijon-style mustard
12	ounces Havarti cheese
2	teaspoons finely chopped walnuts
1	teaspoon snipped parsley or ¼ teaspoon dried parsley flakes
1	teaspoon grated orange peel
1	teaspoon snipped fresh dill or ¼ teaspoon dried dillweed
1	teaspoon snipped fresh basil or ¼ teaspoon dried basil, crushed
½	teaspoon snipped fresh chives
¼	teaspoon fennel seed
	Several dashes ground red pepper
1	beaten egg
	Apple or pear slices
	Assorted crackers

Let folded pastry stand at room temperature for 20 minutes to thaw. Spread mustard over top of cheese. Sprinkle with walnuts, parsley, orange peel, dill, basil, chives, fennel seed, and red pepper. Unfold pastry and center over cheese. Invert cheese and fold two sides over cheese, overlapping edges. Seal seam with water. Trim any excess pastry from ends and fold up. Seal seams with water.

Place, seam-side down, on a lightly greased baking sheet. Use trimmed pastry to cut out shapes of leaves or fruit. Brush bottom of cutouts with water and place on top of pastry-wrapped cheese. Brush entire pastry with egg. Cover and chill for 1 hour.

Preheat the oven to 400°. Bake about 20 minutes or until pastry is nicely browned. Serve warm with apple or pear slices or assorted crackers. Makes 8 to 10 servings.

NICE TO NOTE

—

The delicate mushroom deserves special attention when it comes to choosing, storing, and cleaning. Try to purchase mushrooms within a day or two of using them, especially if you plan to serve them raw. Look for firm, dry mushrooms free of spots or bruises.

Keep mushrooms in a paper bag or open container in the refrigerator, loosely covered with a paper towel that has been moistened ever so slightly.

Wait to clean the mushrooms until you are ready to use them. Though cleaning mushrooms is very important, too much water can make them soggy. Most cultivated button mushrooms are clean enough that a tender wiping with a moist paper towel is all they need.

∾

Roquefort Mousse

If first impressions are lasting, you'll do well to serve this as a first course. Mold the mousse in individual ¼-cup molds. Serve on plates surrounded by pears, apples, and grapes.

16 ounces cream cheese, softened
½ cup crumbled Roquefort or blue cheese (2 ounces)
1 tablespoon minced shallot
 Dash Worcestershire sauce
1 envelope unflavored gelatin
1 tablespoon dry sherry
⅓ cup heavy cream
 Lettuce leaves
 Assorted crackers

In a large bowl, beat cream cheese and Roquefort with an electric mixer on medium speed for 10 to 15 minutes or until very smooth. Add shallot and Worcestershire sauce and beat 5 minutes more.

Meanwhile, in a 1-quart saucepan sprinkle gelatin over sherry. Let soften 5 minutes. Cook and stir over low heat until gelatin dissolves. In another saucepan, heat cream just until hot; do not boil. Add hot cream to warm gelatin mixture. Cool to room temperature.

Add cooled gelatin mixture to cheese mixture and mix well. Pour into an oiled 2½- to 3-cup decorative mold. Cover and chill at least 8 hours. Unmold onto a lettuce-lined plate. Serve with assorted crackers. Makes about 2½ cups.

Goat Cheese Torta

Choose from imported goat cheese, such as Montrachet, or increasingly popular domestic varieties from Texas and Wisconsin.

16 ounces cream cheese, softened
7 to 8 ounces mild goat cheese
2 cloves garlic, minced
4 teaspoons snipped fresh oregano or 1¼ teaspoons dried oregano, crushed
⅛ teaspoon freshly ground pepper
¼ cup prepared pesto
½ cup sun-dried tomatoes packed in oil
1 to 2 tablespoons slivered almonds, toasted
 Fresh oregano or parsley sprig
 Stone ground wheat crackers or thinly sliced baguette

Line a 1-quart loaf or soufflé pan with clear plastic wrap. In a food processor bowl or large mixer bowl, combine cream cheese, goat cheese, garlic, oregano, and pepper. Process or beat with electric mixer until smooth. Spread **one-third** of the cheese mixture in the bottom of the pan. Top with pesto, spreading evenly. Layer with another **one-third** of the cheese mixture.

Drain sun-dried tomatoes, reserving one tomato for garnish. Chop remaining tomatoes. Spread chopped sun-dried tomatoes evenly over cheese mixture in pan. Top with remaining cheese mixture. Cover with plastic wrap and press gently to pack the cheese. Chill several hours.

Uncover cheese; invert onto serving plate. Cut reserved sun-dried tomato into thin slices. Garnish torta with thin slices of sun-dried tomato, the toasted almonds, and fresh oregano or parsley. Serve with stone ground wheat crackers or thinly sliced baguette. Makes 12 to 16 servings.

♪ ♪ ♪

NICE TO NOTE

—

"Torta" is Italian for "cake." This torta joins the ranks of the rich, molded cheesecakes which have become popular as appetizers. They are hostess-friendly as they can be made up to five days in advance. When sliced, they reveal colorfully distinct layers of nuts, herbs, and vegetables.

Fabulous Filled Phyllo

       Cheese Filling (see recipe below)
9   sheets phyllo dough (18x14-inch), thawed if frozen
³/₄ cup butter or margarine, melted

Prepare Cheese Filling. Preheat the oven to 400°. Lightly brush **1 sheet** of phyllo with **some** of the melted butter or margarine. Place another phyllo sheet on top; brush with butter or margarine. Repeat with a third sheet of phyllo and butter or margarine. (Cover the remaining phyllo with waxed paper and overlay with a damp cloth to prevent drying.) Cut the stack of phyllo lengthwise into 2-inch-wide strips.

For **each** triangle, spoon a scant **1 tablespoon** of the Cheese Filling about 1 inch from one end of **each** strip. Fold the end over the filling at a 45-degree angle. Continue folding to form a triangle that encloses filling. Repeat with the remaining phyllo, butter or margarine, and remaining filling.

Place triangles on a baking sheet. Brush tops with remaining butter or margarine. Bake about 8 minutes or until lightly browned. Serve warm. Makes about 24.

Cheese Filling

To ease last-minute preparations, make this filling ahead of time and chill until you're ready to fill the phyllo.

2   tablespoons butter or margarine
2   tablespoons all-purpose flour
¹/₈ teaspoon nutmeg
¹/₂ cup milk
4   ounces mild goat cheese
²/₃ cup shredded Gruyère cheese (about 2¹/₂ ounces)
¹/₄ cup crumbled blue cheese (1 ounce)

In a 1-quart saucepan, melt butter or margarine. Stir in flour and nutmeg. Add milk all at once. Cook and stir over medium heat until thickened and bubbly. Cook and stir for 1 minute more. Let stand until cool.

Meanwhile, in a medium bowl, combine goat cheese, Gruyère cheese, and blue cheese. Pour thickened milk mixture over cheeses and stir until well combined. Makes about 2 cups.

Waldorf Salad in Endive

Stays crisp and fresh several hours in the refrigerator, so feel free to arrange this impressive platter before last-minute party preparations.

5	large heads Belgian endive
4	ounces cream cheese, softened
1	tablespoon fresh lemon juice
2	teaspoons cooking oil
3/4	cup chopped walnuts
1/2	cup finely chopped red apple (unpeeled)
1/2	cup finely chopped Granny Smith apple (unpeeled)
2	tablespoons snipped parsley
3/4	cup crumbled blue cheese (3 ounces)

Separate the leaves of the endive; rinse and pat dry. In a medium bowl, combine the cream cheese, lemon juice, and oil; mix well. Stir in walnuts, apples, and parsley. Gently stir in blue cheese.

Mound **one tablespoon** apple mixture in the base of each endive leaf. Arrange on a large platter in a starburst pattern. Cover and chill until serving time. Makes about 50.

Cheese and Pepper Quesadillas

For variety, try using a red, a yellow, and a green pepper.

3	green peppers, sliced into thin strips
1	medium red onion, thinly sliced
1/4	cup butter or margarine
1/4	teaspoon ground cumin
6	ounces cream cheese, softened
1	cup shredded cheddar cheese (4 ounces)
1	cup shredded Monterey Jack cheese (4 ounces)
1	4-ounce can diced mild green chili peppers
2	tablespoons sliced jalapeño peppers
10	6-inch flour tortillas
	Chili powder
1/2	cup dairy sour cream
1/4	cup salsa
	Cilantro sprigs

Preheat the oven to 425°. In a 10-inch skillet, cook green peppers and onion in butter just until tender. Stir in cumin. Drain, reserving cooking liquid. In a medium bowl, stir together cream cheese, cheddar cheese, Monterey Jack cheese, and **undrained** green chili peppers. Spoon 2 to 3 tablespoons of the cheese mixture onto one side of each tortilla. Top each with some of the green pepper mixture and jalapeño peppers. Fold tortillas in half. Place on lightly greased baking sheet. Brush with reserved cooking liquid. Sprinkle with chili powder. Bake about 7 minutes or until cheese is melted.

Meanwhile, for sauce, stir together sour cream and salsa. To serve, cut tortillas into six wedges. Arrange on serving platter. Garnish with cilantro sprigs. Serve with sauce. Makes 60.

Walnut-Glazed Brie

This is a happy marriage of flavors. The nuts, brown sugar, and coffee liqueur make a delectable topping for the Brie.

²/₃ cup walnuts, finely chopped
¹/₄ cup coffee liqueur
3 tablespoons brown sugar
¹/₂ teaspoon vanilla
1 14-ounce round Brie
    Assorted crackers
    Pear slices

Preheat the oven to 350°. Spread chopped walnuts in a pie pan or 8-inch square baking pan. Bake for 10 to 12 minutes or until toasted, stirring occasionally. Stir in the liqueur, brown sugar, and vanilla; set aside.

Reduce oven temperature to 325°. Remove the top rind of the Brie. Place Brie in a shallow baking dish. Top with the walnut mixture. Bake for 8 to 10 minutes or until the Brie is soft and heated through. Serve immediately with assorted crackers and pear slices. Makes 12 to 15 servings.

Baked Mexican Spinach Dip

1 cup chopped onion
2 tablespoons cooking oil
3 medium tomatoes, peeled, seeded, and chopped (divided)
2 to 4 tablespoons chopped jalapeño peppers
1 10-ounce package frozen chopped spinach, thawed and squeezed dry
2¹/₂ cups shredded Monterey Jack cheese (10 ounces), divided
4 ounces cream cheese, cut into ¹/₂-inch cubes
1 cup light cream
¹/₂ cup sliced ripe olives
1 tablespoon red wine vinegar
    Salt and pepper to taste
    Tortilla chips

Preheat the oven to 400°. In a 10-inch skillet, cook onion in oil until tender. Add **two-thirds** of the chopped tomatoes and all of the jalapeño peppers; cook 2 minutes more. Transfer mixture to a large bowl. Stir in spinach, **2 cups** of the Monterey Jack cheese, cream cheese, cream, olives, vinegar, salt, and pepper. Spoon into a 1¹/₂-quart baking dish. Bake about 35 minutes or until hot and bubbly. Top with remaining Monterey Jack cheese and chopped tomato. Serve with tortilla chips. Makes 6¹/₂ cups.

♪ ♪ ♪

NICE TO NOTE

—

*Baked potatoes can live two lives at your next dinner party. Baked potato skins are wonderful crunchy bites with cocktails and cheesy creamed potatoes complement any beef. Bake the potatoes (1 for each serving) and scoop out the pulp, setting it aside. Cut the skins into one-inch strips with kitchen shears and lay them on a baking sheet. Combine melted butter (¹/₄ to ¹/₂ cup), seasoned salt, freshly-ground pepper, a dash of hot pepper sauce and Worcestershire sauce; sprinkle or brush liberally over the skins. Put in a 475° oven (or broiler if you can stand and watch) until crispy-brown. These will be gone before the first glass is empty!
Mash the reserved potatoes and add 1 tablespoon of butter and 2-3 tablespoons of light cream per potato. Season with salt, pepper, and chopped parsley, chives, or dillweed. Sprinkle grated cheddar cheese over the top and bake at 375° for 15-20 minutes. So simple — so good!*

Dixie Caviar

Try this as a dip with corn chips, or as a salad served on a bed of lettuce or in a hollowed-out tomato.

4	cups frozen or canned black-eyed peas
1	16-ounce can white hominy, drained (optional)
2	medium tomatoes, chopped
1	cup Italian salad dressing
1	cup chopped green pepper
1/2	cup chopped onion
4	green onions, sliced
1	or 2 jalapeño peppers, seeded and chopped
1	or 2 cloves garlic, minced
1/4	cup dairy sour cream or plain yogurt
	Snipped fresh cilantro or parsley
	Tortilla chips or crackers

If using frozen peas, cook according to package directions; drain. If using canned peas, rinse and drain. In a large bowl, combine drained peas, hominy, tomatoes, salad dressing, green pepper, onion, green onions, jalapeño peppers, and garlic. Cover and chill for 1 to 2 days.

Drain mixture, reserving liquid. Partially chop in food processor by pulsing twice. Do not puree. Add back enough of the liquid to make a nice dipping consistency. Top with sour cream and cilantro. Serve cold with tortilla chips or crackers. Makes 2 1/2 quarts.

Cucumber Cocktail Canapés

For that extra special touch, cut the bread into heart, moon, or other decorative shapes with small cookie cutters.

2	medium cucumbers, peeled, halved lengthwise, and seeded
1	teaspoon salt
1/2	cup chopped onion
1/4	cup chopped radishes (optional)
1	tablespoon mayonnaise
	Several dashes ground red pepper
1	loaf sliced party rye or pumpernickel bread
	Snipped fresh dill
	Paprika

Place cucumbers on paper towels. Sprinkle with the salt and let stand about 30 minutes. Press firmly with paper towels to remove excess water. Finely chop cucumbers. In a medium bowl, combine cucumbers, onion, radishes, mayonnaise, and red pepper. Cover and chill.

To serve, spread **one tablespoon** of the cucumber mixture on bread, topping each with fresh dill and paprika. Serve open-faced or topped with an additional bread slice. Makes about 32.

♩ ♩ ♩

NICE TO NOTE

—

Make this once and it will be on your menu lists forever. It's a new twist on Southern favorites and makes a terrific summertime party dish. Black-eyed peas and hominy, typically dinner-table vegetables, are united in this marinated appetizer. Green pepper, garlic and lots of onion give it just the right amount of "bite" and crunch, and the tomatoes, best from the backyard, lend their delicious flavor and color.

♩ ♩ ♩

NICE TO NOTE

—

Sandwiches will stay soft and fresh before a party if you follow this advice: Dampen a cloth or paper towel and wring out to remove excess moisture. Spread over the sandwich tray and add a cover of plastic wrap.

Red and Yellow Pepper Salsa with Croûtes

Photograph on page 23.

4   tablespoons olive oil, divided
2   medium sweet red peppers, cut into julienne strips
1   medium sweet yellow pepper, cut into julienne strips
8   small fresh basil leaves, torn into small pieces, or 1¹/₂ teaspoons dried basil, crushed
1   tablespoon snipped fresh oregano or 1 teaspoon dried oregano, crushed
1   teaspoon snipped fresh thyme or ¹/₄ teaspoon dried thyme, crushed
2   to 4 anchovy fillets, minced
1   tablespoon capers
3   cloves garlic, minced
    Salt and pepper
    Croûtes (see recipe below) or assorted crackers and breadsticks

In a 12-inch skillet, heat **2 tablespoons** of the olive oil over medium heat. Cook sweet pepper strips in olive oil for 3 to 5 minutes or until tender. Set aside. In a medium bowl, combine remaining olive oil, basil, oregano, thyme, anchovies, capers, and garlic. Stir in peppers. Season to taste with salt and pepper. Let stand at room temperature several hours or overnight in refrigerator. Serve at room temperature with croûtes or assorted crackers and breadsticks. Makes about 1¹/₂ cups.

Croûtes

Photograph on page 23.

¹/₂   cup butter, melted
¹/₂   cup olive oil
2   cloves garlic, minced
1   loaf French bread, sliced ¹/₂ inch thick
     Paprika
     Dried basil
     Parmesan cheese

Preheat the oven to 300°. In a small bowl, stir together melted butter, olive oil, and garlic. Brush both sides of bread slices with the butter mixture. Place on a baking sheet. Bake about 20 minutes or until light brown. Sprinkle with paprika, dried basil, and Parmesan cheese. Makes about 30.

Truly Hot Cheddar Dip

3   cups shredded cheddar cheese (12 ounces)
1   cup mayonnaise
1   cup chopped onion
1   to 3 teaspoons crushed red pepper

Preheat the oven to 350°. In a medium bowl, combine cheese, mayonnaise, onion, and red pepper. Transfer to a 1½-quart round baking dish. Bake for 10 to 12 minutes or just until bubbly. Broil 1 to 2 minutes more or until light brown. Makes 3½ cups.

Blue Cheese Wafers

The "dough" for these wafers can be made weeks ahead and frozen. Thaw in the refrigerator several hours before slicing and baking.

2   cups crumbled blue cheese (8 ounces)
1   cup butter or margarine
1½   cups all-purpose flour
1   teaspoon dry mustard
¼   teaspoon salt
1   slightly beaten egg
1   teaspoon water
1   cup chopped pecans

In a food processor bowl or mixer bowl, combine blue cheese and butter. Process or beat with an electric mixer until smooth. Add flour, dry mustard, and salt; process or beat just until blended.

Divide mixture in half. Shape each half into a 1½-inch diameter roll. Stir together egg and water. Coat rolls with egg mixture, then with chopped nuts, pressing gently to help nuts adhere. Wrap in waxed paper or clear plastic wrap and chill 4 to 24 hours.

Preheat the oven to 400°. Cut rolls into ¼-inch slices. Place on an ungreased baking sheet. Bake about 10 minutes or until light brown. Cool. Store in an airtight container. Makes 4 dozen.

Toasted Spice Pecans

We warn you—they're addictive!

2   cups pecan halves
¼   cup butter or margarine
1   egg white
½   cup sugar
1   teaspoon ground cinnamon
⅛   teaspoon ground nutmeg

Preheat the oven to 325°. Spread pecans in a shallow baking pan. Toast in the oven for 10 minutes. Add butter to the baking pan; return to oven until butter is melted. Stir to coat pecans.

Beat egg white until foamy; beat in sugar, cinnamon, and nutmeg. Pour over pecans. Bake 30 minutes more, stirring every 10 minutes. Cool. Store in an airtight container. Makes 2 cups.

Mixed-Up Popcorn

You may have to hide this from your children—and yourself!

6	cups popped popcorn (about $1/3$ cup unpopped)
3	cups bite-size rice squares cereal
2	cups round toasted oat cereal
$1^1/2$	cups salted peanuts
1	cup pecans
1	cup packed brown sugar
$1/2$	cup butter or margarine
$1/4$	cup light corn syrup
1	teaspoon vanilla
$1/4$	teaspoon baking soda

In a large bowl, stir together popcorn, rice cereal, oat cereal, peanuts, and pecans. Transfer to a greased roasting pan.

In a heavy 2- or 3-quart saucepan, combine brown sugar, butter, and corn syrup. Cook and stir over medium heat to boiling. Boil 5 minutes without stirring. Remove from heat; stir in vanilla and baking soda.

Preheat the oven to 250°. Pour the sugar mixture over the popcorn mixture; stir gently to coat. Bake for 1 hour. Cool. Store in an airtight container. Makes about 14 cups.

Cynthia's Curry Dip Allegro

Need some dipper ideas? Try blanched fresh asparagus wrapped in prosciutto, succulent shrimp or snow crab legs, or wonderful garden fresh vegetables.

$1/2$	cup dairy sour cream
$1/2$	cup mayonnaise or salad dressing
2	tablespoons finely chopped onion
2	tablespoons catsup
1	tablespoon curry powder
1	tablespoon Worcestershire sauce
$1/2$	teaspoon hot pepper sauce
	Dash salt

In a small bowl, combine all ingredients. Cover and chill at least 24 hours. Makes $1^1/3$ cups.

◆ ◆ ◆

HEAVEN OR HELL?

—

"When my husband reaches heaven, he is sure to find it a duck blind. As duck season approaches, he becomes more and more like a little boy on Christmas Eve—shopping catalogs for new equipment, setting up scouting visits to find busy flyways, planning hunts with his equally 'duck-struck' buddies. I used to fight it and I admit to a certain amount of 'duck-widow' jealousy. Over the years, however, I have realized how important this fun is to him and I have changed my attitude, even joining him on a few frigid mornings. I decided on my last trip, as I sat in the blind with feet totally numb, that I should show my support from home and leave the hunting to him. I send him off with a smile, my sincere good wishes, and a weekend's supply of this popcorn munchie, voted 'best snack in the blind' by his fellow hunters."

◆ ◆ ◆

SOUPS, SALADS & SAUCES

B.B. King

There is no blues artist better known than Riley B. "B.B." King. His career is full of unforgettable times and remarkable performances. Beginning with his early radio shows at WDIA and his recording debut in 1949, "Blues Boy" King and his famous "Lucille" created a singing-guitar style that galvanized his audiences and made him a favorite wherever the music called "blues" was known. From the bus rides, ten-cent chili, and Beale Street jams of more than forty years ago, he has come to international fame, booking more than 300 shows a year, playing to kings and presidents, recording 50 albums, and winning more than 16 Grammy nominations.

Here in Memphis, where the blues was born, B.B. enjoyed his most thrilling moment. On September 22, 1991, as part of the resurrection of his beloved Beale Street, B.B. King was back home to open his own blues club to a sold-out house of roaring Memphis fans.

B.B. exults: "This club is the culmination of everything I've wanted to do—to come back to my roots and my people here in Memphis."

SOUPS, SALADS & SAUCES

◆ ◆ ◆

SOUPS

◆ ◆ ◆

SALADS

◆ ◆ ◆

SALADS
CONTINUED

◆ ◆ ◆

SAUCES

◆ ◆ ◆

PICTURED OVERLEAF
—
Southern Corn Chowder
(page 61)

◆ ◆ ◆

*S*OUP SATISFIES. ITS FILLING GOODNESS MAKES A ONE-COURSE MEAL or introduces a more elaborate one. Hearty soups, such as stews, gumbos, and chowders need only a crusty bread alongside. Center a luncheon or begin a dinner with a velvety bisque. Cold soups are great summer coolers: tomato-red gazpacho or pale-green cucumber are two beautiful choices when the mercury soars.

Soup is soothing. Chicken noodle has made a name for itself and deservedly so. There's no better prescription for a gray day. A thick potato chowder topped with cheese or a vegetable minestrone would chase away the worst case of winter blues.

Soup is sensational. With so many interesting foods available, it is forever new. Good cooks can take the humblest of ingredients and create a variety of rich and memorable soups. In a pinch, soup can be prepared as a quick meal or stretched to include unexpected arrivals. The variety of soups in *Heart & Soul* should give you an excuse to gather friends around a tureen-centered table.

The true soul-mate of soup is salad: chilled and crunchy, it completes a soup meal like nothing else. It seems to be right with so many things—meat and poultry, pasta, and sandwiches, and yet it is frequently a meal in itself. *Heart & Soul* offers a wide array of salads to to fit any type of menu.

You'll find sauces here, too. They are the crowning touch for salads, vegetables, and all kinds of main dishes and can lift a food from the ordinary to the sublime. ♥

◆ ◆ ◆

STEW STUFFING

—

"Many winters ago, our family gathered at a dear friend's for dinner. As we sat by the fire, DeeDee brought in a tray of bowls filled with her delicious stew. Everyone loved this casual supper, insisting on second helpings. We were completely taken aback when we discovered our real dinner waiting for us in the dining room! We were stuffed later, but no one was sorry for having enjoyed our fill of this savory stew—and not one of us left DeeDee's without the recipe."

◆ ◆ ◆

DeeDee's Minestrone Stew

Round out the meal with a crisp green salad and fresh Italian bread.

1	pound lean ground beef
1	cup chopped onion
1	cup chopped celery
1/2	cup chopped green pepper
6	cups water
1	16-ounce can kidney beans, drained
1	15-ounce can tomato sauce
1 1/2	cups medium noodles
1	cup chopped carrots
4	teaspoons salt
1	tablespoon dried oregano, crushed
1 1/2	teaspoons dried basil, crushed
1 1/2	teaspoons dried thyme, crushed
1/2	to 1 teaspoon pepper

In a 6-quart Dutch oven or stockpot, cook ground beef, onion, celery, and green pepper until meat is brown. Drain. Stir in remaining ingredients. Cover and simmer for 1 hour. Makes 6 main-dish servings.

Home At Six Soup

With a microwave to quick-thaw ground beef and these familiar ingredients on the pantry shelf, this hearty soup can be on the table in a flash.

1½ pounds lean ground beef
1 cup chopped onion
1 28-ounce can whole tomatoes, cut up
1 16-ounce can kidney beans
1 17-ounce can whole kernel corn
1 8-ounce can tomato sauce
1 tablespoon chili powder
½ teaspoon ground cumin
½ teaspoon dried basil, crushed
  Shredded cheddar cheese, guacamole, dairy sour cream, corn chips

In a 6-quart Dutch oven or stockpot, cook ground beef and onion until meat is brown and onion is tender. Drain. Stir in **undrained** tomatoes, **undrained** kidney beans, **undrained** corn, tomato sauce, chili powder, cumin, and basil. Bring to boiling; reduce heat. Cover and simmer for 1 hour. Serve with cheese, guacamole, sour cream, and corn chips for topping. Makes 8 main-dish servings.

Thin Stew Thick Soup

2 pounds beef stew meat
¼ cup all-purpose flour
4 teaspoons salt
½ teaspoon pepper
3 tablespoons shortening
2 cloves garlic, minced
4 potatoes, peeled and cubed
1½ cups water
2 medium onions, sliced
1 medium green pepper, seeded and sliced
2 medium tomatoes, sliced
¼ cup snipped parsley
  Salt and pepper to taste
  French bread or biscuits

Preheat the oven to 325°. Trim fat from meat. Cut into 1-inch cubes. In a plastic or paper bag, combine flour, salt, and pepper. Add meat cubes, a few at a time, shaking to coat. In a 4-quart oven-safe Dutch oven, melt shortening. Add meat and garlic; cook until meat is brown. Add potatoes, water, onions, and green pepper. Cover and bake for 1¼ hours.

Stir in tomatoes and parsley. Cover and bake 20 minutes more or until vegetables are tender. Season with salt and pepper. Serve with French bread or biscuits. Makes 6 to 8 main-dish servings.

♦ ♦ ♦

SUPPER STRETCHER
—

"Thin Stew Thick Soup was a super, flexible, cold-weather meal I served frequently when our boys were growing up. We never knew when a friend or two (or three) might appear for supper and this dish would always stretch. The name originated when several extra guests required some of that stretching, making it more like soup but still so satisfying. It became a standard in our house and when the boys went away to college, they always asked that Thin Stew Thick Soup be waiting when they arrived back home. It was!"

♦ ♦ ♦

My Husband's Navy Bean Soup

Fix it a day in advance. Give the flavors time to blend.

2	pounds dry navy beans
3	quarts water
1¹/₂	pounds ham hocks
2	bay leaves
4	medium onions, chopped
4	carrots, chopped
2	stalks celery, chopped
3	tablespoons butter or margarine
3	to 4 tablespoons tomato paste
2	teaspoons liquid smoke
	Salt and pepper to taste
1	tablespoon honey (optional)

Rinse beans. In a 6-quart Dutch oven or stockpot, bring water to boiling. Add beans, ham hocks, and bay leaves. Bring to boiling; reduce heat. Cover and simmer for 2 hours. Add additional boiling water to soup, if necessary.

Meanwhile, cook onions, carrots, and celery in butter or margarine until tender. Add to bean mixture. Stir in tomato paste, liquid smoke, salt, and pepper. Cook 1 hour more or until creamy. Add honey, if desired. Makes 8 to 10 main-dish servings or 16 to 20 side-dish servings.

Two-Bean Chili

Use ground venison in place of the ground beef for a delicious twist.

1	pound lean ground beef
¹/₂	cup chopped onion
1	16-ounce can kidney beans, drained
1	16-ounce can chili hot beans, drained
1	16-ounce can whole tomatoes, cut up
1	8-ounce can tomato sauce
¹/₄	to ¹/₂ cup dry white wine
4	tablespoons chili powder
1	tablespoon ground cumin
1	teaspoon garlic powder
¹/₂	teaspoon salt
¹/₄	teaspoon pepper
	About 2 cups water
3	cups sliced fresh mushrooms (8 ounces)
1	tablespoon snipped fresh cilantro or parsley

In a 6-quart Dutch oven or stockpot, cook ground beef and onion until meat is brown. Drain. Stir in kidney beans, chili hot beans, **undrained** tomatoes, tomato sauce, wine, chili powder, cumin, garlic powder, salt, and pepper. Cover and simmer for 1¹/₂ hours, adding water during cooking, as necessary, to prevent sticking. Stir in mushrooms and cilantro. Cook 30 minutes more. Makes 4 to 6 main-dish servings.

Lucille's Chili

    2   pounds ground chuck
    1   cup chopped onion
 ³/₄   cup chopped green pepper
    1   clove garlic, minced
    1   16-ounce can whole tomatoes, cut up
    1   16-ounce can kidney beans, drained
    2   8-ounce cans tomato sauce
    1   10-ounce can diced tomatoes and green chilies
    1   jalapeño pepper, seeded and chopped
    1   tablespoon chili powder
    1   tablespoon snipped fresh oregano or 1 teaspoon dried oregano, crushed
    2   teaspoons ground cumin
 1¹/₂ teaspoons snipped fresh basil or ¹/₂ teaspoon dried basil, crushed
 1¹/₂ teaspoons salt
 ¹/₄   teaspoon pepper
        Chopped onion
        Dairy sour cream
        Shredded cheddar cheese

In a 4-quart Dutch oven, cook ground chuck, onion, green pepper, and garlic until meat is brown. Drain well. Add **undrained** tomatoes, drained kidney beans, tomato sauce, **undrained** tomatoes and green chilies, jalapeño pepper, chili powder, oregano, cumin, basil, salt, and pepper. Cook over medium heat for 10 minutes. Reduce heat. Cover and simmer for 1 hour. Serve with additional chopped onion, sour cream, and cheddar cheese for topping. Makes 8 main-dish servings.

Oyster and Artichoke Soup

This soup is delicious even without the oysters!

 ¹/₂   cup butter or margarine
    6   shallots, finely chopped
 ¹/₂   cup chopped celery
    2   cloves garlic, minced
    2   tablespoons all-purpose flour
    3   cups chicken broth or clam juice
    1   14-ounce can artichoke hearts, drained and chopped
    2   tablespoons snipped parsley or 2 teaspoons dried parsley flakes
    2   bay leaves
 ¹/₄   teaspoon dried thyme leaves, crushed
        Dash ground red pepper
        Salt and pepper to taste
   24   shucked oysters

In a 3-quart saucepan, melt butter or margarine. Add shallots, celery, and garlic. Cook over medium heat until tender.

Stir flour into vegetable mixture. Cook and stir over medium heat for 3 minutes. Remove saucepan from heat. Using a wire whisk, stir in chicken broth or clam juice until smooth.

Add artichoke hearts, parsley, bay leaves, thyme, ground red pepper, salt, and pepper. Bring to boiling; reduce heat to low. Cover and simmer for 30 minutes. Remove and discard bay leaves. Add oysters and simmer, uncovered, for 1 to 4 minutes or until oysters begin to curl around the edges. Serve in heated bowls. Makes 8 to 10 side-dish servings.

♦ ♦ ♦

TEN CENTS A BOWL
—

There was a spot on "old" Beale Street run by Sunbeam Mitchell. Here all of the musicians around, including the notable B.B. King, could eat cheap and get a big bowl of the best chili in town. B.B. remembers: "If you had 15 cents at that time, you could eat well: a nickel's worth of crackers and a dime's worth of chili!" "Lucille's Chili," named for B.B.'s famed guitar, is patterned after this memorable feast.

♦ ♦ ♦

Comforting Chicken Noodle Soup

Every good Southern cook needs a recipe for chicken noodle soup.

8	cups chicken broth
1	cup chopped onion
1	cup chopped celery
1	cup chopped carrots
1	clove garlic, minced
2	to 3 cups chopped cooked chicken
2	medium tomatoes, peeled and chopped
1/2	cup uncooked broad egg noodles
1	teaspoon snipped fresh basil or 1/4 teaspoon dried basil, crushed
1/4	to 1/2 teaspoon pepper
1/2	teaspoon snipped fresh thyme or 1/8 teaspoon dried thyme, crushed
1	to 2 tablespoons snipped parsley

In a 6-quart Dutch oven or stockpot, combine chicken broth, onion, celery, carrots, and garlic. Bring to boiling; reduce heat. Simmer, uncovered, for 20 minutes. Add chicken, tomatoes, noodles, basil, pepper, and thyme. Simmer about 8 minutes more or until noodles are tender. Garnish with parsley. Makes 6 to 8 main-dish servings.

Curried Chicken Soup with Wild Rice

1	6-pound stewing chicken, cut up, or 3 pounds chicken breasts
5	cups water
1	cup chopped onion
1	tablespoon snipped fresh marjoram or 1 teaspoon dried marjoram, crushed
1	tablespoon snipped fresh sage or 1 teaspoon dried sage, crushed
1	teaspoon garlic powder
1	cup uncooked wild rice
1/2	cup butter or margarine
1/2	cup all-purpose flour
1	quart light cream
1	to 2 tablespoons curry powder
1/2	to 1 teaspoon ground coriander seed
4	dashes hot pepper sauce
	Pinch ground mace
	Salt and pepper to taste
1/2	cup dry sherry
	Lemon wedges

In a 6-quart Dutch oven or stockpot, combine chicken, water, onion, marjoram, sage, and garlic powder. Cover and bring to boiling. Reduce heat; simmer 2 to 2 1/2 hours for stewing chicken or about 1 hour for chicken breasts or until tender. Remove chicken to cool. Remove meat from bones; coarsely chop chicken. Boil remaining broth, uncovered, until reduced to 2 1/2 cups.

Meanwhile, rinse wild rice. In a 1 1/2-quart saucepan, cook rice in 2 cups boiling water about 40 minutes or until tender. Drain, if necessary.

For roux, in an 8-inch skillet, melt butter or margarine. Stir in flour until well combined. Cook and stir over medium-low heat for 10 minutes or until light brown. Whisk roux into hot broth until well blended. Stir in cream, curry powder, coriander, hot pepper sauce, mace, salt, pepper, chopped chicken, and wild rice. Simmer 5 minutes. Stir in sherry; simmer 2 minutes more. Serve with lemon wedges. Makes 10 to 12 main-dish servings.

Sausage and Duck Gumbo

2 pounds smoked sausage
8 wild or domestic medium ducks
3 stalks celery
1 medium onion, cut up
1/3 cup snipped parsley
1 bay leaf
1/2 cup cooking oil
1 cup all-purpose flour
2 cups chopped onion
2 cups chopped celery
2 cups chopped green pepper
2 10-ounce packages frozen cut okra, thawed
1 tablespoon Worcestershire sauce
2 teaspoons pepper
1/2 teaspoon dried thyme, crushed
Ground red pepper to taste
Hot pepper sauce to taste
Hot cooked rice

In a 10-inch skillet, cook sausage until lightly browned on all sides. Cut into bite-size pieces; set aside. In a 16-quart stockpot, combine ducks, celery stalks, cut-up onion, parsley, and bay leaf. Add enough water to cover (about 6 quarts). Bring to boiling; reduce heat. Cover and simmer about 1 1/2 hours or until ducks are tender. Remove ducks; strain and reserve **4 quarts** of the broth. Discard vegetables. Remove duck meat from bones. Cut meat into bite-size pieces; set aside.

For roux, in the same stockpot, heat oil over medium heat. Stir in flour. Cook and stir about 15 minutes or until roux is dark reddish brown. Slowly stir in chopped onion, chopped celery, green pepper, okra, Worcestershire sauce, pepper, and thyme. Cook and stir until vegetables are tender.

Add reserved 4 quarts duck broth, the duck meat, and sausage. Bring to boiling; reduce heat. Simmer, uncovered, for 3 hours. Season to taste with ground red pepper and hot pepper sauce. Serve over hot cooked rice. Makes about 20 main-dish servings.

Blissful Bisque

1/2 cup butter or margarine
1 medium onion, finely chopped
1 medium carrot, finely chopped
2 tablespoons all-purpose flour
1 teaspoon seafood seasoning
1/4 teaspoon celery salt
1/8 teaspoon white pepper
1 quart light cream or milk
8 to 16 ounces lump crabmeat, cartilage removed
3 tablespoons dry white wine
1 tablespoon snipped parsley
Salt to taste
Ground red pepper

In a 3-quart saucepan, melt butter or margarine. Add onion and carrot and cook until tender. Stir in flour, seafood seasoning, celery salt, and white pepper. Gradually add cream, stirring constantly. Stir in crabmeat, wine, parsley, and salt. Simmer 15 to 20 minutes. Do not boil. Sprinkle each serving with ground red pepper. Serve hot. Makes 6 side-dish servings.

Fancy Pants Soup

Shrimp and artichokes make this an elegant choice when company's coming.

¹/₄ cup butter or margarine
1 cup chopped celery
1 cup chopped carrots
¹/₂ cup sliced green onion
1 clove garlic, minced
1 teaspoon instant chicken bouillon granules
Dash hot pepper sauce
¹/₂ cup all-purpose flour
1 tablespoon cornstarch
1 cup heavy cream
1 quart chicken broth
1 cup tomato puree
1 14-ounce can artichoke hearts, drained and chopped
¹/₄ cup brandy
3 tablespoons snipped parsley
1 pound chopped cooked shrimp

In a 4-quart Dutch oven, melt butter or margarine. Add celery, carrots, green onion, garlic, bouillon granules, and hot pepper sauce. Cook until vegetables are tender. In a small bowl, stir flour and cornstarch into cream until well combined; stir cream mixture into vegetable mixture. Stir in chicken broth, tomato puree, artichoke hearts, brandy, and parsley. Bring to boiling; reduce heat. Simmer for 15 minutes. Stir in shrimp; heat through. Makes 6 side-dish servings.

◆ ◆ ◆

CROUTONS
—

*Cheese-laden croutons
can turn ordinary bowls of soup
into a first-class main course.
It's this simple:*

*Cut a 16-ounce loaf
of **French bread** into ³/₄-inch
cubes. In a 1-quart saucepan,
melt ³/₄ cup **butter or margarine**
over low heat. Stir in 1 cup
shredded **sharp cheddar or
Swiss cheese** and 2 tablespoons
milk until cheese melts.
Remove from heat. Beat 2 **egg
whites** until stiff peaks form.
Fold them into the
cheese mixture.*

*Dip the bread cubes
into the cheese mixture. Place
on a baking sheet and bake in a
350° oven about 10 minutes or
until golden. Float the croutons
in individual bowls of soup.*

◆ ◆ ◆

Spinach and Oyster Soup

2 pounds fresh spinach leaves or 3 10-ounce packages frozen chopped spinach
¹/₂ cup butter or margarine
¹/₂ cup chopped onion
2 cloves garlic, minced
¹/₂ cup all-purpose flour
2¹/₂ pints shucked oysters
6 cups heavy cream
2 cups chicken broth
Salt and pepper to taste

Wash fresh spinach leaves; remove stems. Cook, covered, in a small amount of boiling salted water for 3 to 5 minutes or until tender. (Or, cook frozen spinach according to package directions.) Drain and set aside.

In a 4-quart Dutch oven, melt butter or margarine. Add onion and garlic; cook until tender. Stir in flour until well combined. Add oysters, cream, chicken broth, and cooked spinach. Bring just to boiling; reduce heat. Cook until heated through. Makes 8 to 10 side-dish servings.

Southern Corn Chowder

Photograph on page 51.

1 pound bacon
1 large onion, thinly sliced
8 to 10 medium ears of corn or 1 16-ounce package frozen whole kernel corn
4 cups chicken broth
1 medium potato, cubed
1 or 2 carrots, shredded
$^1/_4$ cup all-purpose flour
$1^1/_2$ cups milk
$1^1/_2$ cups light cream or milk
1 tablespoon lemon juice
3 or 4 dashes hot pepper sauce
Salt and pepper to taste
Instant mashed potato flakes
Fresh bay leaves

Cook bacon until crisp. Drain, reserving drippings. Crumble bacon and set aside. In a 6-quart Dutch oven or stockpot, cook onion in **3 tablespoons** of the bacon drippings. Drain.

If using fresh corn, use a sharp knife to slice just the kernel tops from the ears of corn, then scrape the cobs with the dull edge of the knife. Add the corn, chicken broth, potato, and carrot to the onion in Dutch oven. Bring to boil. Boil 10 minutes or until potato is tender.

For roux, pour enough of the bacon drippings into a 10-inch skillet to reach $^1/_4$ inch. Stir in flour until smooth. Cook and stir over medium-low heat for 10 minutes or until roux is light brown.

Add milk and cream to vegetables in Dutch oven. Heat through. Stir in lemon juice, hot pepper sauce, salt, and pepper. Whisk the roux into the vegetable mixture. Stir in the crumbled bacon. Simmer until thickened and heated through. If desired, add instant potato flakes, 2 tablespoons at a time, until soup is desired consistency. Garnish with fresh bay leaves. Makes 8 to 10 side-dish servings.

Armenian Lemon Soup

Kallen uses the juice of two large lemons to make this soup. Adjust the level of lemon to suit your taste.

6 cups chicken broth
5 tablespoons long grain rice
Salt to taste
3 eggs
$^1/_2$ cup fresh lemon juice
Snipped parsley

In a 3-quart saucepan, bring broth to boiling. Add rice and salt. Cook over medium-low heat about 15 minutes or until rice is tender.

Reduce heat to low. In a medium bowl, beat eggs until light and frothy. Slowly pour lemon juice into eggs, beating constantly until well mixed. Ladle about $1^1/_2$ cups of the hot broth very slowly into egg mixture, stirring constantly. (Ladle enough hot broth to make the egg mixture warm.) Slowly add the warm egg mixture to the remaining broth in the saucepan. Simmer over low heat for 1 to 2 minutes or until heated through. Do not boil. Garnish with snipped parsley. Serve immediately. Makes 6 to 8 side-dish servings.

♦ ♦ ♦

CREAM OF ANY VEGETABLE SOUP
—

Do not despair if you need soup in a hurry and there is no familiar red and white can in the pantry. Soup is always at your fingertips with this easy formula. It uses no special ingredients and can even be a second life for last night's veggies!

• *Cook in 3 tablespoons butter or margarine until crisp-tender:*
2 to 3 cups chopped vegetable of your choice ($1^1/_2$ pounds)
1 cup chopped onion
• *Add and cook until vegetables are tender:*
1 quart chicken broth
3 tablespoons quick-cooking rice
• *Puree in blender or food processor.*
• *Add and heat through:*
1 cup light cream
Seasonings to taste, including salt and white pepper

Suggested seasonings or toppings:
Broccoli—thyme, shredded cheese
Spinach—nutmeg, pernod, or dry vermouth
Carrot—hot pepper sauce, curry powder, or dillweed
Potato—dillweed, leeks, chives, crumbled bacon, cheese
Green beans—savory, basil, or marjoram

♦ ♦ ♦

♦ ♦ ♦

KALLEN'S QUICK FIX
—

"This soup is fabulous when you have a cold. It's quick and very easy to make. I make it a lot when coming in from rehearsals. I'm tired and this really fits the bill. It was taught to my mother by my father's sisters, Rose and Charlotte."

—Kallen Esperian

♦ ♦ ♦

Tomato Dill Soup

2   tablespoons butter or margarine
2   large stalks celery, chopped
2   small carrots, grated
$^1/_4$ cup chopped onion
2   cloves garlic, minced
1   16-ounce can whole tomatoes
2   cups chicken broth
1   $10^1/_2$-ounce can beef consommé
1   8-ounce can tomato sauce
$1^1/_2$ cups diced fully-cooked ham (8 ounces)
3   tablespoons fresh lemon juice
3   bay leaves
1   teaspoon dry mustard
$^1/_2$ teaspoon ground allspice
$^1/_8$ teaspoon sugar
    Garlic salt, seasoned salt, and white pepper to taste
$^1/_2$ cup dairy sour cream
    Snipped fresh dill

In a 3-quart saucepan, melt butter or margarine. Add celery, carrots, onion, and garlic; cook until tender. Add **undrained** tomatoes, chicken broth, beef consommé, tomato sauce, ham, lemon juice, bay leaves, dry mustard, allspice, sugar, garlic salt, seasoned salt, and white pepper. Bring to boiling; reduce heat. Cover and simmer for 2 hours. To serve, ladle into individual bowls. Dollop with sour cream and sprinkle with dill. Makes 6 side-dish servings.

Lightside Potato Soup

This is one comfort food that won't attack your waistline.

4   to 6 large baking potatoes, peeled and cubed
$^1/_2$ cup shredded or sliced carrots
6   cups chicken broth, divided
$1^1/_2$ cups chopped celery
1   cup finely chopped onion
2   tablespoons cooking oil
$1^1/_2$ cups skim milk
2   tablespoons lowfat dairy sour cream
2   tablespoons reduced-calorie margarine
1   tablespoon white wine Worcestershire sauce
2   to 3 tablespoons fresh lemon juice
6   to 10 drops hot pepper sauce
    Salt and pepper to taste
2   to 3 tablespoons instant mashed potato flakes
    Dillweed

In a 6-quart Dutch oven or stockpot, cook potatoes and carrots, covered, in **4 cups** of the chicken broth for 15 to 20 minutes or until tender. Mash **half** of the potatoes and carrots.
    Meanwhile, in a 10-inch skillet, cook celery and onion in cooking oil until tender. Add to potatoes in saucepan. Stir in remaining 2 cups chicken broth, the skim milk, sour cream, margarine, Worcestershire sauce, lemon juice, hot pepper sauce, salt, and pepper. Cook over low heat for 10 minutes. If desired, add potato flakes, 1 tablespoon at a time, until soup is desired consistency. Serve hot or cold. Garnish with dillweed. Makes 4 to 6 side-dish servings.

♦ ♦ ♦

BASIC CHICKEN BROTH
—

When a recipe calls for chicken broth, there are several options open to you. For convenience, use canned ready-to-use chicken broth or add water as directed to condensed broth, instant bouillon granules, or cubes. If you're going for optimum flavor and freshness, make your own.

Cook up a big batch of chicken broth, then freeze in 1- or 2- cup handy portions. The cooked chicken will come in handy for making that Southern kitchen staple, chicken salad.

*In a large stockpot, combine two 3-pound **broiler-fryer chickens**, the **giblets**, 2 medium **carrots**, 2 stalks **celery**, 1 large **parsnip**, and 1 cup chopped **onion**. Using cooking twine, tie together 2 **celery tops**, 3 sprigs **parsley**, and 1 **leek**; add to stockpot. Add enough **cold water** to cover the chicken and vegetables (about 12 cups). Bring to boiling; skim off foam. Add 2 tablespoons **salt** and 12 **black peppercorns**. Reduce heat. Simmer for 1 to $1^1/_2$ hours or until meat falls off the bone. Remove meat and bones from the broth; save meat for another use. Discard tied vegetables. Strain broth through cheesecloth. Makes about 10 cups of broth.*

♦ ♦ ♦

Southern Comforter Potato Soup

6 medium potatoes, peeled and chopped (2 pounds)
1 medium carrot, finely chopped
3 14¹/₂-ounce cans chicken broth
4 slices bacon
2 tablespoons butter or margarine
3 stalks celery, chopped
1 large onion, chopped
2¹/₂ cups light cream
Salt and pepper to taste
Shredded cheese and sliced green onion

In a 4-quart Dutch oven, cook potatoes and carrot in chicken broth for 15 to 20 minutes or until tender. Mash slightly in saucepan.

Meanwhile, in a 10-inch skillet, cook bacon until crisp. Remove bacon, reserving drippings in skillet. Crumble bacon and set aside. Add butter to drippings in skillet and cook celery and onion until tender. Transfer celery and onion to potato mixture in Dutch oven. Stir in cream, salt, and pepper. Cook and stir until heated through. Serve with crumbled bacon, shredded cheese, and green onion for topping. Makes 8 side-dish servings.

Cotton Row Cheese Soup

¹/₄ cup butter or margarine
¹/₂ cup chopped onion
¹/₂ cup grated carrot
¹/₂ cup finely chopped celery
¹/₄ cup all-purpose flour
4 cups milk
4 cups chicken broth
¹/₈ teaspoon baking soda
1 pound Old English cheese
Paprika
Croutons (see recipe, page 60)

In a 4-quart Dutch oven, melt butter or margarine. Add onion, carrot, and celery; cook until tender. Stir in flour until well combined. Stir in milk, chicken broth, and baking soda. Add cheese. Cook and stir over low heat until cheese is melted. Ladle into bowls. Sprinkle with paprika. Serve with Croutons. Makes 6 to 8 side-dish servings.

Cold Cucumber Soup

2 tablespoons butter or margarine
¹/₄ cup chopped onion
2 cups chopped unpeeled cucumber
2 cups chicken broth
¹/₂ cup finely chopped potato
1 tablespoon snipped parsley
¹/₂ to 1 teaspoon dillweed
¹/₂ teaspoon salt
¹/₄ teaspoon dry mustard
¹/₄ teaspoon freshly ground black pepper
1 cup heavy cream
   Snipped chives

In a 2-quart saucepan, melt butter or margarine. Add onion and cook until tender. Stir in cucumber, chicken broth, potato, parsley, dillweed, salt, dry mustard, and pepper. Bring to boiling; reduce heat. Simmer for 15 minutes or until potatoes are tender.

Transfer mixture to a blender container or food processor bowl. Cover and blend or process until smooth. Chill until serving time.

Before serving, stir in cream. Pour into chilled wine glasses. Garnish with snipped chives. Makes 4 side-dish servings.

NICE TO NOTE
—

When serving cold soups, don't forget that pewter Jefferson cups, cocktail glasses, and demitasse cups are ideal for individual portions and make it easy to serve a casual first course to guests who are still enjoying "happy hour."

Gazebo Gazpacho

1¹/₂ cups tomato juice or vegetable juice cocktail
2 medium tomatoes, peeled and finely chopped
¹/₂ cup finely chopped green pepper
¹/₂ cup finely chopped celery
¹/₂ cup finely chopped, seeded cucumber
¹/₄ cup finely chopped onion
¹/₄ cup snipped chives
2 tablespoons olive oil or cooking oil
2 tablespoons red wine vinegar
2 teaspoons snipped parsley
1 teaspoon salt
¹/₂ teaspoon Worcestershire sauce
¹/₄ teaspoon pepper
1 small clove garlic, minced
5 drops hot pepper sauce
   Dairy sour cream
   Snipped chives

In a medium bowl, combine all ingredients except sour cream. Cover and refrigerate several hours or overnight. Serve in chilled cups or bowls. Dollop each serving with sour cream and sprinkle with additional chives. Makes 4 side-dish servings.

Crab and Wild Rice Salad

1   6-ounce box long grain and wild rice
½   bunch broccoli (about 12 ounces)
½   cup sliced carrots
1   pound lump crabmeat, cartilage removed
8   fresh medium mushrooms, sliced
½   cup sliced zucchini
½   cup sliced yellow crookneck squash
½   cup chopped sweet red or green pepper
½   cup sliced green onions
½   cup sliced ripe olives
2   hard-cooked eggs, finely chopped
½   cup plain low-fat yogurt
½   cup calorie-reduced mayonnaise
    Lettuce leaves
    Tomato wedges

Cook rice according to package directions. Cut broccoli into flowerets. Cook broccoli and carrots in a small amount of boiling water for 5 minutes or until crisp-tender; drain.

In a large bowl, combine prepared rice, broccoli, carrots, crabmeat, mushrooms, zucchini, yellow squash, red pepper, onions, olives, and eggs. In a small bowl, stir together yogurt and mayonnaise. Pour over crabmeat mixture; toss lightly. Cover and chill.

To serve, mound mixture on a lettuce-lined platter. Garnish with tomato wedges. Makes 4 to 6 main-dish servings.

Gringo Chicken Salad

4   cups chopped cooked chicken
2   cups shredded sharp cheddar cheese (8 ounces)
1   16-ounce can kidney beans, drained
½   cup chopped onion
½   cup sliced ripe olives
½   cup chopped sweet red or green pepper
½   cup mayonnaise or salad dressing
½   cup low-fat dairy sour cream
1   teaspoon chili powder
½   teaspoon ground cumin
¼   teaspoon dried basil, crushed
    Salt and pepper to taste
    Shredded lettuce
2   medium avocados, seeded, peeled, and sliced
2   medium tomatoes, chopped
    Corn chips

In a large bowl, combine chicken, cheese, kidney beans, onion, olives, and red pepper. In a small bowl, stir together mayonnaise, sour cream, chili powder, cumin, basil, salt, and pepper. Stir into chicken mixture until coated. Cover and chill. Serve on a bed of shredded lettuce topped with avocado slices, chopped tomato, and corn chips. Makes 6 to 8 main-dish servings.

Chicken Cashew Salad

12	chicken breast halves, cooked
2	cups chopped celery
2	8-ounce cans sliced water chestnuts, drained
1	16-ounce can pineapple chunks, drained
¹/₂	cup snipped dates
2	cups mayonnaise or salad dressing
2	tablespoons soy sauce
2	teaspoons curry powder
2	cups whole cashews
	Lettuce, croissants, or pita bread

Remove chicken from bones. Cut chicken into bite-size pieces; chill. In a large bowl, combine celery, water chestnuts, pineapple chunks, dates, and chicken. Stir together mayonnaise, soy sauce, and curry powder. Add to chicken mixture and toss to coat. Cover and chill.

Just before serving, stir in cashews. Serve on a bed of lettuce, croissant, or in pita bread. Makes 12 main-dish servings.

Shrimp and Rigatoni Salad

2¹/₂	pounds fresh or frozen medium shrimp in shells
1	medium onion, quartered
1	lemon, quartered
1	stalk celery
2	teaspoons salt
¹/₂	teaspoon crushed red pepper
1	10-ounce bottle mustard-flavored sandwich and salad sauce
1	8-ounce bottle sweet French salad dressing
1	3-ounce bottle capers
5	small boiling onions, chopped
2	teaspoons lemon juice
1	teaspoon snipped parsley
4	whole cloves
3	bay leaves
¹/₄	teaspoon ground red pepper
8	ounces rigatoni, cooked and drained
1	14-ounce can hearts of palm, drained and sliced
	Salt and pepper to taste

Thaw shrimp, if frozen. In a 6-quart Dutch oven or stockpot, combine 3 quarts water, quartered onion, lemon, celery, salt, and crushed red pepper. Bring to boiling; boil for 10 minutes. Add shrimp; remove from heat. Let stand for 5 minutes. Drain shrimp and run under cold water. Discard vegetables and lemon. Peel and devein shrimp.

In a medium bowl, combine sandwich and salad sauce, sweet salad dressing, **undrained** capers, boiling onions, lemon juice, parsley, cloves, bay leaves, red pepper, and shrimp. Cover and refrigerate overnight. Before serving, remove cloves and bay leaves. Stir in pasta, hearts of palm, salt, and pepper. Makes 6 main-dish servings or 10 to 12 side-dish servings.

Jessica's Shrimp Salad

 3 pounds cooked and peeled shrimp, coarsely chopped
 2 hard-cooked eggs, chopped
 1 stalk celery, finely chopped
 1 large sweet pickle, finely chopped
 $^1/_4$ cup finely chopped vidalia or other sweet onion
 $1^1/_2$ cups mayonnaise or salad dressing
    Avocado slices, tomato wedges, hard-cooked egg wedges

In a large bowl, combine shrimp, chopped eggs, celery, sweet pickle, and onion. Add mayonnaise; toss lightly until coated. Cover and chill. Serve garnished with avocado slices, tomato wedges, and egg wedges. Makes 6 main-dish servings.

Henny Penny Pasta Salad

"In a dish such as this, you can always substitute. A friend of my mother's once shared a similar recipe with me and ended by saying, 'Just add anything good.' Shrimp would be good if you want to make it a little 'dressier.'"

 1 8-ounce package rotini pasta
 1 bunch broccoli (about $1^1/_2$ pounds)
 4 chicken breast halves, cooked
 $^1/_2$ cup chopped sweet red or green pepper
 $^1/_4$ cup sliced ripe olives
 1 tablespoon sliced green onion
 $^1/_2$ cup dairy sour cream
 $^1/_4$ cup mayonnaise or salad dressing
 3 tablespoons white wine vinegar
 2 tablespoons heavy cream
 $1^1/_2$ teaspoons sugar
 1 teaspoon salt
 1 teaspoon dried tarragon, crushed
 $^1/_4$ teaspoon pepper

Cook rotini according to package directions. Rinse under cold water; drain. Cut broccoli into flowerets; cook in a small amount of boiling water for 3 to 5 minutes or until crisp-tender. Drain. Remove chicken from bones; cut chicken into bite-size pieces. In a large bowl, combine pasta, broccoli, chicken, red pepper, ripe olives, and green onion. Toss lightly.

In a small bowl, stir together sour cream, mayonnaise, wine vinegar, cream, sugar, salt, tarragon, and pepper. Pour over pasta mixture and toss. Cover and chill. Makes 4 main-dish servings.

Servin' up JAZZ

KIRK WHALUM

KIRK WHALUM IS A SUPER-TALENTED JAZZ SAXOPHONIST WHO COMES FROM A WELL-KNOWN MEMPHIS FAMILY. HE IS A RHYTHM AND BLUES-BASED MUSICIAN WHOSE HITS INCLUDE "FLOPPY DISK," "AND YOU KNOW THAT," AND "THE PROMISE." WHALUM'S MUSIC HAS ACHIEVED CROSSOVER SUCCESS WITHOUT TURNING ITS BACK ON THOSE PURE JAZZ ROOTS. MEMPHIS TAKES PRIDE IN THE POPULARITY OF THIS HOMETOWN HORN ARTIST WHO IS KNOWN BY JAZZ FANS THE WORLD OVER.

Three-Layer Strawberry Salad

¹/₂ cup butter or margarine
1   cup crushed pretzels
1   cup plus 3 tablespoons sugar, divided
1   6-ounce package strawberry-flavored gelatin
2¹/₂ cups water, divided
1   10-ounce package frozen strawberries or 1¹/₂ cups sliced fresh strawberries
8   ounces cream cheese, softened
1   8-ounce container frozen whipped dessert topping, thawed

Preheat the oven to 350°. In a 1-quart saucepan, melt butter or margarine. Remove from heat and stir in crushed pretzels and **3 tablespoons** of the sugar. Press mixture evenly onto the bottom of a 13x9x2-inch baking dish. Bake for 10 minutes. Cool on a wire rack.

Meanwhile, in a small bowl, dissolve gelatin in **2 cups** boiling water. Stir in the remaining ¹/₂ cup cold water and frozen strawberries. Chill gelatin mixture until partially set.

In a large bowl, stir together the remaining 1 cup sugar and softened cream cheese. Fold in whipped topping. Spoon cream cheese mixture evenly onto the pretzel crust. Spoon gelatin mixture over cream cheese layer. Cover and chill for 2 hours. Cut into squares to serve. Makes 12 side-dish servings.

Frosty Summer Salad

2   cups dairy sour cream
³/₄ cup sugar
¹/₈ teaspoon salt
2   bananas, sliced
     Lemon juice
1   20-ounce can crushed pineapple, drained
¹/₄ cup pitted dark sweet cherries or maraschino cherries, cut into halves
¹/₄ cup chopped nuts

In a bowl, stir together sour cream, sugar, and salt until well mixed. Set aside. Place bananas in another bowl; sprinkle with lemon juice. Stir in drained pineapple, cherries, and nuts. Fold fruit mixture into sour cream mixture. Spoon into muffin pans lined with foil-lined paper bake cups or foil. Freeze until firm. Makes about 16 side-dish servings.

◆ ◆ ◆

SWEET TREAT

—

"I first made this frozen salad for a luncheon given to introduce a new Memphian. It was easy to do and looked beautiful. When the plates went back to the kitchen, I was pleased to notice that everyone finished their serving and I made a note to put the recipe in my permanent file. I was even more tickled when one of my guests asked if she might have a second helping instead of the dessert I had planned!"

◆ ◆ ◆

Artichoke Rice Salad

    2   6-ounce boxes chicken-flavored rice
  3/4   cup chopped green or sweet red pepper
   16   pimiento-stuffed olives, sliced
  1/2   cup sliced green onion
    2   6-ounce jars marinated artichoke hearts
  1/2   cup mayonnaise or salad dressing
    1   teaspoon curry powder

Cook rice according to package directions, omitting butter. Transfer to a large bowl; cool. Add green pepper, olives, and onions. Drain artichoke hearts, reserving liquid. Slice artichoke hearts and add to rice mixture. Mix reserved artichoke liquid, mayonnaise, and curry powder; pour over rice mixture. Toss well. Cover and chill. Makes 12 side-dish servings.

Summer Corn Salad

Photograph on page 168.

    4   cups cut fresh corn or 2 10-ounce packages frozen whole kernel corn
    1   cucumber, peeled and chopped
    1   large tomato, seeded and chopped
    1   purple onion, chopped
  1/2   cup chopped green pepper
  1/2   cup dairy sour cream
    3   tablespoons mayonnaise or salad dressing
    2   tablespoons white wine vinegar
    1   teaspoon salt
  1/2   teaspoon dry mustard
  1/2   teaspoon celery seed
  1/2   teaspoon pepper
        Assorted fresh mixed greens
        Sweet red pepper hearts

In a 2-quart saucepan, cook corn in a small amount of boiling water, covered, for 5 to 7 minutes or until crisp-tender. Drain and cool. In a large bowl, stir together cucumber, tomato, onion, green pepper, and corn.

In a small bowl, combine sour cream, mayonnaise, vinegar, salt, dry mustard, celery seed, and pepper. Spread over top of corn mixture. Cover and chill overnight. Before serving, toss lightly to coat vegetables. Garnish each serving with assorted mixed greens and sweet red pepper hearts. Makes 12 side-dish servings.

◆ ◆ ◆

B.C.
(BEFORE CHILDREN)
AT THE LAKE
—

"In the early years of our marriage my husband and I used to rendezvous with friends from college at Pickwick Lake for an annual 'Houseboat Weekend.' We'd get two big houseboats, tie them together in a secluded cove, and use them as 'home base' for a long weekend of skiing, jet-skiing, lazing in inner tubes, catching up on news, and enjoying the great food and drink brought by each couple.

Cold salads kept in the houseboat refrigerator were always a hit at our large, lively meals, although certain members of the party seemed to be munching at the refrigerator door every time I turned around! Summer corn salad reminds me of those carefree, childless weekends."

◆ ◆ ◆

Marinated Asparagus with Pecans

2 pounds fresh asparagus spears or 3 10-ounce packages frozen asparagus spears
¼ cup sugar
¼ cup white vinegar
¼ cup soy sauce
2 tablespoons cooking oil
¼ cup finely chopped pecans
Lettuce leaves

Snap off and discard tough ends from fresh asparagus. If desired, scrape off scales. Micro-cook in a 13x9x2-inch baking dish with 2 tablespoons **water** on high power for 5 to 7 minutes or until crisp-tender and bright green, rearranging once, or cook, covered, in a small amount of boiling water for 6 to 8 minutes or until crisp-tender. (Or, cook frozen asparagus according to package directions.) Drain; rinse in cold water.

Arrange cooked asparagus in the same 13x9x2-inch baking dish. For marinade, in a small bowl, combine sugar, vinegar, soy sauce, and oil. Stir in pecans. Pour pecan mixture over asparagus. Cover and chill at least 8 hours. To serve, drain asparagus; place on a lettuce leaf-lined platter, drizzling with additional marinade. Makes 6 to 8 servings.

R&B Servin' up

OTIS REDDING

OTIS REDDING CAME TO STAX IN 1962 AND BEGAN TO ROLL WITH THE HITS, WHICH INCLUDED "THESE ARMS OF MINE" AND "TRY A LITTLE TENDERNESS." A HUGE SENSATION OVERSEAS AND AT HOME, REDDING IS PERHAPS MOST FAMOUS FOR "(SITTING ON) THE DOCK OF THE BAY," WHICH HE RECORDED WITH MEMPHIS' OWN BAR-KAYS, JUST THREE DAYS BEFORE HE AND THIS RISING YOUNG BAND WERE KILLED IN A TRAGIC PLANE CRASH.

Roasted Pepper Salad

Make this impressive salad up to a day in advance and refrigerate. Be sure to bring it to room temperature before serving.

2 large green peppers
2 large sweet red peppers
2 large sweet yellow peppers
2 to 4 tablespoons snipped fresh basil or 2 to 4 teaspoons dried basil, crushed
2 tablespoons red wine vinegar
1 or 2 cloves garlic, minced
Salt and freshly ground pepper to taste
6 tablespoons olive oil
Lettuce leaves

Preheat the broiler. Place peppers on a broiler pan 4 inches from heat. Broil, turning often, until charred on all sides. Place in a plastic or paper bag. Close bag tightly. Let stand for 10 minutes. Peel and seed peppers. Cut into ¼-inch-wide strips and place in a medium bowl.

For dressing, in a small bowl combine basil, vinegar, garlic, salt, and pepper. Add olive oil in a steady stream, whisking until blended. Add to peppers; stir well. Let stand for 1 hour before serving. Serve at room temperature over lettuce leaves. Makes 6 to 8 side-dish servings.

Onion Salad

¹/₂ cup water
¹/₂ cup vinegar
¹/₂ cup sugar
1 teaspoon salt
3 or 4 vidalia or mild sweet onions, thinly sliced
¹/₂ cup mayonnaise or salad dressing
1 teaspoon celery seed
3 or 4 tomatoes, cut into thick slices

In a medium bowl, combine water, vinegar, sugar, and salt. Add onions. Cover and soak onions in vinegar mixture in refrigerator for 1 to 4 hours. Drain very well. Stir together mayonnaise and celery seed; add to onion mixture and toss. Serve salad on platter surrounded by tomato slices. Makes 4 to 6 side-dish servings.

Broccoli with a Twist

You'll need the flowerets from two bunches of fresh broccoli for this salad.

1¹/₂ cups mayonnaise or salad dressing
³/₄ cup sugar
2 tablespoons cider vinegar
1 tablespoon lemon juice
5 cups broccoli flowerets
¹/₂ cup raisins
¹/₂ cup chopped pecans, toasted
¹/₂ cup chopped red onion
12 slices bacon, cooked crisp and crumbled

In a small bowl, combine mayonnaise, sugar, vinegar, and lemon juice. Mix well. Cover and chill at least 2 hours.

Place broccoli flowerets in a large bowl. Add raisins, pecans, onion, and bacon. Stir gently to mix. Add mayonnaise mixture; toss lightly to coat. Serve immediately or cover and chill until serving time. Makes 6 side-dish servings.

◆ ◆ ◆

SHOWER SALAD
—

"A dear friend of my mother's gave this recipe to me as part of a kitchen shower gift before my wedding. As the giver was, and is, one of my favorite people, it was among the first things I attempted in my own kitchen and I was thrilled with the result! It remains a favorite summertime dish, made with Vidalia onions and fresh juicy tomato slices. It is a perfect complement to my husband's equally good hamburgers hot off the grill."

◆ ◆ ◆

Garden Glory Salad

1   bunch broccoli (about 1¹/₂ pounds)
1   head cauliflower (about 2 pounds)
1   pound fresh asparagus
    Red and/or green leaf lettuce
4   medium tomatoes, cut into wedges
8   ounces fresh mushrooms
1   green pepper, cut into rings
1   medium zucchini, cut into long strips
1   small red onion, cut into rings
1   avocado, peeled, seeded, and sliced
    Crumbled feta or blue cheese
2   hard-cooked eggs, sliced
1   16-ounce can large pitted ripe olives, drained
1   16-ounce bottle Italian salad dressing

Cut broccoli and cauliflower into flowerets. Cook flowerets and asparagus in a small amount of boiling water about 5 minutes or until crisp-tender. Drain and chill.

Line a large platter with leaf lettuce. Beginning with cooked vegetables, arrange all vegetables in a large mound on platter. Sprinkle with desired amount of cheese. Garnish with egg slices and olives. Pour **half** of the salad dressing over top. Let stand for 10 minutes. Serve with tongs. Pass additional dressing. Makes 8 to 10 side-dish servings.

Tootie's Potato Salad

Definitely best after 24 hours in the refrigerator.

2¹/₂   pounds potatoes
¹/₄   cup snipped parsley
2   hard-cooked eggs, chopped
5   sweet pickles, finely chopped
¹/₄   cup finely chopped onion
¹/₄   cup finely chopped celery
1   cup mayonnaise or salad dressing
¹/₃   cup evaporated milk
        Salt and pepper to taste

In a 6-quart Dutch oven or stockpot, cook potatoes in boiling water for 20 to 25 minutes or just until tender. Drain well. Peel and cut into large cubes. In a large bowl, combine potato cubes, parsley, eggs, pickles, onion, and celery.

In a small bowl, combine mayonnaise, evaporated milk, salt, and pepper. Stir until well mixed. Pour over potato mixture. Toss well. Cover and chill. Serve cold. Makes 15 side-dish servings.

◆ ◆ ◆

PLAYING FAVORITES
—

"My grandmother was fiercely proud of her potato salad which she made with sweet pickle, onion, and a little milk to smooth it out. Mother wasn't one for confrontations, but secretly preferred hers with dill pickle and a bit of yellow mustard for extra 'bite.' I leave out the mustard and put lots of sliced green olives, celery, hard-cooked eggs, and my flavor secret — a little juice from the dill pickles. Potato salad is a standard hit but it has many formulas and a loyal fan club for each one!"

◆ ◆ ◆

Herbed Tomato and Sweet Pepper Salad

2 large sweet red or green peppers
8 medium tomatoes
1 small vidalia or mild sweet onion
$^1/_4$ cup olive oil
2 tablespoons red wine vinegar
1 tablespoon snipped fresh basil or 1 teaspoon dried basil, crushed
1 tablespoon snipped fresh mint or 1 teaspoon dried mint, crushed
1 tablespoon snipped fresh oregano or 1 teaspoon dried oregano, crushed
1 teaspoon capers
1 clove garlic, minced
Salt and freshly ground pepper to taste

To peel peppers, place on a broiler pan 4 inches from heat. Broil, turning often, until charred on all sides. Place peppers in a paper or plastic bag. Close bag tightly. Let stand 10 minutes. Peel and seed peppers. Cut into $^1/_4$-inch-wide strips. Place in a large bowl.

To peel tomatoes, plunge into boiling water for 30 seconds. Immediately dip into cold water. Using a knife, pull skin from tomato. Remove seeds. Cut tomatoes into strips. Add to peppers in bowl.

Slice onion; separate into rings. Add to tomato mixture in bowl. In a small bowl, mix olive oil and wine vinegar. Stir in basil, mint, oregano, capers, garlic, salt, and pepper until well blended. Pour over tomato mixture, tossing to coat. Cover and chill at least 2 hours. Serve cold or at room temperature. Makes 8 to 10 side-dish servings.

Tomato, Bacon, and Basil Salad

5 cups halved cherry tomatoes
6 slices lean bacon, cooked crisp and crumbled
$^1/_3$ cup snipped fresh basil
2 tablespoons red wine vinegar
2 teaspoons sugar
$^1/_2$ teaspoon dry mustard
1 small clove garlic, minced
Salt and pepper to taste
4 tablespoons extra virgin olive oil
Fresh basil sprigs

In a bowl, toss together tomatoes, bacon, and basil. For dressing, in a small bowl combine vinegar, sugar, dry mustard, garlic, salt, and pepper. Add olive oil in a steady stream, whisking until blended. Pour dressing over tomato mixture. Toss lightly. Garnish with additional fresh basil sprigs, if desired. Makes 6 side-dish servings.

Cauliflower Salad

8   cups cauliflower flowerets (2 medium heads)
2   cups shredded sharp cheddar cheese (8 ounces)
¼   cup sliced green onion
¼   teaspoon ground red pepper
      Salt and pepper to taste
      About 1 cup mayonnaise

Cook cauliflower in a small amount of boiling water for 8 to 10 minutes or until tender. Drain well. In a large bowl, combine cauliflower, cheese, onion, red pepper, salt, and pepper. Toss lightly. Add amount of mayonnaise for desired consistency. Toss well. Makes 8 to 10 side-dish servings.

Sunset Symphony Slaw

Perfect for a sunset picnic on the Mississippi River.

6   cups shredded cabbage
½   cup sliced green onion
½   cup chopped green pepper
½   cup chopped sweet red pepper
1   cup sugar
¾   cup cooking oil
½   cup cider vinegar
1   tablespoon salt
1½   teaspoons dried dillweed
1   teaspoon mustard seed
1   teaspoon celery seed

In a large bowl, combine cabbage, onion, green pepper, and red pepper. In a small bowl, stir together sugar, oil, vinegar, salt, dillweed, mustard seed, and celery seed until well blended. Pour over vegetables and toss lightly. Cover and chill. Makes 10 to 12 side-dish servings.

Scott Street Slaw

1   medium head cabbage
3   medium tomatoes
2   medium cucumbers
2   medium green peppers
1   bunch green onions
6   tablespoons mayonnaise or salad dressing
½   cup white wine vinegar
¼   cup sugar
⅛   teaspoon salt
⅛   teaspoon pepper

Cut up all vegetables into bite-size pieces. Toss together in a large bowl. Stir together mayonnaise, wine vinegar, sugar, salt, and pepper until smooth. Pour over vegetables and toss lightly. Makes 12 side-dish servings.

Dinner at Eight Salad

$^1/_2$ cup white wine vinegar
3 tablespoons minced onion
1 tablespoon Dijon-style mustard
$^1/_2$ teaspoon salt
$^1/_2$ teaspoon freshly cracked black peppercorns
$1^1/_2$ cups extra virgin olive oil or salad oil
5 cups mixed torn salad greens (Bibb, romaine, and leaf lettuce)
5 slices bacon, cooked crisp and crumbled
5 tablespoons freshly grated Parmesan cheese
$^1/_4$ cup finely chopped celery
1 cup croutons

For dressing, in a small bowl, combine vinegar, onion, mustard, salt, and cracked peppercorns. Add olive oil in a steady stream, whisking until blended.

In a salad bowl, combine salad greens, bacon, Parmesan cheese, and celery. Add croutons and toss. Drizzle **10 to 12 tablespoons** of the dressing over the salad and toss well. Divide salad among individual salad plates. Makes 4 side-dish servings.

Spinach Salad with Sweet Parsley Dressing

Jarlsberg, a currently popular Scandinavian Swiss cheese, lends a unique nutty flavor to this splendid salad.

$^1/_2$ cup sugar
$^1/_2$ cup white vinegar
2 tablespoons salad oil
1 tablespoon thinly sliced green onion
1 tablespoon snipped parsley
1 teaspoon Worcestershire sauce
1 teaspoon prepared mustard
    Cracked black pepper to taste
1 bunch spinach, torn into bite-size pieces (about 8 ounces)
6 slices bacon, cooked crisp and crumbled
$^1/_2$ cup shredded Jarlsberg cheese
$^1/_4$ cup chopped walnuts

In a screw-top jar, combine sugar, vinegar, oil, onion, parsley, Worcestershire sauce, mustard, and pepper. Cover and shake well. Chill for at least 1 hour.

In a salad bowl, combine spinach, bacon, cheese, and walnuts. Shake dressing and pour over salad. Toss lightly. Makes 6 side-dish servings.

♦ ♦ ♦

SUPPER CLUB
—

"There is a Southern tradition that brings food and friends together once a month that we call 'supper club.' It is an opportunity to try different recipes and taste new wines, catch up a little, and laugh a lot with some of our good friends. I got this recipe from a friend of mine in Louisiana and introduced it to my supper club a couple of years ago. Everyone raved about it and now I'm not allowed to come in the door without it!"

♦ ♦ ♦

Jerry Lee Lewis

"*Crazy Arms.*" "*Whole Lotta Shakin' Goin' On.*" "*Great Balls of Fire.*" It started with these crazy, shakin', fired up hits from Sam Phillips' Sun label, and it continues to this day: a four-gold-record trip through rock and roll stardom as wild as the traveler—Jerry Lee Lewis. His rockabilly piano has kept audiences jumping wherever the stage is big enough for Jerry Lee.

Born deep in rural Louisiana, he came to Memphis on egg money at the age of 21, bringing his "God-given talent" and his southern feel for country, blues, and gospel, pumped up with a boogie beat. He plays with a physical excitement and a stage confidence that leave no doubt—Jerry Lee Lewis is an absolute original, a real "*Killer!*"

Jerry's career was propelled from an unforgettable moment in Sun Studios in 1957 when a one-take, three-minute session produced "*Whole Lotta Shakin',*" a record that hit # 1 on the pop charts and sold over 20 million copies.

It kinda' leaves you "*Breathless.*"

BEVERAGES, BRUNCHES & BREADS

♦ ♦ ♦

BEVERAGES

♦ ♦ ♦

BRUNCHES

♦ ♦ ♦

BREADS

♦ ♦ ♦

PICTURED OVERLEAF

—

*Clockwise from bottom right:
Lila's Biscuits (page 103);
French Breakfast Cakes
(page 101); Elizabeth's
Orange Blossom Muffins
(page 102); and Mimosas
(page 90)*

♦ ♦ ♦

"WHAT CAN WE GET YOU TO DRINK?" BEVERAGES ARE THE FIRST offer of hospitality, a tangible sign of welcome to guests who come for a meal, or just a minute. The Southern seasons put icy drinks in demand for most of the year. Huge tumblers of iced tea, fruit juices and seltzers, and "spirited" concoctions help us cope with the high temperatures and humidity, and are a great excuse for sitting down to sip and chat with a friend. When the cool days do come, we offer hot teas and ciders, hot milks, and coffees. Whatever the weather—or the drink—beverages can lift and recharge us.

When breakfast and lunch came together for brunch, a favorite Southern social custom began. A brunch is a happy occasion given to celebrate a marriage or baptism, send loyal fans off to a big afternoon football game, or just to assemble a congenial group of friends. The day is fresh and the food is warm and inviting. The company is chatty and relaxed—and with these delicious, do-ahead recipes, the host and hostess can be, too!

Bread is the original comfort food. We all know its wonderful, yeasty satisfaction and think of it first when hunger gnaws. It never bores, for it takes many forms and under its name are a multitude of textures, tastes, and shapes. Crusty corn bread to grace a pot of stew, big flat biscuits, chewy French loaves, delicate yeasty luncheon rolls, bran muffins studded with raisins. Who has not tasted—and remembered—the pleasures of bread? ♥

◆ ◆ ◆

TRUE SOUTHERN ICED TEA A.K.A. "SWEET TEA"

—

True Southern Iced Tea, often referred to as Sweet Tea and pronounced by some waitresses as one word, is made "strong enough to stand alone" and sweetened while very hot, then cooled and served in large glasses. Sweetening while it's hot is very important, so as to avoid having a bitter or tasteless brew with a useless layer of undiluted sugar at the bottom of the glass. Sweet or not, all Southern restaurants serve iced tea (even the fancy ones!) and refills are usually free. There are some Southerners who wouldn't drink iced tea without a wedge of lemon and a sprig of mint, especially between April and October.

◆ ◆ ◆

Miss Betty's Iced Tea

*Miss Betty makes tea just the way her East Tennessee farm mother taught her as a child. Like lots of Southern women, she makes a fresh pot **every** day and the cooled tea sits on the stove all day so anyone who happens by can have a quick glass. There is **fresh** iced tea every evening at dinner. It never lasts over a day and to drink tea over 24 hours old would not do.*

3   quarts cold water
5   regular or 2 family-size tea bags
1   cup sugar or to taste
    Ice

In a 4-quart tea kettle or Dutch oven, bring water to a boil. Remove from heat. Add tea bags. Let stand, covered, for 15 minutes. Remove bags. While tea is hot, add sugar. Stir for 30 to 60 seconds or until sugar dissolves. Serve in tall glasses over ice. Makes 12 (8-ounce) servings.

Mint Tea

2 cups boiling water
3 family-size tea bags
2 sprigs fresh mint (10 to 12 leaves)
2 cups pineapple juice
1 cup orange juice
3/4 to 1 cup sugar
1/3 cup fresh lemon juice
    Water
    Fresh pineapple wedges
    Additional mint sprigs

In a 2¹/₂-quart glass pitcher or bowl, pour boiling water over tea bags and mint sprigs; let stand 5 minutes. Remove tea bags and mint. Stir in pineapple juice, orange juice, sugar, lemon juice, and enough water to make 2 quarts. Serve in tall glasses over ice garnished with a fresh pineapple wedge or additional mint sprigs. Makes 8 (8-ounce) servings.

Front Porch Tea

10 cups water, divided
1 cup sugar
2 cups boiling water
2 large family-size tea bags
1 12-ounce can frozen lemonade concentrate, thawed
1 tablespoon vanilla
1 tablespoon almond extract
    Fresh peach slices

To make sugar syrup, in a 1-quart saucepan, combine **2 cups** of the water and the sugar. Cook and stir until sugar dissolves. Set aside. In a 4-quart pitcher or bowl, pour the boiling water over the tea bags. Let stand 5 minutes. Remove tea bags. Add the remaining 8 cups water, the sugar syrup, lemonade concentrate, vanilla, and almond extract. Serve over ice. Garnish with fresh peach slices, if desired. Makes 14 (8-ounce) servings.

The Best Tea Punch

2 cups boiling water
1 family-size tea bag
3 tablespoons sugar
1¹/₂ cups apricot nectar
1 6-ounce can frozen lemonade concentrate, thawed
1 12-ounce can lemon-lime carbonated beverage, chilled
    Lemon slices

In a 2-quart glass pitcher or bowl, pour boiling water over tea bag; let stand 5 minutes. Remove tea bag. Stir in the sugar until dissolved. Stir in apricot nectar and lemonade concentrate. Just before serving, stir in carbonated beverage. Serve over ice. Garnish with lemon slices, if desired. Makes 6 (8-ounce) servings.

Coffee-Ice Cream Punch

A nice "brunch punch," especially on warmer days when hot coffee is not appealing.

1 quart vanilla ice cream
3 cups milk
1/4 cup sugar
1 teaspoon vanilla
3/4 teaspoon ground nutmeg
6 cups freshly brewed coffee, cooled
　 Coffee Ice Cubes
　 Whipped cream

Spoon ice cream by tablespoons into a punch bowl. Add milk, sugar, vanilla, and nutmeg; stir just until combined. Stir in cooled coffee and coffee ice cubes. Ladle into cups. Garnish with whipped cream and, if desired, additional ground nutmeg. Makes 24 (4-ounce) servings.
Coffee Ice Cubes: Pour 2 cups cooled strong coffee into ice cube tray. Freeze.

Poplar Punch

1 6-ounce can frozen orange juice concentrate, thawed
1 6-ounce can frozen lemonade concentrate, thawed
1 quart cranberry juice cocktail
1 quart ginger ale, chilled
1 orange, thinly sliced

Combine orange juice concentrate, lemonade concentrate, and cranberry juice cocktail. Chill. Just before serving, stir in ginger ale. Garnish with orange slices. Makes 12 (6-ounce) servings.

Mimosas

Photograph on page 85.

2 12-ounce cans frozen orange juice concentrate, divided
1 quart fresh strawberries or raspberries
1 750-milliliter bottle dry champagne, chilled

For orange juice and berry ice cubes, prepare **one** can orange juice concentrate according to directions; pour into ice cube trays. Slice strawberries. Place one strawberry slice or one whole raspberry in each section. Freeze overnight.
Just before serving, prepare remaining can of orange juice concentrate according to directions. Stir in champagne. Serve over prepared orange juice and berry ice cubes. Garnish with fresh mint sprigs. Makes about 12 (6-ounce) servings.

● ● ●

STORIES WITH PUNCH
—

"In the days when my husband was in medical training and I taught at a boys' school, I had a wonderful group of friends who were also teachers. We looked forward to the Christmas break when we always got together for a happy morning brunch to enjoy each others' company, trade classroom war stories, and celebrate the season. This punch was a favorite there and was a nice change from the hot "motor oil" brew we had in the teachers' lounge. It is refreshing, creamy good, and seemed to be the perfect accompaniment to our relaxed conversation, sprinkled throughout with laughter."

● ● ●

● ● ●

SNOW MILK
—

"On cold snowy days when I was a child, my younger brother and sister and I would come in from playing outside and my mother would make us "snow milk." It was my favorite drink, since I was allergic to hot chocolate. It was heated milk with sugar, vanilla, and nutmeg. It was such a treat and I always think of it on bitter winter days."

● ● ●

Honey Brunch Mimosas

No Southern brunch would be complete without these, honey bunch!

- 1   6-ounce can frozen lemonade concentrate
- 1/4 cup orange liqueur or frozen orange juice concentrate
- 1/4 cup honey, warmed
- 1   750-milliliter bottle dry champagne, chilled
     Fresh strawberries

In a pitcher, combine lemonade concentrate and orange liqueur or orange juice concentrate. Stir in honey until dissolved. Stir in champagne. Garnish with fresh strawberries, if desired. Makes 6 (6-ounce) servings.

Tequila Cider

And you thought traditional hot apple cider warmed your soul! Use fresh, unpasteurized apple cider, not apple juice, for the fullest flavor.

- 2   quarts fresh apple cider
- 1   cup tequila
- 1/3 cup orange liqueur
- 3   tablespoons fresh lemon juice
- 2   tablespoons sugar (optional)

In a large saucepan, stir together apple cider, tequila, orange liqueur, lemon juice, and, if desired, sugar. Heat over medium-low heat until hot. Serve in mugs. Makes 18 (4-ounce) servings.

Daddy's Bloody Marys

- 1/2   gallon gin
- 1/2   gallon vodka
- 12   46-ounce cans vegetable juice cocktail
- 2   cups lemon juice
- 2   to 4 tablespoons Worcestershire sauce
- 1   to 1 1/2 teaspoons hot pepper sauce
     Salt and pepper to taste
     Celery stalks

In a 6-gallon non-aluminum container, combine gin, vodka, vegetable juice cocktail, lemon juice, Worcestershire sauce, hot pepper sauce, salt, and pepper. Serve in glasses over ice. Garnish with celery stalks. Makes 175 (4-ounce) servings.

Note: For a smaller gathering, in a 2-quart pitcher, combine 1/3 cup gin, 1/3 cup vodka, 1 46-ounce can vegetable juice cocktail, 3 tablespoons lemon juice, 1 teaspoon Worcestershire sauce, 1/8 teaspoon hot pepper sauce, and salt and pepper to taste. Makes 15 (4-ounce) servings.

"Every Christmas Eve, approximately two hundred of my parents' friends drop in for their annual "Bloody Mary" party and share a little cheer to begin the countdown to Santa time. This was a wildly exciting time for me as a star-struck child and I can remember helping Daddy squeeze the lemons and stir the mix with the longest spoon I'd ever used. Then I held the funnel as he poured gallons of the spicy mix into bottle after bottle, ready for the grown-up crowd."

♦ ♦ ♦

Teddy's Toddies

2 cups sugar
1 cup water
3 cups rum
1 cup fresh lime juice
  Lime slices

In a 2-quart saucepan, combine sugar and water. Cook and stir over medium-low heat until sugar dissolves. Cool thoroughly.

Stir in rum and lime juice. Serve over ice. Garnish with lime slices. Makes 8 (6-ounce) servings.

Poinsettia

This is a wonderful Christmas party aperitif. To make individual Poinsettias, pour 1/3 cup champagne into each champagne glass. Add 1/3 cup cranberry juice cocktail and 1 tablespoon orange liqueur.

3 cups champagne, chilled
3 cups cranberry juice cocktail, chilled
1/2 cup orange liqueur

In a 2-quart pitcher, stir together champagne, cranberry juice cocktail, and orange liqueur. Pour into champagne glasses. If desired, drop a few fresh cranberries into each glass. Makes 8 (6-ounce) servings.

Yuletide's Best Eggnog

Fabulous...quite unlike anything you'll get out of a carton.

1 quart milk
6 inches stick cinnamon
6 whole cloves
1 teaspoon vanilla
1/4 teaspoon salt
12 egg yolks
1 1/2 cups sugar
1 cup dark rum
1 cup brandy
1 quart light cream
  Freshly grated nutmeg

In a saucepan, combine milk, cinnamon, cloves, vanilla, and salt. Cook and stir over low heat for 5 minutes. In a large bowl, beat together egg yolks and sugar with a whisk. Gradually stir hot milk mixture into egg yolk mixture. Return entire mixture to saucepan. Cook over medium heat stirring constantly for 2 to 3 minutes or until slightly thickened. **Do not boil.** Cool to room temperature.

Remove stick cinnamon and cloves. (If mixture has curdled, blend 3 to 4 cups at a time in a blender container until smooth before adding rum and brandy.) Stir in rum, brandy, light cream, and nutmeg to taste. Chill several hours or up to 2 days. To serve, pour into glasses and sprinkle with additional nutmeg. Makes 24 (4-ounce) servings.

Poppy Seed-Ham Biscuits

These little biscuits with tender, savory ham filling are right at home with a Bloody Mary, a bowl of soup, or a crisp green salad.

²/₃ cup butter or margarine, softened
¹/₄ cup finely chopped onion
1 tablespoon poppy seed
2¹/₂ teaspoons Dijon-style mustard
4¹/₂ dozen biscuits or tiny, soft party rolls
1 pound shaved country or honey-baked ham

In a small bowl, stir together butter, onion, poppy seed, and mustard until smooth. Cover and refrigerate 24 hours to blend flavors.

Preheat the oven to 350°. Return butter mixture to room temperature to soften. Halve biscuits horizontally. Spread each biscuit bottom with butter mixture. For each serving, place a piece of ham on buttered biscuit bottom; cover with biscuit top. Place biscuits in shallow baking pans. Cover with foil and bake about 10 minutes or just until warm. Makes 4¹/₂ dozen.

Crab-Topped English Muffins

3 to 4 tablespoons butter or margarine
6 English muffins, split
8 ounces cream cheese, softened
1 8-ounce can water chestnuts, drained and finely chopped
4 sliced green onions
2 teaspoons Dijon-style mustard
¹/₂ teaspoon bottled hot pepper sauce
2 eggs, separated
¹/₂ teaspoon salt
¹/₂ teaspoon pepper
2 6-ounce cans crabmeat, drained, flaked, and cartilage removed
1 teaspoon fresh lemon juice
Paprika
Parsley sprigs

Preheat the broiler. Butter each English muffin half. Place on shallow baking sheet and broil until light brown. In a medium bowl, stir together cream cheese, water chestnuts, onions, mustard, hot pepper sauce, egg yolks, salt, and pepper until well combined. Sprinkle crabmeat with lemon juice; fold into cream cheese mixture.

Beat egg whites until stiff peaks form; gently fold into crabmeat mixture. Mound slightly onto toasted English muffins. Broil until golden brown. Sprinkle with paprika. Garnish with parsley sprigs, if desired. Serve immediately. Makes 6 servings.

Honeycomb Egg Casserole

When served, this dish reveals a beautiful puffy texture.

2 cups shredded cheddar cheese (8 ounces)
1 pound bulk pork sausage
6 cups sliced fresh mushrooms (1 pound)
8 eggs
　 Hollandaise Sauce (see recipe, page 82)

Preheat the oven to 375°. Butter a 2-quart casserole. Line with shredded cheese. In a skillet, cook sausage; drain, reserving **2 tablespoons** drippings. Spread cooked sausage over shredded cheese. Cook mushrooms in reserved drippings until tender; drain. Spread mushrooms over sausage. Beat eggs well; pour over mushrooms.

Place baking dish in a larger baking pan on oven rack. Pour boiling water into pan around baking dish to a depth of 1 inch. Bake for 35 to 40 minutes or until puffed and golden. Serve with Hollandaise Sauce. Makes 6 to 8 servings.

Rockin' Rellenos

4 4-ounce cans diced mild or hot green chili peppers, drained
1 cup shredded sharp cheddar cheese (4 ounces)
1 cup shredded Monterey Jack cheese (4 ounces)
2 cups evaporated milk
4 eggs
1/3 cup all-purpose flour
1 teaspoon salt
2 large avocados, seeded, peeled, and sliced

Preheat the oven to 350°. In a greased 12x7¹/₂x2-inch baking dish, layer chili peppers, cheddar cheese, and Monterey Jack cheese. In a blender container, combine evaporated milk, eggs, flour, and salt. Cover and blend until well combined. Pour over chili peppers and cheese. Bake about 45 minutes or until a knife inserted near center comes out clean. Before serving, top with avocado slices. Makes 6 to 8 servings.

Hot Cheese Pudding

16 slices firm-textured white bread
    Butter or margarine
4   cups shredded Monterey Jack or Muenster cheese (1 pound)
4   shallots, minced
5   eggs
1   tablespoon Dijon-style mustard
3   cups milk
1   teaspoon salt
1/4 teaspoon ground red pepper
1/3 cup freshly grated Parmesan cheese
1/4 cup fresh dry bread crumbs
2   tablespoons butter or margarine, cut up

Spread one side of each slice of bread with butter or margarine. In the bottom of a buttered 13x9x2-inch baking dish, place **eight** of the bread slices. Sprinkle with **half** of the Monterey Jack cheese and **half** of the shallots. Repeat layers with remaining bread, Monterey Jack cheese, and shallots.

In a large bowl, beat together eggs and mustard until well blended. Beat in milk, salt, and red pepper. Slowly pour egg mixture over bread layers. Let stand at room temperature for 30 minutes or in the refrigerator overnight.

Preheat the oven to 350°. Combine Parmesan cheese and bread crumbs. Sprinkle over bread mixture. Dot with butter. Bake for 50 to 60 minutes or until knife inserted near center comes out clean. Makes 10 to 12 servings.

Grandma's Breakfast Bread Pudding

1   loaf day-old wheat bread
3   eggs
4   cups sugar
2 1/2 cups milk
1   teaspoon vanilla
1/4 cup butter or margarine
1/4 cup whiskey

Tear stale bread into small pieces. Fill a shallow bowl with water. Dip bread pieces in water until saturated; squeeze water out of each to form a ball. Place balls in a 13x9x2-inch baking dish. In a large bowl, beat together eggs and sugar. Add milk and vanilla and mix well.

Preheat the oven to 350°. In a 3-quart saucepan, melt butter. Stir in sugar mixture and whiskey. Bring to a boil, stirring constantly. Remove from heat; pour over bread in baking dish. Bake for 1 1/2 hours. Makes 12 to 15 servings.

♦ ♦ ♦

BREAD PUDDING FOR BREAKFAST

—

"Part of our Christmas tradition comes from my Aunt Bea who lives in New Orleans. She has a wonderful bread pudding which we look forward to having every Christmas morning. First, we all gather at Mum and Dad's house to exchange gifts. Then, we have our favorite sit-down breakfast starring the bread pudding. It is always lovingly prepared by my grandmother who has had to double the size of the recipe over the years due to the happy growth of our family!"

♦ ♦ ♦

Martha's "Meant To Be" Cheese Danish

When families turn to each other for help, sometimes it's the younger generation that gives. "Martha" is a loving daughter who shared this recipe long-distance with a mother hastily planning a bridge brunch. They're so good they were just "meant to be!"

2	packages (8 rolls each) refrigerated crescent rolls
16	ounces cream cheese, softened
1½	cups sugar, divided
1	egg
1	teaspoon vanilla
½	cup butter or margarine, melted
1	teaspoon ground cinnamon
1	cup chopped pecans

Preheat the oven to 350°. Grease a 13x9x2-inch baking dish. Unroll one can of crescent rolls and press into bottom of dish, pressing perforations together to form a flat sheet of dough. Ease edges of dough slightly up sides of dish. Combine cream cheese, **1 cup** of the sugar, the egg, and vanilla. Spread over crescent roll dough. Unroll remaining can of crescent rolls and place over cream cheese mixture, pinching perforations together. Press edges together to seal.

Combine melted butter, remaining ½ cup sugar, the cinnamon, and pecans. Spread evenly over top layer of crescent roll dough. Bake about 30 minutes or until golden. To serve, cut into rectangles. Makes 16 servings.

Orange Muffins

3	oranges
3	cups all-purpose flour
1	teaspoon baking soda
1	teaspoon baking powder
1	cup butter or margarine
1¾	cups sugar, divided
1	teaspoon vanilla
2	eggs
¾	cup buttermilk
½	cup raisins, finely chopped
¼	cup light corn syrup

Grate peel from **two** of the oranges. Squeeze juice from **all** of the oranges. (You should have **3 tablespoons** peel and ¾ cup juice.) Set peel and juice aside. In a medium bowl, stir together flour, baking soda, and baking powder; set aside.

Preheat the oven to 375°. In a large bowl, beat butter or margarine with an electric mixer until softened. Add **1 cup** of the sugar, vanilla, and grated orange peel. Beat until combined. Add eggs, one at a time, beating until combined. In a small bowl, stir together buttermilk and ½ **cup** of the orange juice. Alternately add flour and orange juice mixture, beating on low to medium speed after each addition just until combined. Fold in chopped raisins.

Grease muffin pans or line with paper bake cups; fill ⅔ full. Bake about 20 minutes or until a toothpick inserted near the centers comes out clean.

Meanwhile, for orange topping, in a medium bowl stir together the remaining ¾ cup sugar, remaining ¼ cup orange juice, and the corn syrup until sugar dissolves. While muffins are still hot, dip tops into orange topping. Makes about 24.

French Breakfast Cakes

Serve these sugar-and-spice muffins for a weekend morning treat with coffee, or make them a special part of a brunch menu. They may be made ahead and frozen. Photograph on page 84.

1^1/$_2$ cups sugar, divided
 2 teaspoons ground cinnamon
1^1/$_2$ cups all-purpose flour
1^1/$_2$ teaspoons baking powder
 ^{1}/$_2$ teaspoon salt
 ^{1}/$_4$ teaspoon ground mace
 ^{1}/$_3$ cup shortening
 1 egg
 ^{1}/$_2$ cup milk
 3 ounces cream cheese, cut into 12 cubes
 ^{1}/$_2$ cup melted butter or margarine

Preheat the oven to 350°. Combine **1 cup** of the sugar and the cinnamon. Set aside. In a small bowl, combine flour, baking powder, salt, and mace. In another bowl beat together shortening, remaining ^{1}/$_2$ cup of the sugar, and the egg. Add flour mixture alternately with milk, stirring just until combined.

Lightly grease muffin pan. Using **half** of the batter, fill muffin cups ^{1}/$_3$ full. Top each with a cube of cream cheese. Top with remaining batter, filling muffin cups ^{2}/$_3$ full. Bake for 20 to 25 minutes or until golden.

Immediately remove from muffin pan. Roll muffins in melted butter, then in sugar-cinnamon mixture, covering entire muffin. Makes 12.

Chocolate Chip-Orange Muffins

1^1/$_2$ cups all-purpose flour
 ^{1}/$_2$ cup sugar
 2 teaspoons baking powder
 ^{1}/$_2$ teaspoon salt
 1 beaten egg
 1 cup milk
 ^{1}/$_4$ cup cooking oil
 1 cup semisweet chocolate pieces
 1 tablespoon finely shredded orange peel
    Powdered sugar

Preheat the oven to 400°. In a mixing bowl, stir together flour, sugar, baking powder, and salt. Make a well in the center. In another bowl, combine beaten egg, milk, and cooking oil. Add egg mixture to flour mixture. Stir just until moistened. Stir in chocolate pieces and orange peel.

Grease muffin pan or line with paper bake cups. Fill cups ^{2}/$_3$ full. Bake about 20 minutes or until golden. Sprinkle with powdered sugar. Makes 12.

Elizabeth's Orange Blossom Muffins

"At holidays, and on occasional Sundays, the usual cereals for breakfast just don't seem right. These muffins, which are a particular favorite of our daughter, Elizabeth, get the day off to a great start." Photograph on page 84.

¹/₂	cup sugar, divided
4	teaspoons all-purpose flour
¹/₂	teaspoon ground cinnamon
¹/₄	teaspoon ground nutmeg
3	tablespoons butter or margarine
2	cups packaged biscuit mix
1	beaten egg
¹/₂	cup orange juice
2	tablespoons cooking oil or melted shortening
¹/₂	cup orange marmalade
¹/₂	cup chopped pecans

For topping, combine ¹/₄ **cup** of the sugar, the flour, cinnamon, and nutmeg. Cut in butter or margarine until mixture resembles coarse crumbs. Set topping aside.

Preheat the oven to 400°. In a bowl, stir together biscuit mix and remaining ¹/₄ cup sugar. Make a well in the center. In another bowl, combine beaten egg, orange juice, and cooking oil. Add egg mixture to dry ingredients. Stir just until moistened. Stir in marmalade and pecans.

Grease muffin pan or line with paper bake cups; fill cups ²/₃ full. Sprinkle topping over each. Bake about 20 minutes or until golden. Makes 12.

Dearie's Bran Muffins

Southern grandmothers are often referred to in fond diminutives such as "Nannie" and "Dearie" and, more often than not, they are fabulous cooks. Count on these muffins to make your family feel pampered like Grandma pampered you.

1	15-ounce box raisin bran cereal
5	cups all-purpose flour
3	cups sugar
5	teaspoons baking soda
2	teaspoons salt
1	teaspoon ground cinnamon
1	teaspoon ground nutmeg
1	teaspoon ground cloves
4	beaten eggs
4	cups buttermilk
1	cup cooking oil
2	teaspoons vanilla
1	cup chopped nuts (optional)

In a very large bowl, stir together cereal, flour, sugar, baking soda, salt, cinnamon, nutmeg, and cloves. In another bowl, combine eggs, buttermilk, oil, and vanilla. Add egg mixture to bran mixture, stirring just until combined. If desired, stir in chopped nuts. (Batter can be stored in a covered container in the refrigerator up to 4 days.)

Preheat the oven to 400°. Grease muffin pan or line with paper bake cups. Fill ²/₃ full. Bake about 15 minutes or until lightly browned. Makes about 40.

Servin' up SWING

JIMMY LUNCEFORD

JIMMY LUNCEFORD WAS A FAMOUS SWING BAND LEADER IN THE 1920S AND '30S AND WAS IN GREAT DEMAND IN THE "FLAPPER ERA." HE ROSE TO INTERNATIONAL STARDOM DURING A TIME WHEN FEW BLACKS RECEIVED SUCH RECOGNITION.

Lila's Biscuits

Lila was the family cook for four generations of hearty Memphis eaters. She served these piping hot biscuits at every supper. Photograph on page 85.

  4   cups all-purpose flour
  1   teaspoon baking powder
 ¹/₂ teaspoon baking soda
  1   teaspoon salt
  1   cup shortening
  2   cups buttermilk
      Orange marmalade, jam, or honey

Preheat the oven to 450°. In a large bowl, stir together flour, baking powder, baking soda, and salt. Cut in shortening until mixture resembles coarse crumbs. Make a well in the center. Add buttermilk. Stir just until the dough sticks together. Form dough into a ball.

On a lightly floured surface, knead dough gently about 10 times. Gently roll dough to ¹/₂-inch thickness. Cut with a floured 2-inch biscuit cutter.

Place on an ungreased baking sheet, close together for soft-sided biscuits or 1-inch apart for crisp-sided ones. Prick biscuits with a fork. Bake for 5 minutes. Reduce oven to 400° and bake 8 to 10 minutes more. Serve with orange marmalade, jam, or honey. Makes about 20.

Baby Butterball Biscuits

Whip up a batch of these little gems for a melt-in-your-mouth treat at any time of day.

  1   cup butter or margarine
  2   cups self-rising flour
  1   cup dairy sour cream

Preheat the oven to 350°. In a bowl, cut butter into flour. Stir in sour cream until well combined. Drop by heaping teaspoons into ungreased 1³/₄-inch muffin cups. Bake for 20 minutes or until firm to the touch. (Biscuits will not brown.) Makes 2¹/₂ dozen.

"Lila was my grandparents' cook for thirty-five years. Her first job as a cook was in the home of my great-grandparents when she was just a teenager. Without an electric mixer or even written recipes, she whipped up family meals and holiday feasts with ease. Just as importantly, she always laughed at my grandfather's jokes. It didn't take guests too many visits to figure out that if they mentioned their favorite dishes in Lila's presence, she would do her best to 'surprise' them the next time they came. At every supper, she served freshly baked biscuits. They were small and flat. Any leftover biscuits were presented with sausage at breakfast the next morning."

◆ ◆ ◆

Crusty Corn Bread

This recipe is a family favorite that has stood the test of several generations.

- ¹/₂   cup cooking oil, divided
- 2   beaten eggs
- 1   cup dairy sour cream
- 1   cup cream-style corn
- ¹/₂   teaspoon salt
- 1   cup self-rising cornmeal

Preheat the oven to 400°. Place ¹/₄ **cup** of the oil in a 10-inch oven-safe skillet. Place skillet in the preheating oven. Meanwhile, in a medium bowl, combine eggs, sour cream, cream-style corn, the remaining ¹/₄ cup oil, and salt. Add self-rising cornmeal to the egg mixture and stir just until moistened and smooth (**do not overbeat**).

Pour batter into the **hot** skillet. Bake about 30 minutes or until a toothpick inserted near the center comes out clean. Makes 6 to 8 servings.

Devil in Disguise Corn Bread

For best results, use a cast-iron skillet.

- 1¹/₂   cups self-rising cornmeal
- 1   cup yellow cream-style corn
- 1   cup buttermilk
- 1   cup shredded sharp cheddar cheese (4 ounces)
- 2   beaten eggs
- ¹/₂   cup cooking oil
- ¹/₂   cup chopped onion
- 2   to 4 jalapeño peppers, seeded and chopped
- 1   tablespoon shortening

Preheat the oven to 400°. Melt the shortening in a 10-inch oven-safe skillet by placing skillet in the preheating oven for 5 to 7 minutes. Meanwhile, in a medium bowl, stir together cornmeal, corn, buttermilk, cheese, eggs, oil, onion, and peppers just until combined. Pour batter into the **hot** skillet. Bake for 35 to 40 minutes or until golden brown. (Or, grease muffin pan; fill cups ²/₃ full. Bake in a 400° oven for 18 to 20 minutes or until golden brown.) Serve warm. Makes 8 servings (or about 12 muffins).

Servin' up **JAZZ**

NAOMI MOODY

NAOMI GREW UP HEAVILY STEEPED IN THE BLACK MUSIC TRADITION. HER FATHER, NAT D. WILLIAMS, WAS THE FIRST DISC JOCKEY ON MEMPHIS' FIRST ALL-BLACK RADIO STATION, WDIA, WHERE B.B. KING GOT HIS FIRST BIG BREAK. INTERNATIONALLY RECOGNIZED IN THE FIELDS OF JAZZ AND OPERA, SHE IS KNOWN WORLD-WIDE FOR HER PERFORMANCE OF BESS IN "PORGY AND BESS."

Country Corn Bread

1 cup cornmeal
$^1/_2$ teaspoon baking powder
$^1/_2$ teaspoon salt
2 beaten eggs
1 cup cream-style corn
1 cup milk
$^1/_2$ cup cooking oil
$1^1/_2$ cups shredded sharp cheddar cheese (6 ounces)
1 10-ounce package frozen chopped broccoli, cooked and well-drained (optional)

Preheat the oven to 350°. In a medium bowl, stir together cornmeal, baking powder, and salt. Make a well in the center.

In another medium bowl, combine eggs, cream-style corn, milk, and oil. Add egg mixture all at once to the cornmeal mixture. Stir just until moistened and smooth **(do not overbeat)**. Fold in cheese and, if desired, broccoli.

Pour batter into a greased 9-inch square baking pan. Bake about 1 hour or until a toothpick inserted near the center comes out clean. Makes 9 servings.

Apricot-Pecan Bread

12 fresh apricots, halved, pitted, and peeled, or 1 16-ounce can apricot halves, drained
$1^1/_2$ cups all-purpose flour
1 teaspoon baking soda
$^1/_2$ teaspoon salt
$^1/_2$ teaspoon ground cinnamon
$^1/_2$ teaspoon ground ginger
$^1/_2$ teaspoon ground allspice
$^1/_4$ teaspoon baking powder
$^1/_2$ cup butter or margarine, softened
1 cup plus 2 tablespoons sugar
2 eggs
$^1/_3$ cup chopped pecans

Preheat the oven to 325°. In a food processor bowl, process apricots until pureed; set aside. In a medium bowl, stir together flour, baking soda, salt, cinnamon, ginger, allspice, and baking powder.

In a large bowl, beat together butter and sugar with an electric mixer until well combined. Add eggs and **1 cup** of the apricot puree. Add flour mixture and beat just until moistened. Stir in pecans.

Pour into a greased 9x5x3-inch loaf pan. Bake about 45 minutes or until a toothpick inserted near center of loaf comes out clean. Cool in pan on rack for 10 minutes. Remove; cool completely. Makes 1 loaf (12 servings).

Zucchini Bread

This easy, moist bread is quicker to make than most. Just mix everything in one bowl. Makes two so you can take one to a friend!

3	eggs
1	cup cooking oil
2	cups sugar
2	teaspoons vanilla
1	teaspoon salt
1	teaspoon baking soda
1	teaspoon cinnamon
1/4	teaspoon baking powder
2	cups shredded zucchini
3	cups flour
1/2	cup chopped walnuts

Preheat the oven to 350°. In a large bowl, beat together eggs and oil. Stir in sugar, vanilla, salt, baking soda, cinnamon, and baking powder. Add zucchini. Stir in flour and walnuts just until combined. Pour into 2 greased and floured 8x4x2-inch loaf pans. Bake for 1 hour or until a toothpick inserted near center comes out clean. Cool in pan 10 minutes. Remove from pan; cool completely. Makes 2 loaves (18 servings).

Orange Poppy Seed Bread

3	cups all-purpose flour
2 1/4	cups sugar
2	tablespoons poppy seed
1 1/2	teaspoons baking powder
1/2	teaspoon salt
3	eggs
1 1/2	cups milk
1	cup cooking oil
2	tablespoons finely shredded orange peel
1 1/2	teaspoons vanilla, divided
1	teaspoon almond extract, divided
3/4	cup sifted powdered sugar
1/4	cup orange juice

Preheat the oven to 350°. In a large bowl, stir together flour, sugar, poppy seed, baking powder, and salt. Add eggs, milk, oil, orange peel, **1 teaspoon** of the vanilla, and **1/2 teaspoon** of the almond extract. Beat with an electric mixer on medium speed for 2 minutes.

Pour batter into 2 greased 8x4x2-inch loaf pans. Bake about 1 hour or until a toothpick inserted near the centers comes out clean. Meanwhile, for glaze, in a medium bowl, stir together powdered sugar, orange juice, the remaining 1/2 teaspoon vanilla, and remaining 1/2 teaspoon almond extract until smooth.

Using a long-tined fork, poke holes in tops of baked loaves. Pour glaze over loaves. Cool loaves in pans for 10 minutes. Remove bread from pans. Cool thoroughly on wire racks. Makes 2 loaves (18 servings).

Cream Cheese Pastries

1	cup dairy sour cream
1¼	cups sugar, divided
½	cup butter or margarine, cut up
1	teaspoon salt
2	packages active dry yeast
½	cup warm water (110° to 115°)
3	eggs, divided
4	cups all-purpose flour
16	ounces cream cheese, softened
4	teaspoons vanilla, divided
2	cups sifted powdered sugar
¼	cup milk
2	tablespoons brown sugar
1	teaspoon ground cinnamon
½	cup slivered almonds, toasted

In a 1-quart saucepan, heat sour cream, ½ **cup** of the sugar, butter or margarine, and salt just until warm (115° to 120°) and butter is almost melted, stirring constantly. In a large bowl, soften yeast in the warm water. Stir in sour cream mixture, **two** of the eggs, and flour; beat well. Cover and refrigerate overnight.

For filling, in a small bowl, beat together the remaining egg, softened cream cheese, the remaining 3/4 cup sugar, and **2 teaspoons** of the vanilla until well combined. Set filling aside.

Divide dough into thirds. On a lightly floured surface, roll each portion of dough into a 12x8-inch rectangle. Spread **one-third** of the filling on **each** rectangle of dough. Roll up each rectangle, jelly-roll style, from a long side. Pinch seams and ends together to seal. Place pastries, seam sides down, on greased baking sheets. Using kitchen shears, make V-shaped snips at 2-inch intervals in the top of each pastry. Cover and let rise in a warm place about 1 hour or until double.

Preheat the oven to 375°. Bake pastries for 12 to 15 minutes or until golden. Meanwhile, for cinnamon glaze, in a small bowl stir together powdered sugar, milk, brown sugar, remaining 2 teaspoons vanilla, and cinnamon. Drizzle over tops of pastries, then sprinkle with toasted almonds. Makes 3 pastries (24 servings).

R&B Servin' up

DAVID PORTER

HONORED BY THE SMITHSONIAN INSTITUTE AND THE CANNES FILM FESTIVAL, AND HOLDER OF NUMEROUS GOLD RECORDS, DAVID PORTER, ALONG WITH ISAAC HAYES, MADE UP THE GREATEST SONG-WRITING TEAM IN THE HISTORY OF SOUL. THEIR MONSTER HITS INCLUDE "SOUL MAN," "WHEN SOMETHING IS WRONG WITH MY BABY," AND "HOLD ON, I'M COMING."

ENTRÉES

Sam Phillips

Go-getter. Visionary. Super-star. Soul man. Sam Phillips, founder of Sun Record Company, has always "known" people and the music that would touch them. His pioneer days in the recording industry propelled Elvis Presley, Jerry Lee Lewis, Charlie Rich, and many others to stardom and changed the world of popular music forever. Sam instinctively knew how to draw genius from his performers and in his famous Sun Studios, created a relaxed environment that encouraged the unconventional and original.

"Boys, we've got a 'take!'" These are the words that young artists anxiously waited to hear him utter. Sam says, "For as long as I live, I'll always remember the ecstasy and disbelief on their faces when I prophesied that we had just finished recording a 'hit.'

"My most memorable moment was Elvis' first concert at the Overton Park Shell in 1954. Slim Whitman was the headliner and we had Elvis open the show for him. Elvis Presley simply stole the show." Sorry, Slim.

The rest, as they say, is history.

ENTRÉES

◆ ◆ ◆

MEAT
PAGE 116

◆ ◆ ◆

POULTRY
PAGE 136

◆ ◆ ◆

FISH & SEAFOOD
PAGE 152

◆ ◆ ◆

BARBECUE & GRILLING
PAGE 168

◆ ◆ ◆

PICTURED OVERLEAF

—

Clockwise from top right: Jalapeño Southern Fried Chicken (page 138); Spicy Peppered Beef (page 124); and Prune and Apricot Stuffed Pork Roast (page 131)

◆ ◆ ◆

MEAT

◆ ◆ ◆

PICTURED AT LEFT

—

*Bistro Beef Burgundy
(page 125)*

◆ ◆ ◆

Mary Jenkins

◆ ◆ ◆

*A*s the "King's" cook for 18 years, Mary Jenkins had many opportunities to see Elvis Presley up close and witness the everyday home life of the "legend." She knew his likes and dislikes and spent almost two decades providing his favorite foods on demand, though his hours were erratic and his mealtimes unpredictable. Mary knew that Elvis' food tastes were simple and reflected his Southern background. Perhaps it was the hectic, urban pace of concerts, press appearances, and recording dates that drew him to the comfort of basic, familiar foods when he was at home at Graceland. Mary Jenkins recalls watching television with Elvis on Sunday mornings as he enjoyed her sausage, scrambled eggs, homemade biscuits, and coffee, and she tells of two- or three-week food attachments to Southern goodies like corn bread and well-seasoned greens. Elvis once returned from a concert tour requesting the duplication of a new food favorite — a peanut butter-banana sandwich grilled in butter. This stayed at the top of his chart along with his #1 dessert choice, banana pudding. After Elvis' death in 1977, Mary Jenkins stayed on at Graceland with other Presley family members and has published a cookbook memoir, Elvis, Memories Beyond Graceland's Gates.

117

Anniversary Veal Ragout

1/2	cup all-purpose flour
1	teaspoon paprika
1/2	teaspoon salt or to taste
1/2	teaspoon white pepper
2	pounds boneless veal round steak, cut into 1-inch cubes
6	tablespoons butter, divided
8	small new potatoes
2	cups fresh or canned Italian plum tomatoes, seeded and coarsely chopped
2	cups chicken broth
1/2	cup finely sliced onion
10	whole peeled shallots
1/4	cup snipped cilantro
1/4	cup snipped fresh basil or 1 tablespoon dried basil, crushed
2	cloves garlic, minced
4	teaspoons finely shredded orange peel
2	teaspoons finely shredded lemon peel
1	pound fresh mushrooms, sliced in half
1 1/2	cups heavy cream
	Fresh basil sprigs

Preheat the oven to 350°. In a small bowl, combine flour, paprika, salt, and white pepper. Add veal cubes, a few at a time, stirring to coat. In a 3- or 4-quart oven-safe Dutch oven, melt **4 tablespoons** of the butter. Add veal and cook over medium heat about 5 minutes, stirring frequently to prevent browning. Remove from heat.

Add potatoes, tomatoes, chicken broth, onion, shallots, cilantro, basil, garlic, orange peel, and lemon peel. Bring to boiling. Cover and bake for 1 to 1 1/4 hours or until veal is tender.

Meanwhile, in an 8-inch skillet, melt remaining 2 tablespoons butter. Add mushroom halves. Cook until tender; set aside.

Remove stew from oven. Ladle **2 cups** of the hot liquid into a small saucepan. Add cream in a slow steady stream, whisking constantly. Simmer, uncovered, for 5 minutes, stirring constantly. Return mixture to Dutch oven on stovetop; cook about 5 minutes or until heated through. Transfer to a serving dish or individual bowls and serve immediately. Garnish with basil sprigs. Makes 6 to 8 servings.

Rack of Lamb with a Mustard Crust

Have your butcher crack the chops at the base of the rack for easier carving.

1	2-pound rack of lamb (8 to 10 chops)
3/4	cup Dijon-style mustard
3	tablespoons soy sauce
2	tablespoons olive oil
1	tablespoon snipped fresh rosemary or 1 teaspoon dried rosemary, crushed
1	teaspoon pepper
1	clove garlic, minced

Preheat the oven to 400°. Trim fat from lamb. In a small bowl, stir together mustard, soy sauce, olive oil, rosemary, pepper, and garlic to make a paste. Coat lamb with the paste. Place rack, rib side down, in a shallow roasting pan. Roast about 30 minutes for medium (160°) or 45 minutes for well-done (170°). Makes 4 servings.

♦ ♦ ♦

**CHAMPAGNE
AND
UNDERSTANDING**
—

"My husband, an M.D., had been working fourteen-hour days for months and had promised to spend a special anniversary evening at our favorite restaurant. At six o'clock, as I wondered when I'd hear his car in the driveway, the telephone rang. An emergency case would keep him at the hospital until 9:30. Our reservation could not be changed. Frustrated and disappointed at first, I suddenly had a fun idea. I had wanted to try a new veal ragout and I decided that this was the night. List in hand, I dashed out to pick up bread, dessert, and champagne. Once home, I transformed our big den coffee table with linen, crystal, and silver candlesticks and set to work on the veal. When my fatigued husband straggled in at ten o'clock and saw the champagne on ice and dinner ready to enjoy in the comfort of home, he was overcome. The veal was a big hit. As we lingered over coffee and French pastries, he promised he had never enjoyed a meal — or a moment — more."

♦ ♦ ♦

Lamb with Bordelaise Sauce

2	5-ounce lamb chops, cut 1 inch thick
1/4	cup dry red wine
4	teaspoons soy sauce
1	tablespoon water
2	teaspoons onion powder
1	teaspoon garlic salt
1/2	teaspoon dried rosemary, crushed
1/4	teaspoon dried thyme, crushed
	Dash pepper
	Bordelaise Sauce (see recipe below)

Trim excess fat from lamb chops. Place lamb chops in a plastic bag set into a shallow dish. For marinade, in a small bowl, stir together wine, soy sauce, water, onion powder, garlic salt, rosemary, thyme, and pepper. Pour marinade over lamb chops. Close bag. Marinate in the refrigerator for 4 to 8 hours, turning bag occasionally.

Preheat the broiler. Drain lamb, reserving marinade. Place chops on the unheated rack of a broiler pan. Broil 5 inches from heat about 6 minutes on each side or until tender, brushing chops often with marinade. Serve with Bordelaise Sauce. Makes 2 servings.

Bordelaise Sauce

1	tablespoon butter or margarine
4	ounces sliced fresh mushrooms (1 1/2 cups)
1	tablespoon all-purpose flour
1/2	cup water
1/4	cup dry red wine
1	tablespoon thinly sliced green onion
2	teaspoons instant beef bouillon granules
1	teaspoon dried tarragon, crushed
1	teaspoon lemon juice
1/2	teaspoon dried thyme, crushed
1	bay leaf

In a 1-quart saucepan, melt butter or margarine. Add mushrooms. Cook and stir over medium-high heat for 4 to 5 minutes or until tender. Stir in flour. Add water and wine all at once; stir until smooth. Stir in green onion, beef bouillon granules, tarragon, lemon juice, thyme, and bay leaf. Cook and stir over medium heat until thickened and bubbly. Remove bay leaf before serving. Makes about 1/2 cup.

Congratulations
on the new baby!
♡, Gra...

POULTRY

♦ ♦ ♦

PICTURED AT LEFT
—
New Mommy Roast Chicken
(page 141)

♦ ♦ ♦

Billy Gibbons/ZZ Top

The moment was an auspicious summer night in 1971 at the Overton Park Shell. The "Memphis Country Blues Festival" was treating blues fans to the well-known sounds of Furry Lewis, Bukka White, and other traditional bluesmen from the Delta. An obscure band from Texas took the stage and gave the blues a new power that stunned the audience that night and is still electrifying listeners today. ZZ Top has a dynamic presence and a huge rock sound with a touch of "citified" blues. Billy Gibbons, Dusty Hill, and Frank Beard have really "cooked" in Memphis since that first amazing performance, and they have forged a Texas-Tennessee connection. They love Memphis — its music, its people, its food — and when they're here to taste it all, they bring a little Texas magic in return. Billy says: "there's something creative in the air, from low-down blues to high-tech jazz and all points in between...Memphis' got it." Billy is a powerhouse in the kitchen as well as on stage and submitted this fun-loving example of his Texas cookery. Only the brave need apply...
Billy's Border Chicken
• *12 ounces **jalapeño peppers**, pickled as hot as you can handle*
• *2 cups **milk** (Longhorn, if possible)*
• *1 range **chicken**, cleaned and plucked*
• ***Flour** seasoned with **salt** and **paprika** to taste*
Drain the jalapeños and remove seeds. Hold on to the juice. Use a blender to grind the peppers and some of the juice. Pour in the milk. Use this mixture to soak the chicken for at least four hours. Drain the chicken. Coat it with the seasoned flour. Fry it up for a Southwestern border treat.

OULTRY, A LONG-STANDING FIXTURE IN SOUTHERN CUISINE, HAS found new favor in this age of speed and health-conscious cooking. Turkey breasts and cutlets have joined boneless chicken as centerpieces of conveniently quick and interesting dishes. They are delicious — sautéed or grilled, alone or teamed with pasta, light sauces, vegetables, and fresh herbs. Unusual ingredients and ethnic recipes abound.

Still, the old-fashioned ways are hard to beat. Fried chicken jealously guards its place in the heart of many a Southern cook, and who could forget the crispy goodness of a whole roast chicken or turkey with Grandmother's corn bread dressing and pan gravy? Mid-South children still beg for chicken pot pie for supper. Their fathers bring in the riches of the field, as their grandfathers did before them, for delectable game bird dinners of duck and dove, prepared in a manner generations old. These represent a tradition of fine Southern cooking that will not — and should not — pass away. ♥

♦ ♦ ♦

DELICIOUS STORIES

—

"I will never forget the wonderful, promising smell of fried chicken that wafted toward me through the late afternoon air as I walked home from school and cut across the neighbor's yard to my back door. Not only did it mean that I would soon sit down to my favorite supper of chicken, rice and gravy, and chocolate brownies, but also that I would find Mary Frances in the kitchen and, if I begged, she was sure to tell me more of her stories that I recall were as delicious as that chicken."

♦ ♦ ♦

Jalapeño Southern Fried Chicken

The best fried chicken ever! The sauce turns this into dinner party fare. Photograph on page 113.

5	cups buttermilk
2	large cloves garlic, minced
2	medium jalapeño peppers, minced
5	to 6 pounds chicken breast halves
1½	cups self-rising flour
2	teaspoons finely shredded orange peel
1	teaspoon salt
½	teaspoon dried basil, crushed
¼	teaspoon ground red pepper
½	cup butter or margarine
½	cup honey
	Cooking oil for frying
	Jalapeño pepper slices

Combine buttermilk, garlic, and **half** of the minced jalapeño pepper. Place chicken pieces in a large bowl; pour buttermilk mixture over. Cover and chill for 1½ to 2 hours.

In a medium bowl, combine self-rising flour, orange peel, salt, basil, and red pepper. Drain chicken. Coat chicken in flour mixture, shaking off excess. Place coated chicken pieces on waxed paper; let stand at room temperature 20 minutes.

For sauce, in a heavy 1½-quart saucepan, melt butter over low heat. Add remaining minced jalapeño pepper. Cook and stir for 1 minute. Stir in honey. Bring to boiling; reduce heat. Simmer for 15 minutes. Remove from heat. Cover and keep warm.

Meanwhile, in a heavy 12-inch skillet, heat ½ to ¾ inch of cooking oil to 375°. Add chicken in batches (do not crowd) and fry for 5 to 7 minutes per side or until crisp, golden brown. Drain on paper towels. Transfer to platter. Garnish with jalapeño slices. Pass honey-jalapeño sauce. Makes 10 to 12 servings.

Lebanese Chicken and Rice

A hearty, unique dish with a Mideastern flavor.

2	2¹/₂- to 3-pound broiler-fryer chickens, cut up
1¹/₂	pounds lean ground beef
2	teaspoons ground allspice
1	teaspoon salt
1	teaspoon pepper
³/₄	cup pine nuts
2	cups long grain rice
	Paprika

Skin and rinse chicken. In an 8-quart stockpot or 2 4-quart Dutch ovens, combine chicken and 6 cups water. Bring to boiling; reduce heat. Cover and simmer for 40 minutes. Remove chicken; strain broth, reserving **5 cups**. Remove chicken from bones in large pieces. Place chicken in a single layer in a 15x10x1-inch baking pan.

Preheat the oven to 350°. In a skillet, brown ground beef; drain. Stir in allspice, salt, and pepper. Spread pine nuts evenly in a baking pan. Bake for 3 to 5 minutes or until toasted. Stir into beef mixture.

In a large saucepan, combine rice, **4¹/₂ cups** of the reserved chicken broth, and the beef mixture. Bring to boiling, stirring often. Reduce heat; cover and simmer about 20 minutes or until rice is tender, stirring once or twice.

Sprinkle chicken pieces with paprika. Pour remaining ¹/₂ cup of the chicken broth over chicken. Broil until lightly brown.

To serve, place rice in center of a large platter surrounded by chicken pieces. Makes 12 servings.

Breast of Chicken in Tarragon Cream

This is classic French with a tarragon flavor that doesn't overpower your taste buds.

¹/₄	cup all-purpose flour
¹/₂	teaspoon salt
¹/₂	teaspoon pepper
3	tablespoons butter or margarine
6	chicken breast halves, skinned and boned
2	cups sliced fresh mushrooms
³/₄	cup heavy cream
1¹/₂	teaspoons dried tarragon, crushed
3	tablespoons dry white wine
	Hot cooked rice
	Parsley sprigs or sautéed mushrooms caps

In a paper or plastic bag, combine flour, salt, and pepper. Add chicken, a few pieces at a time. Shake to coat well; shake off excess. In a 12-inch skillet, melt butter or margarine. Add chicken and cook over medium heat until lightly browned. Add mushrooms; cover and cook over medium heat for 10 minutes. Add cream and tarragon. Bring to a gentle boil; reduce heat. Cover and simmer over low heat for 10 minutes.

Transfer chicken to a serving platter; keep warm. Stir wine into cream mixture in skillet. Bring to boiling; reduce heat. Simmer, uncovered, over low heat until liquid is reduced to desired consistency. Serve chicken over rice. Spoon sauce on top. Garnish with parsley sprigs or sautéed mushroom caps. Makes 6 servings.

Breast of Chicken Athenia

A pesto and pine nut mixture bakes beneath the skin of these chicken breasts. On top of that, the glorious sauce. Exquisite!

6   chicken breast halves
³/₄   cup shredded Swiss cheese (3 ounces)
³/₄   cup pine nuts or sliced almonds
¹/₃   cup prepared pesto
      Salt and pepper
1   tablespoon all-purpose flour
1   tablespoon cooking oil
2   cups chicken broth
      Fresh basil leaves

Preheat the oven to 350°. Without removing skin from chicken, bone chicken breasts. Combine Swiss cheese, pine nuts, and pesto. Place some of the pesto mixture in the pocket between the skin and meat of each chicken breast. Form breasts into oval shapes and place in an oven-safe skillet or Dutch oven. Sprinkle with salt and pepper. Bake, uncovered, about 30 minutes or until lightly browned.

For roux, in a small heavy skillet, combine flour and oil until smooth. Cook and stir over low heat about 15 minutes or until dark brown. Set aside.

Remove chicken from skillet or Dutch oven; keep warm. Place skillet or Dutch oven over medium heat. Add chicken broth and cook for 5 minutes, scraping any browned bits from bottom of pan. Stir in roux. Cook and stir until thickened. Serve sauce over chicken. Garnish with basil leaves. Makes 6 servings.

Layered Chicken and Artichoke Casserole

1   10-ounce package frozen chopped spinach
1   8-ounce can sliced water chestnuts, drained
6   large chicken breast halves, skinned
1   cup dry sherry, divided
1   bay leaf
2   tablespoons butter or margarine
8   ounces sliced fresh mushrooms (3 cups)
¹/₂   cup sliced green onions
1   clove garlic, minced
³/₄   cup mayonnaise
1   cup freshly grated Parmesan cheese, divided
¹/₂   cup dairy sour cream
1   14-ounce can artichoke hearts, drained and chopped

Cook spinach according to package directions; drain, squeezing out excess liquid. Stir in water chestnuts. Set spinach mixture aside.

Meanwhile, preheat the oven to 350°. In a 12-inch skillet, arrange chicken breasts. Add ¹/₂ **cup** of the sherry and the bay leaf. Bring to boiling; reduce heat. Cover and simmer for 18 to 20 minutes or until tender and no longer pink. Drain and set chicken aside.

In the same skillet, melt butter or margarine. Add mushrooms, green onions, and garlic. Cook and stir over medium-high heat for 4 to 5 minutes or until mushrooms and onion are tender; set aside.

In a medium bowl, stir together mayonnaise, ¹/₂ **cup** of the Parmesan cheese, sour cream, and the remaining ¹/₂ cup sherry.

To assemble, spread spinach mixture evenly in the bottom of a 13x9x2-inch baking dish. Top with chicken breasts, artichokes, and mushroom-green onion mixture. Spread mayonnaise mixture over top. Sprinkle with the remaining ¹/₂ cup Parmesan cheese. Bake about 20 minutes or until heated through. Makes 6 servings.

♪♪♪

NICE TO NOTE
—

If you have spent any time at all in a Southern kitchen, or spent any time around someone who has, you are familiar with the term "roux," the time-tested thickener for many gumbos, soups, and sauces. It is a simple recipe: equal parts butter or oil and flour. But there is a 3-fold secret to making a good roux. Cook it slowly (sometimes upwards of half an hour if it's a large amount), stir the whole while, and call it done when it turns the color of an old copper penny.

∞

New Mommy Roast Chicken

This chicken has another life as a gourmet picnic star in the company of goat cheese, a crusty French baguette, and a bottle of Chardonnay. It is pictured on page 136.

1   3- to 4-pound broiler-fryer chicken
    Salt and pepper
$^1/_2$ lemon, cut into 4 wedges
$^1/_2$ medium onion, cut into 4 wedges
6   cloves garlic, peeled
$^1/_4$ cup butter or margarine, cut up
    Snipped parsley, quartered shallots, sautéed sweet potato slices

Preheat the oven to 475°. Rinse chicken and pat dry. Sprinkle cavity of chicken with salt and pepper. Place lemon wedges, onion wedges, garlic, and cut-up butter in cavity. Skewer neck skin to back; tie legs to tail. Place, breast side down, in a foil-lined shallow roasting pan. Sprinkle outside of chicken with salt and pepper.

Roast, uncovered, for 45 minutes or until meat is no longer pink and drumsticks move easily in sockets. Garnish with parsley, shallots, and sweet potato slices. Makes 6 servings.

Curried Apricot Chicken

Do you have a baby in the house? If you're in a hurry, a jar of baby apricots can substitute for the puree.

8   chicken breast halves
6   tablespoons all-purpose flour
1   to 2 tablespoons curry powder
$^1/_2$ teaspoon salt
$^1/_4$ cup cooking oil
1   cup water
$^1/_2$ cup sliced green onions
$^1/_2$ cup pureed cooked apricots or 1 4-ounce jar apricot baby food
2   tablespoons lemon juice
1   tablespoon sugar
2   teaspoons soy sauce
1   teaspoon instant beef bouillon granules
$^1/_4$ teaspoon ground red pepper
$^1/_4$ cup snipped parsley

Remove skin from chicken breasts. In a paper or plastic bag, combine flour, curry powder, and salt. Add chicken, a few pieces at a time. Shake to coat well. In a 10-inch skillet, brown chicken, half at a time, in cooking oil. Place in a 15x11$^1/_2$x2-inch baking dish.

Preheat oven to 350°. In a 1-quart saucepan, combine water, green onions, pureed apricots, lemon juice, sugar, soy sauce, bouillon granules, and red pepper. Bring to boiling. Pour over chicken. Bake, covered, about 45 minutes or until tender. Sprinkle chicken with parsley. Makes 8 servings.

◆◆◆

BABY GIFTS
—

"I have made this for new mothers for years, because it's not too spicy for a nursing mother, yet it has enough personality for everyone in the family to enjoy. Served with salad, bread, and dessert, it's light enough to be considered sinless and ample enough to accommodate the whole household, including grandmothers and baby nurses."

Rooted deep in the tradition of Southern hospitality is the custom of taking food on special occasions. Friends and neighbors bearing cakes and casseroles are as customary at Southern births as are flowers and cards. New mothers always appreciate the gift of food, for very few of them have the time or energy to cook, and that stuffed chicken or chocolate pound cake may do more for her spirits than any other baby gift!

◆◆◆

Chicken with Black Beans

NICE TO NOTE

For a party menu with South-of-the-border flavor, try this recipe, substituting yellow saffron rice for the white rice. Round out the menu with a citrus-avocado salad and "Fit and Fabulous Flan" on page 243 for dessert.

∽

    Cooking oil
¹/₂ cup chopped onion
2   cloves garlic, minced
2   16-ounce cans black beans, rinsed and drained
1   16-ounce can tomatoes, drained
1   8-ounce can tomato sauce
1   4-ounce can chopped green chili peppers, drained
2   tablespoons white wine vinegar
4   teaspoons chili powder, divided
1   tablespoon ground cumin
1   teaspoon ground coriander
1   cup all-purpose flour
¹/₂ teaspoon salt
6   chicken breast halves, skinned and boned
3   cups hot cooked rice
    Plain yogurt or dairy sour cream
    Prepared salsa
    Sliced green onion
    Chopped tomatoes
    Shredded cheddar cheese

In a 3-quart saucepan, heat **1 tablespoon** cooking oil. Add onion and garlic and cook until onion is tender. Stir in black beans, tomatoes, tomato sauce, chili peppers, vinegar, **3 teaspoons** of the chili powder, the cumin, and coriander. Bring to boiling; reduce heat. Simmer, uncovered, for 25 minutes or until mixture is reduced to sauce consistency.

In a paper or plastic bag, combine flour, salt, and the remaining 1 teaspoon chili powder. Add chicken breast halves, two at a time, and shake until well coated. Shake off excess flour mixture.

Preheat the oven to 400°. In a 10-inch skillet, heat ¹/₂ inch of cooking oil. Cook chicken over medium-high heat for 4 to 5 minutes per side or until browned. Drain on paper towels. Transfer chicken to a 12x7¹/₂x2-inch baking dish. Top with black bean mixture. Bake, uncovered, for 20 minutes or until beans are heated through.

To serve, spread **¹/₂ cup** rice on each plate. Top with a chicken breast half and some of the black bean mixture. Garnish with yogurt or sour cream, salsa, green onion, tomatoes, and cheese. Makes 6 servings.

Light and Easy Italian Chicken

Add pasta, hot or cold, bread, and wine and you have an easy meal so right for a hard day.

6   chicken breast halves, skinned and boned
¹/₂ cup reduced-calorie Italian salad dressing
¹/₄ teaspoon cracked black pepper
1   teaspoon snipped fresh tarragon or basil, or ¹/₂ teaspoon dried tarragon or basil, crushed
¹/₃ cup grated Parmesan cheese
    Fresh tarragon or basil sprigs

Preheat the oven to 350°. Place chicken in a 12x7¹/₂x2-inch baking dish. Fill dish with about ¹/₄ inch water. Pour dressing over chicken. Sprinkle with cracked black pepper, then tarragon or basil. Sprinkle with Parmesan cheese. Bake about 20 minutes or until tender. Garnish with fresh tarragon or basil sprigs. Makes 6 servings.

Raspberry Chicken

Fresh, fascinating flavors make this chicken brand-new.

4   chicken breast halves, skinned and boned
¼   cup all-purpose flour
2   tablespoons butter or margarine
1   tablespoon cooking oil
2   tablespoons finely chopped shallots
½   cup chicken broth
⅓   cup raspberry vinegar
½   cup heavy cream
1   tablespoon crème de cassis
    Freshly ground pepper to taste
    Fresh red raspberries

Place each chicken breast half between 2 pieces of clear plastic wrap. Working from center to edges, pound lightly with the flat side of a meat mallet until ¼ inch thick. Remove plastic wrap. Lightly press both sides of chicken pieces into flour; shake off excess.

In a 12-inch skillet, heat butter and oil over medium heat. Add chicken and cook about 3 minutes per side or until lightly browned and cooked through.

Remove chicken from skillet; set aside. Add shallots to skillet and cook over low heat about 5 minutes or until tender. Add chicken broth. Bring to boiling. Cook over high heat, uncovered, for 10 to 15 minutes or until reduced by half. Add vinegar and cook over high heat until the consistency of heavy cream. Stir in cream and crème de cassis; cook over medium heat until thickened, stirring frequently. Season with pepper.

Add chicken to sauce in skillet. Heat through. To serve, place chicken on serving plates; spoon sauce over chicken. Garnish with fresh raspberries. Makes 4 servings.

Chicken Breast Tenderloins in Brandy Cream

An elegant choice for a dinner party, it can be prepared ahead of time up to the point where the cream is added.

2   tablespoons butter or margarine
1   pound boneless, skinless chicken breast tenders (12 to 16 pieces)
¾   cup chicken broth
½   cup heavy cream
4   large fresh mushrooms, sliced
¼   cup brandy
1   tablespoon snipped parsley
    Salt and freshly ground pepper to taste
    Cooked wild rice

In a 12-inch heavy skillet, melt butter. Add chicken and cook until golden. Add chicken broth. Bring to boiling; reduce heat. Cover and simmer for 15 minutes.

Pour cream over chicken; cover and cook 5 to 10 minutes more, stirring occasionally. Do not boil. Add mushrooms; cook 5 minutes more, shaking skillet occasionally so juices splash over mushrooms. Stir in brandy, parsley, salt, and pepper. Heat through. Serve with wild rice. Makes 4 servings.

NICE TO NOTE

Vinegar is no longer reserved solely for salad dressings and pickling. In this era of concern over fat and sodium, vinegar can be a flavorful accent to all kinds of foods without adding salt or calories. White vinegar and cider vinegar, long staples in our pantries, have been joined on the shelf by wine vinegars, rice vinegar, balsamic vinegar, and vinegars infused with fruits and herbs. Each has its own distinct flavor and use. Fruit and herb vinegars are both fun and easy to make and are wonderful, inexpensive homemade gifts.

∞

Duck and Wild Rice Amandine

If the duck hunters come home empty-handed, try this with chicken or turkey.

2 medium ducks
3 stalks celery
1 onion, halved
1 teaspoon garlic salt
1/2 teaspoon pepper
1 bay leaf
1 6-ounce package long grain and wild rice
2 cups sliced fresh mushrooms
1/2 cup chopped onion
1/2 cup butter or margarine
1/4 cup all-purpose flour
1 1/2 cups light cream
1/4 cup dry white wine
4 slices bacon, cooked crisp and crumbled
2 tablespoons snipped parsley
3 tablespoons slivered almonds

In a 6-quart Dutch oven or stockpot, combine ducks, celery, onion, and enough water to cover. Add garlic salt, pepper, and bay leaf. Bring to boiling; reduce heat. Simmer for 1 hour. Remove ducks. Skim fat and strain broth, reserving **1 1/2 cups** of the broth. Remove meat from bones; cube meat.

Meanwhile, cook rice according to package directions. In a 10-inch skillet, cook mushrooms and onion in butter or margarine until tender. Stir in flour, then the reserved broth. Cook and stir until thickened.

In a medium bowl, combine rice, duck, mushroom mixture, cream, wine, bacon, and parsley. Transfer to a greased 2-quart casserole. Sprinkle with almonds. Cover and bake in a 350° oven for 20 minutes. Uncover and bake 5 to 10 minutes more or until very hot. Makes 6 servings.

Chicken Presto

6 chicken breast halves, skinned and boned
2 tablespoons soy sauce
1 tablespoon water
1 tablespoon cooking oil
1 tablespoon sesame oil
1 1/2 cups sliced fresh mushrooms
1 cup long grain rice
1/2 cup chopped onion
1 teaspoon celery seed
3 cups chicken broth
3/4 cup frozen peas

Cut chicken into thin strips. Place in a bowl. Stir in soy sauce and water. Cover and chill for 30 minutes.

In a 12-inch skillet, heat cooking oil and sesame oil. Stir-fry chicken for 2 minutes. Add mushrooms, rice, onion, and celery seed. Stir-fry 2 minutes more. Add chicken broth. Bring to boiling; reduce heat. Cover and simmer for 20 minutes. Add peas; simmer 10 minutes more or until rice is tender. Makes 6 servings.

Chicken Mediterranean

This is the perfect dish for a cold evening at home by the fire. Its best accompaniments are good friends and laughter.

8	chicken breast halves, skinned and boned
	Salt and pepper
¼	cup olive oil
¾	cup finely chopped onion
1	tablespoon minced garlic
1	28-ounce can tomatoes
2	cups coarsely chopped sweet red pepper
1	cup chicken broth
1	cup dry white wine
3	tablespoons tomato paste
½	cup sliced ripe olives
½	cup sliced green olives
1½	teaspoons dried basil, crushed
1½	teaspoons dried oregano, crushed
¼ to ½	teaspoon crushed red pepper
1	bay leaf
2	small zucchini, sliced ¼ inch thick

Season chicken with salt and pepper. In a heavy 12-inch skillet, heat olive oil. Add chicken; cook over medium-high heat for 4 to 5 minutes per side or until browned. Remove chicken; pour off all but **1 tablespoon** of the olive oil. Add onion and garlic and cook until tender.

Drain tomatoes, reserving **1 cup** of the liquid. Add tomatoes, reserved liquid, sweet red pepper, chicken broth, wine, and tomato paste, stirring until well combined. Stir in ripe olives, green olives, basil, oregano, crushed red pepper, and bay leaf. Add chicken. Cover and cook over low heat for 30 to 40 minutes or until chicken is tender. Add zucchini; cover and cook for 5 minutes. Uncover and cook 5 minutes more. Season to taste with salt and pepper. Makes 8 servings.

Creole Chicken Cordon Bleu

"Tasso" is Cajun smoked ham. If it isn't available in your area, substitute the wonderful Italian ham, prosciutto, or Canadian bacon for an equally fine flavor.

6	chicken breast halves, skinned and boned
2	teaspoons creole seasoning
3	tablespoons butter or margarine
1½	cups heavy cream
¾	cup chopped tasso, prosciutto, or Canadian bacon
¼	cup sliced green onions
2	teaspoons pepper
1	cup freshly grated Parmesan cheese, divided
6	cups cooked rice

Preheat the oven to 350°. Dust chicken breasts with creole seasoning. To blacken chicken, in a large heavy oven-safe skillet, melt butter or margarine over high heat. Add chicken breasts and blacken for 3 minutes on one side and 2 minutes on the other. Move skillet to the oven and bake about 5 minutes or until chicken is tender.

In a 1-quart saucepan, combine cream, tasso, green onions, and pepper. Cook over medium heat until slightly thickened. Stir in ¾ **cup** of the Parmesan cheese.

To serve, place 1 cup rice on each plate. Top with chicken breast and sauce. Sprinkle with remaining Parmesan cheese. Makes 6 servings.

Chicken in Phyllo

18   18x12-inch sheets frozen phyllo dough (12 to 15 ounces), thawed
³/₄   cup butter, melted
6   medium chicken breasts halves, skinned and boned, and pounded ¹/₄ inch thick
      Salt and pepper
      Basil Butter, Tarragon Butter, or Garlic Butter
2   tablespoons grated Parmesan cheese

Preheat the oven to 350°. To assemble bundles, unfold phyllo. Place 1 sheet of phyllo on a waxed-paper-lined work surface; brush with some of the ³/₄ cup melted butter. Top with a second sheet of phyllo; brush with more melted butter and top with a third sheet of phyllo. (Cover remaining phyllo with waxed paper overlayed with a damp towel to prevent drying out; set aside.)

Sprinkle chicken with salt and pepper. Place 1 chicken breast half diagonally across and near the end of one corner of the phyllo stack. Spoon **1 tablespoon** of the Basil, Tarragon, or Garlic Butter on top. Fold bottom corner of phyllo up and over herb butter; fold in side corners. Roll chicken in remaining length of phyllo rectangle to form a bundle. Repeat making bundles with the remaining phyllo dough, melted butter, chicken breast halves, and herb butter.

Butter a 15x10x1-inch baking pan. Place bundles in pan. Brush top of bundles with remaining melted butter; sprinkle with Parmesan cheese. Bake about 40 minutes or until golden. Makes 6 servings.

Basil Butter: In a small bowl, stir together ¹/₂ cup **butter**, softened, and 1¹/₂ teaspoons dried **basil**, crushed.

Tarragon Butter: In a small bowl, stir together ¹/₂ cup **butter**, softened; 2 **shallots**, finely chopped; and 1 teaspoon dried **tarragon**, crushed.

Garlic Butter: In a small bowl, stir together ¹/₂ cup **butter**, softened, and 2 cloves **garlic**, minced.

Chicken with Tomato-Basil Sauce

The sauce is even better when made a few days ahead, refrigerated, and warmed just before serving.

6   chicken breast halves, skinned and boned
2   beaten eggs
1   cup Italian-seasoned bread crumbs
¹/₂   cup olive oil, divided
      Freshly grated Parmesan cheese
1   cup chopped onion
1   clove garlic, minced
1¹/₂ pounds tomatoes, chopped
¹/₂   cup snipped fresh basil
¹/₂   teaspoon sugar
      Salt and pepper to taste

Soak chicken breasts in beaten eggs in the refrigerator for 2 to 3 hours. Remove chicken and roll in bread crumbs. Preheat the oven to 350°. In a 12-inch skillet, heat ¹/₄ **cup** of the olive oil. Cook chicken, uncovered, over medium heat for 5 to 7 minutes per side or until lightly browned. Place in a shallow baking dish. Bake about 20 minutes or until tender. Sprinkle generously with Parmesan cheese.

Meanwhile, for sauce, in a 2-quart saucepan cook onion and garlic in the remaining ¹/₄ cup olive oil until tender. Add tomatoes, basil, sugar, salt, and pepper. Bring to boiling; cook over medium-high heat for 2 to 3 minutes. Reduce heat to medium-low and cook 20 minutes more. Serve sauce over chicken. Makes 6 servings.

♪ ♪ ♪

NICE TO NOTE
—

Basil had its beginnings in ancient Greece where its use was prohibited by anyone other than the royal family. Today, Southerners can grow (and use) any of the many varieties of the herb without fear of imprisonment! Its warm, pungent flavor is increasingly popular in Italian dishes, soups, and stews.

While even a breath of cold air can wither this tender annual, our long growing season and warm temperatures make basil an ideal addition to any Southern garden. Just remember to bring it in before the first frost.

Chicken and Sausage Sauté

6   chicken breast halves, skinned and boned
    Salt and freshly ground pepper
$^1/_2$ cup all-purpose flour
2   tablespoon olive oil
2   medium zucchini, cut into 1-inch-long julienne strips
1   pound fresh sweet Italian sausage links
1   tablespoon butter or margarine
$^1/_4$ teaspoon crushed red pepper
$^1/_2$ cup dry white wine
$^1/_2$ cup chicken broth
1   7-ounce jar roasted red bell peppers, drained and finely sliced
2   large cloves garlic, minced
1   teaspoon dried oregano, crushed
1   teaspoon dried basil, crushed
1   tablespoon snipped parsley

Cut chicken into thin bite-size strips. Sprinkle with salt and freshly ground pepper. Roll chicken pieces in flour to coat. Set chicken aside.

In a 12-inch skillet, heat olive oil. Add zucchini; cook and stir over medium-high heat for 1 to 2 minutes or until slightly browned. Remove zucchini from skillet and set aside. Add sausage links to skillet and cook over medium heat until brown. Remove sausage from skillet; drain, reserving **1 tablespoon** drippings in skillet. Set sausage aside.

Add butter or margarine and crushed red pepper to drippings in skillet. Heat until butter is melted. Add chicken. Cook and stir for 2 to 3 minutes or until no longer pink. Add wine; bring to boiling. Boil, uncovered, for 2 minutes.

Cut sausage into $^1/_4$-inch-thick slices. Add sliced sausage, chicken broth, roasted red bell peppers, garlic, oregano, and basil. Bring to boiling; reduce heat. Cover and simmer over low heat for 20 minutes. Add zucchini and simmer 2 minutes more. Sprinkle with parsley. Makes 6 servings.

Family Favorite Chicken

2   eggs
1   cup milk
8   chicken breasts halves, skinned, boned, and cut into bite-size pieces
1   to 1$^1/_2$ cups dry seasoned bread crumbs
    Cooking oil
3   cups shredded cheddar cheese (12 ounces)
3   cups shredded mozzarella cheese (12 ounces)
1   cup chicken broth

In a large bowl, beat together eggs and milk. Add chicken to milk mixture. Cover and refrigerate for 6 to 12 hours.

Drain chicken; discard milk mixture. Roll chicken pieces in bread crumbs until coated. In a 12-inch skillet, heat **2 tablespoons** cooking oil. (Add more oil as necessary during cooking.) Add **half** of the chicken; cook and stir over medium-high heat for 3 to 4 minutes or until no longer pink. Remove chicken from skillet and drain on paper towels. Repeat cooking and draining the remaining chicken.

Preheat the oven to 350°. In a greased 3-quart casserole, layer **half** of the chicken, **half** of the cheddar cheese, and **half** of the mozzarella cheese. Repeat layering the remaining chicken and cheese. Pour chicken broth over the top. Cover and bake for 40 to 45 minutes or until heated through. Makes 8 servings.

Country-Style Chicken Pie

Talk about comfort food!

2 carrots, bias-sliced into $^1/_4$-inch-thick slices
1 medium potato, peeled and cubed
1 medium onion, cut into bite-size pieces
$^1/_2$ cup fresh or frozen peas
6 tablespoons butter or margarine
6 tablespoons all-purpose flour
$2^1/_2$ cups chicken broth
$1^1/_2$ cups heavy cream
1 teaspoon salt
$^1/_2$ teaspoon pepper
$^1/_2$ teaspoon dried thyme, crushed
$^1/_8$ to $^1/_4$ teaspoon ground sage
4 cups cubed cooked chicken or turkey
Pastry for single crust pie

Preheat the oven to 425°. In a 2-quart saucepan, cook carrots, potato, onion, and peas in a small amount of water, covered, about 10 minutes or until crisp-tender. Drain well.

Meanwhile, in another 2-quart saucepan melt butter or margarine. Add flour; cook and stir until mixture is golden brown. Slowly add chicken broth, cream, salt, pepper, thyme, and sage. Cook and stir for 5 minutes or until thickened and smooth.

Place chicken in a 3-quart casserole. Top with cooked vegetables and sauce; stir gently to combine. Place pastry over casserole. Flute edges of pastry and cut slits in top for steam to escape. Bake for 25 to 30 minutes or until golden brown. Makes 8 servings.

Chicken and Crab Rosemary

$^1/_2$ cup plus 1 tablespoon butter or margarine, divided
$^1/_2$ cup dry bread crumbs
2 tablespoons finely chopped onion
7 tablespoons all-purpose flour
1 teaspoon salt
1 teaspoon freshly ground pepper
$1^1/_2$ cups chicken broth
1 tablespoon snipped fresh rosemary or 1 teaspoon dried rosemary, crushed
3 cups cubed cooked chicken
2 cups dairy sour cream
1 cup lump crabmeat, cartilage removed
Hot cooked rice or pasta

In an 8-inch skillet, melt **1 tablespoon** of the butter or margarine. Add bread crumbs; cook and stir over medium heat until golden. Remove from heat and set aside.

Preheat the oven to 350°. In a 2-quart saucepan, melt the remaining $^1/_2$ cup butter or margarine. Add onion and cook over medium heat until tender. Stir in flour, salt, and pepper. Add chicken broth and rosemary. Cook and stir over medium heat until thickened and bubbly. Cook and stir for 1 minute more. Remove from heat.

Stir chicken, sour cream, and crabmeat into thickened broth mixture. Transfer to a 2-quart casserole. Sprinkle with the buttered bread crumbs. Bake for 30 minutes. Serve with rice or pasta. Makes 6 to 8 servings.

Chicken Enchiladas with Crema Fresca

1   cup dairy sour cream
1   cup heavy cream
16 to 20 10-inch flour tortillas
4   cups coarsely chopped cooked chicken
2   cups shredded Monterey Jack cheese (8 ounces)
1   cup chopped onion
    Bottled picante sauce

For crema fresca, in a small bowl, combine sour cream and heavy cream. Cover and let stand at room temperature for 8 hours. Chill for 24 hours.

Preheat the oven to 350°. Dip a tortilla in boiling water for 1 second. Place **¼ cup** chicken on tortilla; top with **2 tablespoons** cheese and **1 tablespoon** onion. Roll up carefully and place, seam side down, in a greased 13x9x2-inch baking dish. Repeat with remaining tortillas, chicken, cheese, and onion. Cover and bake for 25 to 30 minutes or until heated through. Dollop crema fresca over tortillas. Top with picante sauce. Makes 8 to 10 servings.

Chicken-Filled Bundles

1   package (8 rolls) refrigerated crescent rolls
3   ounces cream cheese with chives, softened
2   tablespoons butter or margarine, softened
2   cups cubed cooked chicken breast or turkey breast
2   tablespoons butter or margarine, melted
½   cup crushed seasoned croutons
    Cheese Sauce (see recipe below)

Preheat the oven to 350°. Divide crescent roll dough into 4 rectangles, pinching diagonal seam together. With a rolling pin, slightly flatten rectangles. In a bowl, stir together cream cheese and the softened butter. Stir in cooked chicken. Place **one-fourth** of the mixture on one side of each dough rectangle. Fold in half and pinch to seal seams. Brush bundles with melted butter or margarine. Roll in crushed croutons. Place in a shallow baking dish. Bake for 25 to 30 minutes or until golden. Serve with Cheese Sauce. Makes 4 servings.

Cheese Sauce

2   tablespoons butter or margarine
2   tablespoons all-purpose flour
⅛   teaspoon salt
1   cup milk
½   cup shredded American cheese
1   tablespoon finely chopped onion
½   teaspoon Worcestershire sauce
    Dash pepper

In a 1-quart saucepan, melt butter or margarine over low heat. Stir in flour and salt. Add milk; cook and stir until thickened and bubbly. Add cheese, onion, Worcestershire sauce, and pepper. Cook until cheese is melted. Makes about 1¼ cups.

Chicken and Spinach Filled Crepes

1	pound fresh spinach or one 10-ounce package chopped spinach
10	tablespoons butter or margarine, divided
8	ounces sliced fresh mushrooms (3 cups)
$^1/_2$	cup all-purpose flour
2	teaspoons salt, divided
	Dash white pepper
2	cups milk
1	cup chicken broth
$1^1/_2$	cups finely shredded Swiss cheese (6 ounces), divided
2	tablespoons cooking oil
$^1/_2$	cup chopped onion
2	tablespoons pine nuts, toasted
$^1/_2$	teaspoon finely shredded lemon peel
$^1/_2$	teaspoon dried chervil, crushed
$3^1/_2$	cups chopped cooked chicken
12	Crepes (see recipe below)

Wash fresh spinach; remove stems. In a 3-quart saucepan, cook spinach in a small amount of boiling salted water for 3 to 5 minutes or until tender. Drain spinach, squeezing out excess liquid; chop spinach. (Or, cook frozen spinach according to package directions. Drain, squeezing out excess liquid.) Set aside.

For sauce, in a 10-inch skillet, melt **2 tablespoons** of the butter or margarine. Add mushrooms; cook and stir over medium-high heat for 4 to 5 minutes or until tender. Remove from heat and set aside. In a 1-quart saucepan, melt **4 tablespoons** of the remaining butter or margarine. Stir in flour, **1 teaspoon** of the salt, and white pepper. Add milk and chicken broth. Cook and stir over medium heat until thickened and bubbly. Cook and stir for 1 minute more. Stir in **1 cup** of the Swiss cheese until melted. Stir in mushrooms. Set sauce aside.

For filling, in a 12-inch skillet, heat the remaining 4 tablespoons butter or margarine and cooking oil. Add onion and cook over medium heat until tender. Stir in pine nuts, the remaining 1 teaspoon of the salt, lemon peel, and chervil. Stir in chicken, cooked spinach, and 1 cup of the sauce.

Preheat the oven to 350°. Spoon about $^1/_3$ **cup** of the filling down the center of the unbrowned side of each crepe. Roll up crepes. Place crepes, seam side down, in a buttered 12x7$^1/_2$x2-inch baking dish. Spread the remaining sauce over the top of the crepes. Sprinkle with the remaining $^1/_2$ cup Swiss cheese. Bake for 30 to 35 minutes or until heated through and cheese is lightly browned. Makes 6 servings.

Crepes

To freeze crepes for future use, stack crepes with 2 layers of waxed paper between crepes. Thaw, covered, at room temperature for one hour before using.

$1^1/_2$	cups milk
1	cup all-purpose flour
2	eggs
1	tablespoon cooking oil
$^1/_4$	teaspoon salt

In a bowl, combine milk, flour, eggs, oil, and salt. Beat with a rotary beater until well mixed. Heat a lightly greased 6-inch skillet. Remove from heat. Spoon in **2 tablespoons** of the batter; lift and tilt the skillet to spread batter. Return to heat; brown on one side only. Invert pan over paper towel; remove crepe. Repeat with remaining batter, greasing skillet occasionally. Makes 18.

ROCKABILLY
Servin' up

CARL PERKINS

BEST KNOWN FOR HIS ROCKABILLY MEGAHIT, "BLUE SUEDE SHOES," CARL PERKINS GOT HIS START WITH SAM PHILLIPS AT SUN STUDIOS. FROM A POOR RURAL BACKGROUND, PERKINS HAS SAID HE HAD THE MUSIC IN HIM EVEN AS A CHILD. IT JUST TOOK SAM PHILLIPS TO BRING IT OUT.

Turkey Tetrazzini

3 quarts turkey broth* or water, salted
8 ounces thin spaghetti or fettuccine
7 tablespoons butter or margarine, divided
8 ounces sliced fresh mushrooms (3 cups)
3 tablespoons all-purpose flour
1 cup turkey broth* or chicken broth
1/2 cup light cream
2 slightly beaten egg yolks
2 to 3 cups chopped cooked turkey
1/4 cup grated Parmesan cheese

In a 6-quart Dutch oven or stockpot, bring turkey broth or salted water to boiling. Add pasta and cook for 8 to 10 minutes or until tender but still firm. Drain and toss with **3 tablespoons** of the butter or margarine; set aside.

In a 10-inch skillet, melt **1 tablespoon** of the remaining butter or margarine. Add mushrooms; cook and stir over medium-high heat for 4 to 5 minutes or until tender. Set mushrooms aside.

In a 2-quart heavy saucepan, melt the remaining 3 tablespoons butter or margarine. Stir in flour until smooth. Cook over medium heat for 5 minutes, stirring constantly. Reduce heat to low. Cook and stir until roux is a light reddish brown. Remove from heat.

In a small bowl, stir together 1 cup turkey broth or chicken broth, light cream, and egg yolks. Return roux to medium heat. Slowly pour broth mixture into roux; cook and stir until thickened. Stir in turkey and cooked mushrooms. Add cooked pasta. Gently toss until coated. Transfer to a serving dish and sprinkle with Parmesan cheese. Serve immediately. Makes 6 servings.

*To make turkey broth from turkey carcass, break or cut turkey carcass in half. Place in a 6-quart Dutch oven or stockpot with 3 1/2 quarts water; turkey giblets, if desired; 1 onion, quartered; and 2 teaspoons salt. Bring to boiling; reduce heat. Cover and simmer for 1 1/2 hours. Strain broth.

Note: To make ahead, transfer pasta-turkey mixture to a freezer-safe and oven-safe serving dish. Sprinkle with Parmesan cheese. Cover, label, and freeze. To serve, thaw 24 hours ahead in the refrigerator. Preheat the oven to 350°. Bake about 50 minutes or until heated through.

◆ ◆ ◆

CREATIVE RECYCLING

—

"Christmas season at our house begins with the Thanksgiving turkey! I buy a huge bird, planning to have enough left over for this favorite dish that is the centerpiece of the buffet table at our tree-trimming party. Not only is this event fun for the children and their friends, it is also fun for me—I feel childlike in my anticipation of the rest of the holiday season. The children usually break a fifth of our ornaments, and the adults usually drink about a fifth of something while gluing them back and listening to Luciano and the Vienna Boys' Choir. The tetrazzini gives me the chance to exercise the trait (obsession?) my mother and grandmother passed down to me, namely using everything, wasting nothing. My ancestors were the original recyclers!"

◆ ◆ ◆

FISH & SEAFOOD

♦ ♦ ♦

PICTURED AT LEFT
—
Jazzy Orange Roughy
(page 154)

♦ ♦ ♦

Jazz-y Memphians

♦ ♦ ♦

The night air on Beale Street swings with the sounds of great live music. But wait — this is not blues, or rock, or soul. This is jazz — a Memphis music legacy all too often overlooked. It's been said that blues is taken to its highest artistic expression in jazz. Its emotion, its message is there, but it's told in a different language — up-tempo, uptown, sophisticated. We are proud of the jazz giants that call Memphis home. They are world class. Legendary pianist Phineas Newborn died in 1989 but lives on in the performances of brilliant followers such as Harold Mabern, James Williams, Mulgrew Miller, and Donald Brown. Harold Mabern grew up beside saxophonist George Coleman, another jazz genius, and has gone on to become "a living piano legend," as acclaimed in The New Yorker. *Williams, three-time winner of* Downbeat *magazine's Critics' Poll, earned international acclaim for his artistry with Art Blakey and the Jazz Messengers and went on to more first-rate recording and live performance, leaving the Jazz Messengers' bench to the very able Donald Brown. Mulgrew Miller has played these same rare circles and is also hailed by critics. Herman Green, saxophonist, and Kirk Whalum, trumpeter, add to Memphis' impact on the jazz scene, and there are many others. Performing, recording, producing, they stay on an endless round of engagements and Memphis may not see her own too often, but we are listening with pride and we do not forget. To all of them we say, "Come home often."*

*T*HE SOUTH HAS ALWAYS BEEN WELL-SUPPLIED BY THE GULF OF Mexico and our many freshwater lakes and streams. Southern cooks have used this bounty to develop distinctive regional recipes. With the advent of rapid shipping (Federal Express was *born* in Memphis), these same cooks gained access to a wider variety of fresh seafood. They have applied their traditional recipes and created new variations to take advantage of their broader opportunities. No matter the season, no matter the seasonings, seafood represents a rich source for the palate and a healthy alternative to meat, whether it's used as an appetizer or entrée.

Think seafood. Think of shrimp and scallops, salmon, swordfish, and tuna. Think of baked or broiled fillets napped with sauce, delectable crabmeat casseroles, and perfectly grilled shrimp. From fresh water or salt, fish and shellfish are full of nutrients and flavor and deserve to be involved more often in our everyday diets.

When Memphians plan a special party, they often borrow from the sea. Almost everyone loves shrimp and guests line up three deep at the shrimp table, proving the popularity of this shellfish. No less popular at any gathering are steamed crabs, grilled fish, and delicate scallops fresh out of a cooler from the coast or the great seafood departments of today's markets.

We may be landlocked, but our tastebuds are always ready for coastal dainties. *Heart & Soul* invites you to sample our version of the best the water has to offer. ♥

JAZZ
Servin' up

CALVIN NEWBORN

INTERNATIONALLY KNOWN JAZZ GUITARIST AND THE BROTHER OF LATE LEGENDARY PIANIST PHINEAS NEWBORN, CALVIN HAS PLAYED ALL OVER THE WORLD WITH ACCLAIMED PERFORMERS INCLUDING LIONEL HAMPTON, FATHA HINES, AND RAY CHARLES. HE BRINGS A SPECIAL "BLUESY" TOUCH OF THE SOUTH TO HIS JAZZ AND IS A FAVORITE OF AUDIENCES EVERYWHERE.

~

Jazzy Orange Roughy

This colorful, low-calorie dish is pictured on page 152.

2	fresh or frozen orange roughy fillets (about 6 ounces each)
	Salt and pepper
2$^1/_2$	teaspoons snipped fresh basil or $^3/_4$ teaspoon dried basil, crushed
1$^1/_2$	teaspoons snipped fresh oregano or $^1/_2$ teaspoon dried oregano, crushed
1	large clove garlic, minced
$^1/_2$	green pepper, thinly sliced
$^1/_2$	sweet yellow pepper, thinly sliced
$^1/_2$	sweet red pepper, thinly sliced
1	small onion, thinly sliced
2	to 3 tablespoons olive oil
2	tablespoons slivered almonds, toasted (optional)
	Orange or lemon wedges

Thaw fish, if frozen. Preheat the oven to 275°. Pat fillets dry with a paper towel and place in a shallow baking dish. Season generously with salt and pepper. Sprinkle fillets with basil, oregano, and garlic. Bake for 45 minutes or until fish flakes easily.

Meanwhile, in a medium skillet, cook green pepper, yellow pepper, red pepper, and onion in olive oil until crisp-tender. Arrange pepper mixture over cooked fish. Sprinkle with almonds. Broil for 3 minutes or until lightly browned. Garnish with orange or lemon wedges. Makes 2 servings.

Orange Roughy Thermidor

4	fresh or frozen orange roughy fillets (about 6 ounces each)
1¹/₂	cups milk
¹/₄	teaspoon pepper
3	tablespoons butter or margarine, melted
3	tablespoons all-purpose flour
1	cup shredded cheddar cheese (4 ounces)
¹/₄	cup fresh lemon juice
1	tablespoon snipped parsley
1	teaspoon paprika
	Hot cooked rice

Thaw fish, if frozen. Preheat the oven to 350°. Cut fillets in half lengthwise. Roll up each fillet piece, jelly-roll style, starting from the narrow end; secure with a toothpick. Place in a lightly greased 13x9x2-inch baking pan. Pour milk around fillet rolls; sprinkle fillets with pepper. Cover and bake about 30 minutes or until fish flakes easily with a fork. Drain fish, reserving milk.

In a 1-quart saucepan, melt butter or margarine. Stir in flour. Add the reserved milk all at once. Cook and stir over medium heat until thickened and bubbly. Cook and stir for 1 minute more. Add cheese; cook and stir over low heat until melted. Stir in lemon juice.

Pour cheese sauce over fish in baking pan. Sprinkle with parsley and paprika. Broil 6 inches from heat for 2 to 3 minutes or until lightly browned. Serve fish rolls and sauce over hot cooked rice. Makes 4 servings.

Red Snapper with Toasted Pecan Butter

Fans of Criolla's Restaurant at Grayton Beach near Destin, Florida, consider this to be the best fish on the planet!

4	fresh or frozen red snapper fillets (about 6 ounces each)
¹/₂	cup all-purpose flour
4	teaspoons paprika
2	teaspoons garlic powder
1¹/₂	teaspoons salt
¹/₄	teaspoon ground thyme
¹/₄	teaspoon plus ¹/₈ teaspoon ground red pepper, divided
¹/₂	cup milk
¹/₄	cup peanut oil
²/₃	cup pecans
¹/₈	teaspoon white pepper
¹/₄	cup butter
2	tablespoons finely snipped parsley
1	tablespoon fresh lemon juice

Thaw fish, if frozen. In a medium bowl, combine flour, paprika, garlic powder, salt, thyme, and ¹/₄ **teaspoon** of the red pepper. Dip each fillet in milk, then in the flour mixture. In a 12-inch skillet, heat peanut oil over medium heat. Add fillets and cook for 6 minutes, turning once, until golden brown. Remove fillets and keep warm.

For pecan butter, toss pecans with white pepper and the remaining ¹/₈ teaspoon red pepper. In an 8-inch skillet, melt butter. Add seasoned pecans; cook about 3 minutes or until lightly browned. Remove from heat. Stir in parsley and lemon juice.

Transfer red snapper fillets to dinner plates. Spoon pecan butter over fillets and serve immediately. Makes 4 servings.

Criolla's Restaurant, Grayton Beach, FL

♪♪♪

NICE TO NOTE
—

With the current trend toward lower fat and calories, both shellfish and fin fish have enjoyed a renaissance. In preparing fish, however, many cooks feel that they're in "uncharted waters." Perhaps the following tips will help to de-mystify our marine friends a bit.

• Look for freshness. The eyes of whole fish should bulge slightly and the scales should be shiny and firmly attached. The flesh should be firm to the touch. The odor of fresh fish is mild. (If it smells bad, it probably is!)

• Never refreeze fish. Be sure you know if what you are buying has been previously frozen.

• Cook fish as soon as possible after purchasing or catching it. Bought from the market, it can be kept safely for up to 2 days, well-wrapped, in the coldest part of the refrigerator.

• When thawing frozen fish, always defrost the fish in the refrigerator, never at room temperature. Allow 24 hours for 1 pound of fish. Larger fish will take longer.

• Figure on 4 to 6 ounces of fish or seafood per person, excluding bones or shells.

• As a general guideline, fish should cook about 10 minutes per inch at the thickest part.

Red Snapper with Fresh Tomatoes

4   fresh or frozen red snapper fillets (about 6 ounces each)
1/4 cup butter or margarine
1   green pepper, seeded and thinly sliced
2   stalks celery, coarsely chopped
1   small onion, thinly sliced
4   medium tomatoes, peeled, seeded, and chopped
2   tablespoons snipped Italian parsley
1   teaspoon salt
1   teaspoon freshly ground pepper
1   teaspoon dried basil, crushed
1   teaspoon dried oregano, crushed
1   clove garlic, minced
    Salt and freshly ground pepper

Thaw fish, if frozen. Preheat the oven to 350°. In a 12-inch skillet, melt butter or margarine. Add green pepper, celery, and onion. Cook until vegetables are crisp-tender. Add tomatoes, parsley, salt, pepper, basil, oregano, and garlic. Cook 5 minutes more, stirring occasionally.

In a 13x9x2-inch baking dish, arrange the fillets in a single layer. Sprinkle with additional salt and freshly ground pepper. Spoon tomato mixture over fillets. Bake for 20 to 30 minutes or until fish flakes easily with a fork. Makes 4 servings.

Swordfish with Tomatoes and Olives

This is very fresh-tasting; perfect for a moonlit dinner. Serve at your own risk!

1   pound fresh or frozen 1-inch-thick swordfish steaks, cut into 4 pieces
6   tablespoons olive oil
6   cloves garlic, thinly sliced
1 1/2 cups sliced fresh mushrooms (4 ounces)
1/2 cup finely chopped onion
     Salt and freshly ground pepper
1/3 cup snipped fresh basil
1/4 cup snipped fresh oregano
2   tablespoons snipped fresh mint
1 3/4 cups drained canned Italian plum tomatoes, chopped
1/2 teaspoon crushed red pepper
2/3 cup Greek ripe olives
2   tablespoons capers
6   ounces hot cooked orzo or vermicelli

Thaw fish, if frozen. In a heavy 12-inch skillet, heat oil over low heat. Add garlic and cook about 10 minutes or until pale golden, stirring occasionally. Remove garlic with a slotted spoon and place in a small bowl; set aside.

Increase heat to medium and cook mushrooms until tender; remove with slotted spoon and add to garlic in bowl. Add onion to skillet and cook for 2 minutes. Add fish and sear on both sides. Remove skillet from heat. Season fish with salt and pepper.

In a small bowl, combine basil, oregano, and mint. Add **all but 2 tablespoons** of the herb mixture to fish. Return skillet to heat. Cook fish over low heat for 3 to 5 minutes per side or until fish flakes easily with a fork. Remove fish to serving platter; keep warm.

Add tomatoes and crushed red pepper to skillet. Cook over high heat for 1 minute. Add olives, capers, and the reserved mushrooms and garlic. Heat mixture through. Place orzo or vermicelli on individual plates. Top each with a fish portion. Spoon tomato mixture over fish. Sprinkle with remaining 2 tablespoons herbs. Makes 4 servings.

NICE TO NOTE
—

If your market does not have the fish that you require for a recipe, bear in mind that substitutions can be made. Medium firm fish such as red snapper, orange roughy, and sole can be interchanged for one another, as can firm-fleshed choices such as swordfish, shark, and tuna.

∞

Best-Ever Fried Catfish with Fresh Tartar Sauce

Southern cooks know that soaking the fish in vinegar makes it tender, white, and flaky.

	Fresh Tartar Sauce (see recipe below)
6	fresh or frozen catfish fillets (2 to 2¹/₂ pounds total)
4	cups water
¹/₄	cup vinegar
3	tablespoons salt
1¹/₂	cups cornmeal
¹/₂	cup all-purpose flour
2	teaspoons seasoned salt
1	teaspoon salt
¹/₂	teaspoon onion powder
	Cooking oil

Prepare Fresh Tartar Sauce. Cover and chill at least 1 hour. Thaw fish, if frozen. In a large bowl, combine water, vinegar, and salt. Soak catfish in vinegar mixture for 4 to 5 hours in the refrigerator. Drain.

In a plastic bag, combine cornmeal, flour, seasoned salt, salt, and onion powder. Shake to mix. Add catfish, one at a time, and shake until completely coated.

In a heavy 12-inch skillet or Dutch oven, pour oil to a depth of 2 to 3 inches. Heat oil to 375°. Fry catfish for 4 to 5 minutes per side or until golden brown. Drain well. Serve immediately with Fresh Tartar Sauce. Makes 4 to 6 servings.

Fresh Tartar Sauce

1	cup mayonnaise
2	tablespoons fresh lemon juice
	Dash hot pepper sauce
¹/₄	cup finely chopped dill pickle
2	tablespoons finely chopped onion
2	tablespoons snipped parsley
2	tablespoons capers
1	tablespoon chopped pimiento
	Salt and pepper to taste

In a small bowl, combine mayonnaise, lemon juice, and hot pepper sauce. Add dill pickle, onion, parsley, capers, pimiento, salt, and pepper. Stir well. Cover and chill at least 1 hour before serving. Makes about 1²/₃ cups.

Memphis Heart and Sole

Not exactly soul food, but your heart will love it!

6	fresh or frozen sole fillets (about 4 ounces each)
4	medium tomatoes, peeled and thinly sliced
1/2	teaspoon dried basil, crushed
1/2	cup fine dry bread crumbs
1/2	teaspoon salt
1/2	teaspoon freshly ground pepper
3/4	cup dry white wine
1/2	cup butter or margarine
1	tablespoon fresh lime juice
1/2	cup freshly grated Parmesan cheese

Thaw fish, if frozen. Arrange tomato slices evenly in the bottom of a 13x9x2-inch baking dish. Sprinkle basil over tomatoes. Top with bread crumbs. Arrange fillets over bread crumbs. Sprinkle with salt and pepper.

Preheat the oven to 400°. In a 1-quart saucepan, combine wine, butter, and lime juice. Cook over medium heat until butter melts. Pour over fillets. Sprinkle with Parmesan cheese. Bake for 15 to 20 minutes or until fish flakes easily with a fork. Makes 6 servings.

Fillet of Sole Stuffed with Crabmeat

6	fresh or frozen sole fillets (about 4 ounces each)
3	slices Swiss cheese, halved lengthwise (about 4 ounces)
8	ounces lump crabmeat, cartilage removed
1	tablespoon snipped fresh basil or 1 teaspoon dried basil crushed
4	tablespoons butter or margarine, divided
1/4	cup chopped mushrooms
2	teaspoons chopped shallots
3	tablespoons dry white wine
2	teaspoons lemon juice, divided
3	tablespoons all-purpose flour
1	cup clam juice
1/2	cup light cream
	Salt to taste
	Paprika
1	tablespoon snipped parsley

Thaw fish, if frozen. Place fillets on a work surface, skin side up. Top each fillet with 1/2 **slice** of the Swiss cheese, **3 tablespoons** of the crabmeat, and 1/2 **teaspoon** of the fresh basil. Roll up fillets and place, seam side down, in a shallow baking dish.

Preheat the oven to 400°. For sauce, in a heavy skillet, melt **2 tablespoons** of the butter or margarine over medium heat. Add mushrooms, shallots, wine, and **1 teaspoon** of the lemon juice. Cook until liquid evaporates. Add remaining 2 tablespoons butter and heat until melted. Stir in flour until well combined. Stir in clam juice. Cook and stir until thick and bubbly. Add cream, the remaining 1 teaspoon lemon juice, and salt. Pour sauce over fish rolls; sprinkle lightly with paprika.

Cover and bake for 16 to 20 minutes or until fish flakes easily. Carefully remove fish rolls to serving plates. Spoon sauce over fish and sprinkle with snipped parsley. Makes 6 servings.

♦ ♦ ♦

GONE FISHIN'
—

"Even though fish and seafood have become extremely popular in these fitness-conscious times, they have always been a mainstay in our family's gatherings. Freshwater fish from Mississippi's lakes and ponds, and seafood from the Gulf Coast—all caught by one of the many eager fishermen in my family—are mealtime favorites and mean home to me."

♦ ♦ ♦

Salmone Ala Limone Panna Sala

   4   fresh or frozen salmon fillets (8 to 10 ounces each), skinned
1³/₄   cups dry white wine, divided
 ³/₄   cup water
 ¹/₂   cup plus 1 tablespoon fresh lemon juice, divided
   1   teaspoon salt
 ¹/₂   teaspoon white pepper
 ¹/₂   cup butter or margarine
   8   green onions, thinly sliced
 ¹/₄   cup finely snipped parsley
   1   clove garlic, minced
        Pinch of saffron
   1   cup heavy cream
        Salt and white pepper to taste
        Parsley sprigs and lemon slices

Thaw fish, if frozen. To poach salmon, in a 12-inch skillet, combine ³/₄ **cup** of the wine, water, **1 tablespoon** of the lemon juice, salt, and white pepper. Bring to boiling. Add the salmon fillets. Return just to boiling; reduce heat. Cover and simmer gently over low heat for 4 to 6 minutes per ¹/₂-inch thickness or until salmon flakes easily with a fork. Transfer salmon to a platter. Cover loosely with foil to keep warm while preparing the sauce.

For sauce, in a 1-quart saucepan, melt butter or margarine. Stir in green onions, the remaining ¹/₂ cup lemon juice, parsley, garlic, and saffron. Cook and stir over medium-high heat until onion is tender. Pour the remaining 1 cup wine into the skillet. Using a metal spatula or wire whisk, scrape up any browned bits from bottom of pan. Bring to boiling. Boil until mixture is reduced by half. Pour in cream. Cook and stir until slightly thickened. Season to taste with additional salt and white pepper.

To serve, spoon sauce onto dinner plates. Place salmon on top. Garnish with parsley sprigs and a lemon slice. Makes 4 servings.

Ronnie Grisanti & Sons
3rd Generation of Grisanti

Salmon Au Poivre

   4   fresh or frozen salmon fillets (about 10 ounces each), skinned
   2   cups dry white wine, divided
1¹/₂   cups water
   1   teaspoon dried dillweed
   1   teaspoon dried tarragon, crushed
   1   teaspoon fennel seed
   1   teaspoon white pepper
 ¹/₂   teaspoon green peppercorns
   2   cups heavy cream
        Pinch salt

Thaw fish, if frozen. In a 4-quart Dutch oven, combine **1¹/₂ cups** of the wine, the water, dillweed, tarragon, fennel seed, and white pepper. Bring to boiling. Gently lower salmon into cooking liquid. Cover and simmer for 10 to 12 minutes or until fish flakes easily. Carefully remove fish to serving platter; keep warm. Discard cooking liquid.

For sauce, in the same Dutch oven, combine remaining ¹/₂ cup wine and the green peppercorns. Bring to boiling; boil until wine has almost evaporated. Stir in cream. Bring to boiling; reduce heat. Simmer until thickened. Season with salt. Spoon sauce over salmon and serve immediately. Makes 4 servings.

Poached Salmon with Tarragon-Mustard Sauce

Few meals say "spring" like salmon, asparagus, and new potatoes. Why not celebrate the arrival of the first robin with this menu?

4   fresh or frozen 1-inch-thick salmon fillets (about 6 ounces each), skinned
1   cup plus 2 tablespoons heavy cream, divided
1¼   cups dry white wine
2   shallots, sliced
¼   cup butter or margarine, cut into pieces
2   tablespoons Dijon-style mustard
1   teaspoon snipped fresh tarragon or ¼ teaspoon dried tarragon, crushed
¼   teaspoon cracked black pepper

Thaw fish, if frozen. In a small bowl, whisk **2 tablespoons** of the heavy cream until soft peaks form; cover and refrigerate.

In a 12-inch skillet, combine wine and shallots. Bring to boiling. Boil about 5 minutes or until liquid is reduced by half. Add the remaining 1 cup heavy cream and bring to boiling; reduce heat to low. Add the salmon fillets. Cover and simmer for 10 to 12 minutes or until fish flakes easily with a fork. With a spatula, transfer salmon to a platter. Cover loosely with foil to keep warm while preparing the sauce.

For sauce, bring poaching liquid in the skillet to boiling. Boil over high heat about 5 minutes or until mixture is reduced to ¾ **cup**. Reduce heat to low. Gradually add butter, whisking until melted. Stir in mustard, tarragon, and cracked pepper. Remove sauce from heat. Fold in chilled whipped cream. To serve, spoon sauce over fish. Makes 4 servings.

Mustard-Crusted Red Snapper

4   fresh or frozen red snapper fillets (6 to 8 ounces each)
    Salt and pepper
½   cup olive oil
¼   cup finely chopped onion
3   large cloves garlic, minced
⅓   cup coarse-grained mustard
½   cup all-purpose flour
¼   cup unsalted butter

Thaw fish, if frozen. Score skin side of fillets and season both sides with salt and pepper. Brush skin side of fillets with a small amount of the olive oil. In a small bowl, combine onion and garlic. Press **4 teaspoons** of the onion mixture into the scored skin of each fillet. Spread **4 teaspoons** of the mustard over the onion mixture, coating evenly.

Gently coat fillets with flour, shaking off excess. In a 12-inch skillet, heat the remaining oil and the butter over medium-high heat until hot, but not smoking. Cook fillets, skin side down, for 3 to 4 minutes or until golden brown and crusty. Carefully turn and cook 4 to 5 minutes more or until fish flakes easily with a fork. Makes 4 servings.

Shrimp Creole

Memphis and New Orleans share, among other things, muggy heat, the Mississippi, and a love of Shrimp Creole.

1¹/₂ pounds fresh or frozen peeled and deveined shrimp
8 slices lean bacon
1 cup chopped onion
¹/₂ cup finely sliced celery
¹/₂ green pepper, cut into julienne strips
2 cloves garlic, thinly sliced
1 tablespoon all-purpose flour
1 28-ounce can Italian plum tomatoes
1 8-ounce can tomato juice
1 bay leaf
1¹/₄ cups chicken broth
1 tablespoon paprika
2 teaspoons Worcestershire sauce
¹/₄ to ¹/₂ teaspoon ground red pepper
   Salt and pepper to taste
   Hot cooked rice

Thaw shrimp, if frozen. In a 6-quart Dutch oven or stockpot, cook bacon over medium heat until crisp. Drain, reserving drippings in Dutch oven or stockpot. Crumble bacon and set aside. Cook onion, celery, green pepper, and garlic in bacon drippings over medium-low heat until vegetables are tender. Add flour; cook and stir for several minutes.

Drain tomatoes, reserving **1 cup** liquid. Chop tomatoes. Add tomatoes and reserved liquid, tomato juice, bay leaf, chicken broth, paprika, Worcestershire sauce, and red pepper to Dutch oven. Bring to boiling; reduce heat and simmer about 30 minutes or until desired consistency, stirring occasionally. Add shrimp, salt, and pepper. Cook and stir for 3 to 4 minutes or until shrimp turn pink. Discard bay leaf. Serve over rice and top with crumbled bacon. Makes 6 servings.

Criolla's Barbecue Shrimp

Serve with plenty of French bread for dipping into the fabulous sauce.

1 pound fresh or frozen peeled and deveined large shrimp
¹/₈ teaspoon salt
¹/₂ cup butter or margarine
1 tablespoon water
1 tablespoon fresh lemon juice
1 tablespoon Worcestershire sauce
1¹/₂ teaspoons freshly ground pepper
   French bread

Thaw shrimp, if frozen. Sprinkle salt over shrimp. In a 10-inch skillet, melt butter or margarine. Add shrimp, water, lemon juice, Worcestershire sauce, and pepper. Cook over medium-high heat, shaking pan constantly, for 1 to 3 minutes or until shrimp turn pink. If desired, season to taste with additional freshly ground pepper. Serve with French bread for dipping in sauce. Makes 2 to 4 servings.

Criolla's Restaurant, Grayton Beach, FL

◆ ◆ ◆

ROUX TOUT DE SUITE

—

Essential to a multitude of Creole or Cajun dishes is a roux, that tan-to-brown paste made by browning equal amounts of flour and oil. Traditionalists will claim that the only way to prepare a roux is to use a black iron skillet and to stand forever over a low fire, stirring constantly until the desired color and depth of flavor is achieved. With the advent of the microwave, however, it is now possible to make a roux in a large glass measuring cup in just minutes. Gumbos, étouffées, and jambalayas are relatively easy when the roux is done so quickly.

In a 4-cup glass measure, stir together ²/₃ cup cooking oil and ²/₃ cup all-purpose flour. Microcook on High, uncovered, for 6 to 7 minutes or until the roux is light brown. Stir. Microcook 30 seconds to 1 minute more or until dark brown. This makes enough roux to thicken 3 to 4 quarts of soup or stew. Freeze any remaining roux for future use.

◆ ◆ ◆

Herbed Shrimp with Basil Mayonnaise

Try this as a first course or as the centerpiece of a light summer supper. These shrimp are great on the grill, too. The smoky crispness that grilling gives the shrimp perfectly complements the piquant herb mayonnaise.

2	pounds fresh or frozen peeled and deveined large shrimp
³/₄	cup olive oil
2	tablespoons fresh lemon juice
1	tablespoon snipped parsley
2	cloves garlic, crushed
1	teaspoon salt
¹/₂	teaspoon dried oregano, crushed
¹/₄	teaspoon freshly ground pepper
	Basil Mayonnaise (see recipe below)
	Lemon slices
	Parsley sprigs

Thaw shrimp, if frozen. For marinade, in a 13x9x2-inch baking dish combine olive oil, lemon juice, parsley, garlic, salt, oregano, and pepper. Thread shrimp on skewers and arrange in baking dish. Marinate in the refrigerator for 2 hours, turning every 30 minutes.

Meanwhile, prepare Basil Mayonnaise. Transfer skewered shrimp to broiler pan; broil (or grill directly over medium coals) for 3 minutes on each side or until shrimp turn pink. Arrange on platter. Garnish with lemon slices and parsley sprigs. Serve with Basil Mayonnaise. Makes 6 servings.

Basil Mayonnaise

2	egg yolks
1	tablespoon white wine vinegar
1	tablespoon Dijon-style mustard
¹/₄	teaspoon salt
¹/₄	teaspoon white pepper
1	cup olive oil
3	tablespoons lemon juice
2	cups firmly packed fresh basil leaves
1	clove garlic, crushed

In a small bowl or food processor bowl, combine egg yolks, vinegar, mustard, salt, and white pepper. Beat with an electric mixer on medium speed or process until combined. With mixer or processor running, add olive oil in a slow steady stream, stopping occasionally to scrape sides of bowl. While continuing to mix or process, add lemon juice and, if necessary, more salt and white pepper to taste. Transfer mayonnaise to a medium bowl.

In the food processor bowl or a blender container, combine **1 cup** of the mayonnaise, the basil leaves, and garlic. Cover and process or blend until smooth. Whisk basil mixture into remaining mayonnaise, adding more lemon juice, if desired. Cover and store in the refrigerator up to 2 weeks. Makes about 2¹/₂ cups.

Baked Shrimp Douglas

If you use jumbo shrimp in this dish, add a few minutes to the baking time.

- 2 pounds fresh or frozen medium shrimp
- 1/2 cup butter or margarine, melted
- 1/3 cup Worcestershire sauce
- 3 tablespoons olive oil
- 1 teaspoon dried rosemary, crushed
- 1 teaspoon garlic salt
- 1/2 teaspoon salt
- 1/2 teaspoon celery salt
- 1/2 teaspoon dried oregano, crushed
- 1/2 teaspoon dried thyme, crushed
- 1/2 teaspoon paprika
- 1/4 teaspoon ground red pepper
- 1 clove garlic, minced

Thaw shrimp, if frozen. Peel and devein shrimp. Preheat the oven to 350°. Combine shrimp, butter, Worcestershire sauce, olive oil, rosemary, garlic salt, salt, celery salt, oregano, thyme, paprika, red pepper, and garlic. Transfer to a 13x9x2-inch baking dish. Bake, uncovered, about 20 minutes or until shrimp turn pink. Makes 6 servings.

Shrimp Ratatouille on a Roll

This makes a satisfying late-night supper and would be ideal to have planned for traveling guests who arrive after the dinner hour and are ready for "a little something."

- 1 pound fresh or frozen peeled and deveined shrimp
- 1 medium eggplant (about 1 pound), cut into 1/2-inch cubes
- 2 medium zucchini (about 1 pound total), cut into 1/2-inch cubes
- 1 medium green pepper, coarsely chopped
- 1/2 cup chopped onion
- 3 cloves garlic, minced
- 1/4 cup olive oil
- 1 16-ounce can whole tomatoes
- 3 tablespoons tomato paste
- 1 tablespoon red wine vinegar
- 2 teaspoons salt
- 1 1/2 teaspoons snipped fresh basil or 1/2 teaspoon dried basil, crushed
- 1/2 teaspoon pepper
- 1/2 teaspoon ground red pepper
- 1 16-ounce loaf Italian or French bread or 6 individual French rolls
- 1 1/2 cups shredded mozzarella cheese (6 ounces)

Thaw shrimp, if frozen. In a 4-quart Dutch oven, cook eggplant, zucchini, green pepper, onion, and garlic in olive oil for 5 minutes. Drain tomatoes, reserving **2 tablespoons** liquid. Chop tomatoes. Add tomatoes and reserved liquid, tomato paste, red wine vinegar, salt, basil, pepper, and red pepper. Cover and simmer for 25 minutes, stirring occasionally.

Preheat the oven to 350°. Meanwhile, slice top crust from bread. Hollow out loaf of bread, leaving a 1-inch border. Place bread on baking sheet in oven for 5 minutes to warm.

Stir shrimp into tomato mixture. Cover and simmer about 4 minutes or until shrimp are pink. Spoon shrimp mixture into hollowed out bread; sprinkle with mozzarella cheese. Broil for 1 to 2 minutes or just until cheese is bubbly and lightly browned. Makes 6 servings.

Seafood Casserole

     6 tablespoons butter or margarine, divided
     6 tablespoons all-purpose flour
   1/2 teaspoon salt
   1/4 to 1/2 teaspoon freshly ground pepper
        Dash ground red pepper
  1 3/4 cups milk
   1/4 cup dry white wine
     1 cup shredded cheddar cheese (4 ounces), divided
     1 cup sliced fresh mushrooms
    12 ounces peeled and deveined medium shrimp, cooked
    12 ounces lump crabmeat, cartilage removed

Preheat the oven to 350°. In a 2-quart saucepan, melt **4 tablespoons** of the butter or margarine. Stir in flour, salt, freshly ground pepper, and ground red pepper. Add milk and wine all at once. Cook and stir over medium heat until thickened and bubbly. Add 3/4 **cup** of the cheese. Cook and stir over low heat until melted. Remove from heat and set aside.

In an 8-inch skillet, melt the remaining 2 tablespoons butter or margarine. Add mushrooms. Cook and stir over medium heat for 4 to 5 minutes or until tender.

Stir mushrooms, cooked shrimp, and crabmeat into cheese mixture. Pour into a 2-quart casserole. Sprinkle with the remaining 1/4 cup cheese. Bake for 20 to 30 minutes or until hot and bubbly. Makes 4 to 6 servings.

Southern Scallops in Lemon Butter Sauce

     1 pound fresh or frozen bay scallops
     7 tablespoons unsalted butter, divided
     2 teaspoons Cajun Creole seasoning
     1 cup sliced fresh mushrooms
   3/4 cup sliced green onions
   1/2 cup chicken broth
     2 tablespoons fresh lemon juice
     1 tablespoon snipped parsley
        Hot cooked rice or crusty French bread

Thaw scallops, if frozen. In a 12-inch skilet, melt **4 tablespoons** of the butter over medium heat. Remove from heat. Add scallops and stir to coat well with the butter. Sprinkle Cajun seasoning over scallops and stir to coat evenly. Return skillet to medium-high heat and cook about 2 minutes or just until scallops are opaque. Remove scallops with a slotted spoon and set aside.

Add **1 tablespoon** of the remaining butter to skillet and return to medium heat. Add mushrooms and onions. Cook about 4 minutes or until tender. Remove vegetables with a slotted spoon and set aside.

Increase heat to high. Stir in chicken broth and lemon juice, scraping up any browned bits from bottom of skillet. Bring to boiling; boil for 3 minutes. Cut remaining 2 tablespoons butter into small pieces; stir a few pieces at a time into skillet until all butter is melted and sauce is smooth, about 1 minute. Stir in parsley, reserved scallops, and reserved vegetables. Return to boiling. Remove from heat immediately. Serve over hot cooked rice or in bowls with crusty French bread for dipping. Makes 2 to 4 servings.

Sea Scallops with Red Pepper Cream Sauce

  2 pounds fresh or frozen sea scallops
  9 tablespoons butter or margarine, divided
  2 large sweet red peppers, seeded and chopped
 1/2 cup chopped onion
  2 cloves garlic, minced
  1 teaspoon Hungarian paprika
 1/4 to 1/2 teaspoon crushed red pepper
 1/4 cup dry white wine
 3/4 cup heavy cream
 1/2 teaspoon salt
     Freshly ground pepper and salt to taste
     Parsley sprigs

Thaw scallops, if frozen. In a 12-inch skillet, melt **6 tablespoons** of the butter or margarine. Add sweet red peppers, onion, garlic, paprika, and crushed red pepper. Cook, stirring occasionally, over medium-low heat about 15 minutes or until vegetables are tender. Stir in wine and cook 5 minutes more, stirring frequently.

Stir cream into mixture in skillet. Bring to boiling; remove from heat. Transfer mixture to a blender container or food processor bowl. Cover and blend or process until pureed. Strain mixture through a fine sieve. Transfer cream mixture to a 1-quart saucepan. Stir in salt. Keep warm over low heat while preparing the scallops.

To prepare scallops, in the same skillet, melt the remaining 3 tablespoons butter or margarine. Add scallops. Season with freshly ground pepper and additional salt. Cook, stirring frequently, over medium heat for 1 to 3 minutes or until scallops are opaque.

To serve, spoon sauce onto a serving plate. Arrange scallops on top and garnish with parsley sprigs. Makes 6 servings.

Crabmeat Amandine

Served in small portions, this makes a wonderful first course. For a complete meal, be more generous with servings and add French bread and your favorite green salad.

 1/2 cup butter or margarine
  3 green onions, finely sliced
  3 tablespoons fresh lemon juice
  1 pound lump crabmeat, cartilage removed
  2 tablespoons snipped parsley
     White pepper
     Hot pepper sauce
 1/4 cup slivered almonds, toasted

In a 10-inch skillet, melt butter or margarine. Add onions and lemon juice. Cook and stir over medium heat for 1 minute. Add crabmeat and parsley to onion mixture, stirring gently to avoid breaking up crabmeat. Season to taste with white pepper and hot pepper sauce. Cook over medium heat just until heated through. Stir in almonds. Makes 4 main-dish servings or 8 appetizer servings.

Elegant Crabmeat Casserole

Make early in the day for an impressive "I slaved all day over a hot stove" effect!

1¹/₂   cups shell macaroni (6 ounces)
 ¹/₄   cup butter or margarine
  3   tablespoons finely chopped onion
 ¹/₄   cup all-purpose flour
  2   cups heavy cream
 ¹/₃   cup dry white wine
       Salt and pepper to taste
  1   pound lump crabmeat, cartilage removed
  1   14-ounce can quartered artichoke hearts, drained
  2   tablespoons lemon juice
  1   cup shredded Gruyère cheese (4 ounces)
 ¹/₄   teaspoon paprika

In a 6-quart Dutch oven or stockpot, cook macaroni in 3 quarts boiling salted water for 8 to 12 minutes (depending on size of shells) or until almost tender. Drain well. In a 3-quart saucepan, melt butter over low heat. Add onion and cook until tender. Stir in flour until well combined. Add cream, whisking vigorously. Cook over medium heat, stirring until sauce comes to a boil. Remove from heat and add wine, salt, and pepper.

Preheat the oven to 350°. In a large bowl, combine crabmeat, artichoke hearts, and lemon juice. Stir in cooked macaroni. Add cream sauce and stir gently but thoroughly. Spoon mixture into a greased 3-quart casserole. Sprinkle with shredded cheese and paprika. Bake for 45 minutes. Makes 6 servings.

Crab Rolls

A perfect luncheon dish or light summer entrée.

  3   French-style rolls, 6 to 7 inches long
       Butter or margarine, melted
  3   green onions, sliced
 ¹/₄   cup mayonnaise
  2   tablespoons dairy sour cream
  1   pound lump crabmeat, cartilage removed
  1   cup finely shredded Gruyère cheese (4 ounces)
       Ground red pepper
       Fresh lemon juice
       Ground nutmeg

Preheat the broiler. Cut rolls in half lengthwise. Brush cut surfaces with melted butter or margarine. Place, cut side up, on a baking sheet. Broil until lightly toasted.

Reduce oven temperature to 400°. In a medium bowl, stir together green onions, mayonnaise, and sour cream. Add crabmeat and Gruyère cheese. Toss until combined. Season to taste with ground red pepper, lemon juice, and nutmeg. Spoon crab mixture onto cut surfaces of toasted rolls. Bake for 5 to 10 minutes or until heated through. Makes 3 servings.

Note: To make ahead, prepare crab mixture as directed above, except do not stir in green onions. Cover and refrigerate for up to 6 hours before serving. To serve, stir onion into crab mixture, toast rolls, and continue as above.

CLASSICS
Servin' up

ALAN BALTER

ALAN BALTER BECAME MUSIC DIRECTOR AND CONDUCTOR OF THE MEMPHIS SYMPHONY ORCHESTRA IN 1984 AFTER SERVING AS PRINCIPAL CLARINETIST AND ASSISTANT CONDUCTOR OF THE ATLANTA SYMPHONY UNDER ROBERT SHAW. HE HAS BEEN INVITED TO CONDUCT THE SYMPHONIES OF ST. LOUIS, OAKLAND, BUFFALO, AND SAN DIEGO. HE HAS CONDUCTED NATIONALLY AND INTERNATIONALLY BROADCAST PERFORMANCES. ALAN BALTER HAS DRAMATICALLY EXPANDED THE SYMPHONY PERFORMANCE SCHEDULE AND HAS BROUGHT THE MEMPHIS SYMPHONY TO AN UNPRECEDENTED LEVEL OF ACCOMPLISHMENT.

Crab Cakes with Spicy Tomato Tartar Sauce

Spicy Tomato Tartar Sauce (see recipe below)
- 6 tablespoons butter or margarine
- $^1/_2$ cup all-purpose flour
- $^1/_2$ teaspoon salt
- $^1/_4$ teaspoon pepper
- 2 cups milk
- 1 pound lump crabmeat, cartilage removed
- $^1/_2$ cup finely chopped sweet red pepper
- $^1/_2$ cup finely chopped sweet yellow pepper
- $^1/_2$ cup finely chopped celery
- $^1/_4$ cup finely sliced green onions
- 2 teaspoons lemon juice
- 1 teaspoon dry mustard
- $^1/_8$ to $^1/_4$ teaspoon ground red pepper
- 3 cups fine dry bread crumbs, divided
- $^1/_2$ cup cooking oil

Prepare Spicy Tomato Tartar Sauce. Cover and chill at least 1 hour or overnight.

In a 1$^1/_2$-quart saucepan, melt butter over low heat. Stir in flour, salt, and pepper until well combined. Gradually stir in milk. Cook and stir until thickened and bubbly. Cook and stir 2 minutes more. Set aside.

In a large bowl, combine crabmeat, sweet red pepper, yellow pepper, celery, onions, lemon juice, dry mustard, and ground red pepper. Stir in sauce. Cool thoroughly. Stir in **1 cup** of the bread crumbs. Using $^1/_4$ **cup** of the mixture for each, shape into $^1/_2$-inch-thick cakes. Thoroughly coat cakes with the remaining 2 cups bread crumbs.

In a 12-inch skillet, heat **2 tablespoons** of the cooking oil over medium-high heat. Cook crab cakes for 3 to 5 minutes per side or until golden. Add more oil to skillet as needed to cook remaining crab cakes. Drain on paper towels. Serve with Spicy Tomato Tartar Sauce. Makes 4 or 5 servings.

Spicy Tomato Tartar Sauce

- 2 cups mayonnaise
- 2 tomatoes, peeled, seeded, and chopped
- 10 cornichons, chopped
- 1 4-ounce can chopped green chili peppers, drained
- $^1/_4$ cup lemon juice
- $^1/_4$ cup finely chopped onion
- 2 tablespoons capers, minced
- $^1/_2$ teaspoon salt
- $^1/_2$ teaspoon pepper

In a medium bowl, stir together all ingredients. Cover and chill at least 1 hour before serving. Makes about 5 cups.

BARBECUE & GRILLING

◆ ◆ ◆

PICTURED AT LEFT

—

*Summer Corn Salad (page 69)
and Holiday Ribs (page 176)*

◆ ◆ ◆

Isaac Hayes

◆ ◆ ◆

It was a fateful day when Isaac Hayes first found his way to "Soulsville, U.S.A.," Stax Recording Studio. He moved to Memphis from Covington, Tennessee, as a teenager and launched a career that put his name in lights across the country. He played keyboard for Otis Redding, Carla Thomas, and other Stax stars and, in the '60s, moved into songwriting to produce a string of hits now being resurrected by new artists. (A nine-volume set of Stax singles released and nominated for a Grammy in 1992 has stirred fresh interest in the hot times and tunes of Isaac's days at Stax.) Teaming up with David Porter, Isaac Hayes wrote Sam and Dave's power-packed hits "Hold On, I'm Coming," "Soul Man," and "When Something is Wrong With My Baby." Later, he worked independently and turned up gold on several albums before striking it rich in Hollywood, writing and singing the Oscar-winning theme to the movie "Shaft." Isaac now lives in Atlanta when he is not on the road with the acting angle of his career, and his hits, old and new, continue to win him honors. His two hits "Shaft" and "Deja Vu" (recorded by Dionne Warwick) recently earned him two songwriter awards recognizing songs with more than a million radio plays.

*O*UR EARLIEST FOREBEARS DISCOVERED THAT FIRE MADE A HUGE improvement in the taste of meat. Today, we continue to refine the techniques and enjoy the unbeatable flavors of outdoor grilling. It may no longer include saber-toothed tiger, but the long list of meats, seafood, and fowl offers many choices adaptable to outdoor cooking with wondrous results. Not only does grilling outside produce delicious meals, it is also fun for the chef and for guests and family.

Go simple with hamburgers and chicken, which are tested family-pleasers, or put on a beef tenderloin, leg of lamb, or salmon for a special occasion. Whether your preference is for wild duck or farm-raised chicken, shish-kebab or the great American sirloin, the grill can impart a delightful flavor to meat that indoor cooking simply cannot duplicate. Perhaps it is because grilling evokes happy family times and the carefree days of summer: picnics, backyard parties, and Friday night burgers. Maybe it's the taste of the great outdoors, or the happy fact that it's usually Dad who does the cooking!

Whatever the reason, grilling has become a family sport in many Memphis households and pork barbecuing is almost a religion. True barbecue comes from long, slow, basted cooking, producing a meat of incredible tenderness and taste that has made Memphis famous. Find your recipe, fire up the grill, and feast on the best of outdoor cooking. ♥

NICE TO NOTE

Except where otherwise noted, our recipes have been developed and tested for use with charcoal grills. Gas grills may produce a different result. Please consult manufacturer's directions for approximate cooking times and instructions for gas grills. Grilling time can vary with the cut of meat, grill position, weather, coal temperature, and degree of doneness desired.

∞

Flank Steak Tournedos

For gourmets on the go, this recipe takes under 30 minutes from start to finish if you have your butcher tenderize the meat to ¹/₄-inch thickness for you.

1	2-pound beef flank steak
1	teaspoon all-purpose Greek seasoning
1	teaspoon freshly ground pepper
4	cloves garlic, minced
¹/₄	cup snipped parsley
8	ounces bacon, cooked and drained

Place flank steak on a cutting board. Working from the center to the edges, pound with the coarse-tooth side of a meat mallet to a 16x12-inch rectangle or to about ¹/₄-inch thickness. Score one side of steak, using a sharp knife to make shallow cuts diagonally across steak in a diamond pattern. Sprinkle with Greek seasoning and pepper.

Spread garlic, then parsley over scored side of steak. Place the slices of cooked bacon lengthwise on the steak. Starting from a narrow end, roll up steak, jelly-roll style. Skewer with toothpicks at 1-inch intervals. Cut the roll between the toothpicks into twelve 1-inch slices.

Place tournedos on cooking grid. Grill, covered, directly over medium coals for 12 to 14 minutes for medium doneness, turning halfway through grilling time. Makes 6 servings.

Rudy's Rib Eye Steaks

Seasoned pepper
6 cloves garlic, minced
6 beef rib eye steaks, cut 1¼ to 1½ inches thick
2 cups soy sauce
½ cup Worcestershire sauce
2 cups hickory chips

Generously sprinkle seasoned pepper over steaks. Spread **1 clove** of the minced garlic over the surface of **each** steak; press garlic into meat. In a 13x9x2-inch baking dish, arrange steaks in a single layer. Pour soy sauce and Worcestershire sauce over steaks. Cover and marinate in the refrigerator for 1 to 8 hours, turning steaks occasionally.

At least 30 minutes before grilling, soak hickory chips in enough water to cover. Drain hickory chips and place on preheated coals. Drain steaks, reserving marinade. Place steaks on cooking grid. Spoon **2 tablespoons** of the reserved marinade onto each steak. Grill, covered, directly over medium coals for 9 to 11 minutes for medium-rare, 10 to 12 minutes for medium, or 12 to 13 minutes for well-done, turning steaks and spooning an additional **2 tablespoons** of the marinade on steaks halfway through grilling time. Makes 6 servings.

Marinated Flank Steak

The meat can also be cut up and skewered for kebabs, alternating with vegetables such as onions, tomatoes, sweet peppers, and mushrooms.

2 tablespoons soy sauce
2 tablespoons dry sherry
2 tablespoons sugar
2 teaspoons salt
¼ teaspoon ground cinnamon
1 1-pound beef flank steak

For marinade, combine soy sauce, sherry, sugar, salt, and cinnamon. Place steak in a plastic bag set into a shallow dish. Pour marinade over steak. Close bag. Marinate in the refrigerator for 1½ hours, turning bag 2 or 3 times to distribute marinade.

Drain steak. Place steak on cooking grid. Grill, covered, directly over medium coals for 10 to 15 minutes for rare, 15 to 18 minutes for medium-rare, or 18 to 20 minutes for medium. To serve, slice steak diagonally across the grain into thin slices. Makes 4 servings.

Fabulous Flank Steaks

2	1- to 1½-pound beef flank steaks
³/₄	cup cooking oil
³/₄	cup soy sauce
¹/₂	cup wine vinegar
¹/₃	cup fresh lemon juice
¹/₄	to ¹/₂ cup snipped parsley
¹/₄	cup Worcestershire sauce
3	cloves garlic, minced
1	teaspoon salt
1	teaspoon pepper

In a 13x9x2-inch baking dish, arrange flank steaks. For marinade, in a medium bowl, stir together oil, soy sauce, vinegar, lemon juice, parsley, Worcestershire sauce, garlic, salt, and pepper. Pour marinade over flank steaks. Cover and marinate in the refrigerator overnight, turning steaks occasionally.

Drain steaks; discard marinade. Place steaks on cooking grid. Grill, covered, directly over medium coals for 10 to 15 minutes for rare, 15 to 18 minutes for medium-rare, or 18 to 20 minutes for medium. To serve, slice diagonally across the grain. Makes 8 to 12 servings.

Daddy's Shish-K-Bob

1	cup bottled clear Italian salad dressing
3	tablespoons cracked black pepper
3	tablespoons Worcestershire sauce
1	tablespoon garlic salt
2½	pounds boneless beef top sirloin, cut into 1½-inch cubes
3	large tomatoes, cut into 1½-inch wedges
3	green peppers, seeded and cut into 1½-inch slices
2	red onions, cut into 1½-inch wedges

For marinade, combine Italian salad dressing, cracked black pepper, Worcestershire sauce, and garlic salt. Place beef cubes in a plastic bag set into a shallow dish. Pour marinade over beef. Close bag. Marinate in the refrigerator at least 3 hours.

Drain meat, reserving marinade. Thread meat on skewers. Thread tomatoes, green peppers, and onions on skewers, threading only one type of vegetable on each skewer to allow for different cooking times.

Place meat kebabs on cooking grid. Grill, covered, directly over medium coals for 15 to 18 minutes for medium rare and 18 to 22 minutes for medium, turning occasionally. Meanwhile, grill vegetable kebabs on outer edges of grid for 10 to 12 minutes or until vegetables are tender, turning halfway through grilling time and brushing occasionally with reserved marinade. Makes 10 servings.

♪ ♪ ♪

NICE TO NOTE

—

Determine doneness of steaks and other meats with bones by making a small slit near the bone and checking color; for boneless cuts, make a small slit near the center. Use a meat thermometer to accurately determine the doneness of large cuts of meat.

∾

♦ ♦ ♦

SHISH-K-BOBBY

—

"My father loved to prepare this 'Shish-K-Bob' on Saturday or Sunday evenings. My memory is of four freshly-bathed, wet-headed children around a pint-size table in our den, watching 'The Wonderful World of Walt Disney' or 'I Love Lucy' as Daddy cooked dinner. When everything was ready, he would announce, 'Shisk-K-Bobby!' and our plates would appear. With one eye on Lucy, we watched as he proceeded to cut everyone's meat into bite-size pieces. By the time he completed this task, his food would be cold. Now we carry on this tradition with our own children, except that they watch Disney videos—and I have the cold food!"

♦ ♦ ♦

Palmer Burgers

These simple burgers were a hit at a multi-family getaway at nearby Chickasaw State Park, and the recipe came home as a favorite souvenir of the trip.

  2   pounds lean ground beef
  3   tablespoons steak sauce
  1   tablespoon dried tarragon, crushed
  1   tablespoon bottled Italian salad dressing
  1   tablespoon Worcestershire sauce
      Dash garlic powder
      Seasoned salt and coarsely ground pepper to taste
      Kaiser rolls or large hamburger buns

In a large bowl, mix together ground beef, steak sauce, tarragon, Italian salad dressing, Worcestershire sauce, garlic powder, seasoned salt, and pepper. Shape into 6 ($^3/_4$-inch) patties. Place patties on cooking grid. Grill, covered, directly over medium coals for 12 to 14 minutes for medium-rare, 14 to 16 minutes for medium, or 16 to 18 minutes for well-done. Serve on split kaiser rolls or large hamburger buns. Makes 6 servings.

Grilled Lamb, Squash, and Melon Shish Kebabs

To make tiny appetizer kebabs, thread one lamb cube on each of 30 soaked toothpicks, omitting zucchini and mushrooms. Grill in a disposable aluminum pan on an uncovered grid for 7 to 9 minutes, adding a melon cube to each toothpick during the last minute.

  $^1/_2$ cup olive oil
  $^1/_3$ cup red wine vinegar
  4   teaspoons snipped fresh rosemary or $1^1/_2$ teaspoons dried rosemary, crushed
  $1^1/_2$ teaspoons pepper
  1   clove garlic, minced
  1   pound boneless lamb round steak or sirloin steak, cut into 1-inch cubes
  1   medium zucchini, sliced $^1/_2$ inch thick
  12   large fresh mushrooms
  8   1-inch cubes cantaloupe

For marinade, combine olive oil, vinegar, rosemary, pepper, and garlic. Place lamb in a plastic bag set into a shallow dish. Pour marinade over meat. Close bag. Marinate in the refrigerator for 2 hours, turning bag once to distribute marinade.

Drain lamb, reserving marinade. On four 12-inch skewers alternately thread meat, zucchini, and mushrooms. Place kebabs on cooking grid. Grill, uncovered, directly over medium coals for 7 to 9 minutes for rare, 10 to 13 minutes for medium, or 14 to 17 minutes for medium-well, turning halfway through grilling time. Brush with reserved marinade several times during grilling. Add 2 cubes of melon to end of each skewer during last minute of grilling. Makes 4 servings.

Dudley's Butterflied Leg of Lamb

1¹/₂   cups olive oil
1   cup soy sauce
1   6- to 8-pound leg of lamb, boned and butterflied
       Garlic pepper seasoning

For marinade, combine olive oil and soy sauce. Place lamb, fat side up, in a plastic bag set into a shallow dish. Pour marinade over meat. Generously sprinkle lamb with garlic pepper seasoning. Close bag. Marinate in the refrigerator for 12 to 24 hours, turning and sprinkling with additional garlic pepper seasoning halfway through marinating time.

Drain lamb, reserving marinade. Insert a meat thermometer near center of lamb. Place lamb, fat side down, on cooking grid. Grill, covered, directly over medium coals for 20 to 30 minutes, basting often with marinade. Turn and grill 15 to 20 minutes more or until meat thermometer reads 150° (medium-rare), basting often. (Thinner leg portions should be 160° to 170° for medium-well.) To serve, cut into ¹/₄-inch slices. Makes 12 to 16 servings.

◆ ◆ ◆

H APPY E VER A FTER

—

"My mother was served this wonderful lamb at a party and knew at first bite that it was made for my husband to cook. On her next visit, she presented Dudley with the recipe. He cooked it and loved the results, as she knew he would. It has been on the menu for every mother-in-law visit since! This recipe gives Mother her serving medium-well, Dudley can have his on the rare side, and the whole family is perfectly content."

◆ ◆ ◆

Plastered Porkers' Shoulder

The Plastered Porkers are a fun-loving, championship team in the Memphis in May Barbecue Contest.

4   cups vinegar
³/₄   cup butter or margarine, divided
4¹/₄   cups catsup, divided
1   tablespoon ground red pepper
1   tablespoon pepper
1   6- to 8-pound pork shoulder arm roast
       Salt
       Garlic powder
       Pepper
¹/₂   cup chopped onion
¹/₂   cup packed brown sugar
2   tablespoons lemon juice
1   tablespoon prepared mustard
3   cloves garlic, minced

For basting sauce, in a 2-quart saucepan, combine vinegar, ¹/₄ **cup** of the butter or margarine, ¹/₄ **cup** of the catsup, ground red pepper, and pepper. Bring to boiling. Remove from heat and set aside.

Generously sprinkle roast with salt, garlic powder, and pepper. Rub seasonings into the surface of the roast.

Place roast on cooking grid. Grill, covered, directly over very slow coals for 3 hours.* Vent holes should remain open during entire grilling time. Add coals as needed every 45 minutes to 1 hour to maintain grilling temperature.

Turn roast and grill 5 hours more, brushing with basting sauce every hour. Meanwhile, for final sauce, in a 3-quart saucepan combine remaining 4 cups catsup, remaining ¹/₂ cup butter or margarine, onion, brown sugar, lemon juice, mustard, and garlic. Bring to boiling; reduce heat. Simmer, uncovered, over medium-low heat for 15 minutes. Serve final sauce with roast. Makes 10 to 14 servings.

*Note: The coals should be 10 to 12 inches from the grid. If grill is too shallow to allow for this, arrange preheated coals in a circle or on sides, leaving a hole in the center. Test for medium-slow heat over the center. Place roast in center of cooking grid. Grill, covered, for 3 hours. Turn meat and grill 5 hours more, basting every hour. Add coals as needed every 45 minutes to 1 hour to maintain grilling temperature.

The King's Grilled Tenders

Many feel that tenders are the royalty of pork cuts.

1¹/₂   cups cooking oil
³/₄   cup soy sauce
¹/₂   cup red wine vinegar
¹/₃   cup fresh lemon juice
¹/₄   cup Worcestershire sauce
2   tablespoons dry mustard
2   tablespoons snipped parsley
1   tablespoon pepper
2   cloves garlic, minced
3   1-pound pork tenderloins

For marinade, combine oil, soy sauce, vinegar, lemon juice, Worcestershire sauce, dry mustard, parsley, pepper, and garlic. Cover and refrigerate for 3 hours.

Place tenderloins in a plastic bag set into a shallow dish. Pour marinade over meat. Close bag. Marinate in the refrigerator overnight, turning bag occasionally to distribute marinade.

Drain tenderloins. Place tenderloins on cooking grid. Grill, covered, directly over medium coals for 14 to 20 minutes or until no pink remains. Slice to serve. Makes 10 to 12 servings.

Ben's Barbecue Sauce

Not designed for basting, this sauce goes on chicken or steak after grilling. Make plenty so you'll have enough left over for dipping French bread.

¹/₄   cup butter or margarine
1¹/₂   cups finely chopped celery
¹/₂   cup chopped onion
2   cloves garlic, minced
1¹/₂   cups water
1   cup catsup
¹/₂   cup cider vinegar
¹/₄   cup Worcestershire sauce
5   teaspoons fresh lemon juice
1   teaspoon pepper
1   teaspoon paprika
2   bay leaves
1   tablespoon chili powder

In a 2-quart saucepan, melt butter or margarine. Add celery, onion, and garlic and cook until tender. Stir in water, catsup, vinegar, Worcestershire sauce, lemon juice, pepper, paprika, and bay leaves. Bring to boiling; reduce heat. Simmer, uncovered, for 15 minutes, stirring often. Remove from heat.

Stir about **2 tablespoons** of the sauce into the chili powder to make a paste. Stir chili powder mixture into remaining sauce. Cool for 1 hour at room temperature. Remove and discard bay leaves. Cover and refrigerate at least 1 day before serving. To serve, reheat sauce. Serve over grilled chicken or steak. Makes about 3¹/₂ cups.

♩ ♩ ♩

NICE TO NOTE
—

John Wills, two-time Grand Champion of the Memphis in May International Barbecue Contest and owner of the barbecue establishment that bears his name, explains what sets Memphis barbecue apart: "When Texans think of barbecue, they think of beef-specifically beef brisket, slow-cooked but sliced. We think only of pork—shoulder or ribs." The shoulders are cooked 14 to 16 hours in the pit until the meat is literally falling from the bone. They must be removed to the counter with a special shovel, lest a morsel of the prize be lost. The meat is then pulled—with hands and hands only—from the bone. A few chops of the knife ready it for sandwiches. Most Memphis barbecue is served topped with slaw on a bun. Spicy baked beans flavored with bits of barbecue and a loaf of onion rings complete this meal in the famed Memphis tradition.

Devilishly Delicious Barbecued Pork Loin

1	cup catsup
¼	cup butter or margarine
¼	cup packed brown sugar
3	tablespoons Worcestershire sauce
2	tablespoons soy sauce
1	tablespoon onion powder
1	tablespoon vinegar
1	2- to 3-pound pork loin roast
	Seasoned salt
	Lemon-pepper seasoning
	Caraway seed

For sauce, in a 1-quart saucepan, combine catsup, butter or margarine, brown sugar, Worcestershire sauce, soy sauce, onion powder, and vinegar. Bring to boiling; reduce heat. Simmer, uncovered, over medium-low heat for 15 minutes. If desired, stir in additional catsup to taste and to make sauce red in color. Set aside.

Place pork loin roast on a large piece of heavy foil. Generously sprinkle with seasoned salt, lemon-pepper seasoning, and caraway seed. Bring up long edges of foil and, leaving a little space for expansion of steam, seal loosely with a double fold. Fold short ends to seal.

Place roast on cooking grid. Grill, covered, directly over medium coals for 1 to 1¼ hours per pound or until no longer pink. Brush with sauce during the last 15 minutes of grilling. Makes 8 to 12 servings.

Holiday Ribs

*Memphians are **serious** about barbecue all year long. Rib smoke is heavenly even when mingled with snow in the air! This recipe is a good example of "dry" ribs. Photograph on page 168.*

4	to 5 pounds pork loin back ribs (2 slabs)
1	cup fresh lemon juice, divided
5	tablespoons ground cumin, divided
10	teaspoons chili powder, divided
5	teaspoons seasoned salt, divided
½	teaspoon ground red pepper
2½	cups white vinegar
¾	cup cooking oil

Lay ribs on a piece of heavy foil that is large enough to wrap meat. Rub the meaty side of each slab of ribs with 1½ **tablespoons** of the lemon juice. Sprinkle **each** slab with 1 tablespoon of the cumin, **2 teaspoons** of the chili powder, **1 teaspoon** of the seasoned salt, and ¼ **teaspoon** of the ground red pepper. Wrap ribs and refrigerate overnight.

For basting sauce, combine vinegar, oil, remaining lemon juice, 3 tablespoons cumin, 6 teaspoons chili powder, and 3 teaspoons seasoned salt. Stir well.

In a covered grill, arrange preheated coals in a circle or on sides, leaving a hole in the center. Test for medium-slow heat over the center. Place ribs in center of cooking grid or on rib rack. Grill, covered, for 5 to 6 hours or until tender, turning and basting with sauce every 30 minutes. Add coals every 45 to 60 minutes to maintain grilling temperature. Makes 4 or 5 servings.

♪♪♪

NICE TO NOTE

—

While there are many schools of thought on eating ribs, the "dry" method is considered unique to the Memphis area. This involves rubbing the meat with a mixture of spices that seeps in and adds flavor during cooking. Barbecue enthusiasts will argue about sauces, marinades, and cooking methods, but "the rub" wins most popularity contests in the Mid-South. Once you have become a dry-rub convert, it's hard to eat ribs that drip.

◆ ◆ ◆

DADDY'S HOME

—

"We always knew when my hard-working dad was at home when I was a child— smoke would be rising from the barbecue grill! He took barbecue seriously and he was good at it. He would put his wonderful ribs on for all the standard holidays and even began adding them to the traditional turkey and ham on Thanksgiving and Christmas tables. I might add that even if there was leftover turkey, the ribs would be gone! No matter what else was on the menu, it just wouldn't be a holiday in our family without my daddy's ribs."

◆ ◆ ◆

Grandpa's Ribs

1½ cups cooking oil
½ cup white vinegar
¼ cup Worcestershire sauce
2 tablespoons lemon juice
  Garlic salt
  Cracked black pepper
4 to 6 pounds pork loin back ribs
  Desired barbecue sauce

For basting sauce, in a medium bowl, combine oil, vinegar, Worcestershire sauce, and lemon juice. Sprinkle garlic salt and cracked black pepper over ribs.

Place ribs, meaty side up, on cooking grid. Grill, covered, directly over slow coals.* Grill for 1½ hours or until tender, turning and brushing with basting sauce every 15 minutes. Vent holes should remain open during entire grilling time. Add coals as needed every 45 minutes to 1 hour to maintain grilling temperature.

Brush with desired barbecue sauce and grill 10 minutes more, turning and brushing with barbecue sauce after 5 minutes. To serve, slice between ribs. Makes 4 to 6 servings.

*Note: The coals should be 10 to 12 inches from the grid. If grill is too shallow to allow for this, arrange preheated coals in a circle or on sides, leaving a hole in the center. Test for medium-slow heat over the center. Place ribs in center of cooking grid. Grill, covered, for 5 to 6 hours or until tender, turning and basting every 15 minutes. Add coals as needed every 45 minutes to 1 hour to maintain grilling temperature. Ten minutes before serving, spread coals in a single layer. Brush ribs with barbecue sauce and grill directly over coals for 10 minutes more, turning and brushing with barbecue sauce after 5 minutes.

Randy's Yummy Ribs

These "wet" ribs slow-cook with sauce inside a foil packet on the grill. Don't skimp on the sauce. The ribs should practically swim in it. P.S...This sauce is equally yummy on pork or chicken!

1 cup butter or margarine
1 cup packed brown sugar
1 28-ounce bottle vinegar-based marinade or basting sauce
1 8-ounce can tomato sauce
1 6-ounce jar prepared mustard
3 tablespoons soy sauce
3 tablespoons Worcestershire sauce
6 pounds pork loin back ribs or pork spareribs
  Ground red pepper

For sauce, in a saucepan, melt butter or margarine. Add brown sugar, marinade, tomato sauce, mustard, soy sauce, and Worcestershire sauce. Simmer 10 minutes.

Place ribs on cooking grid or rib rack. Grill, covered, directly over medium coals for 15 minutes per side or until brown. Remove ribs to a large sheet of heavy foil. Generously cover ribs with sauce. Sprinkle with red pepper. Close up foil and seal. Return foil-wrapped ribs to grid and grill, covered, directly over slow coals about 2 hours or until tender, adding coals every 45 to 60 minutes to maintain grilling temperature.

Remove ribs from foil. Place ribs directly on cooking grid. Baste with sauce and grill 5 to 10 minutes more on each side. Serve ribs with remaining sauce. Makes 6 servings.

Cox's Memphis in May Ribs

This Memphis in May 1991 Grand Champion of the World Championship Barbecue Cooking Contest is rib-stickin' good in Memphis—or anywhere! Make the barbecue sauce 2 to 4 weeks in advance for the best flavor.

2	cups white vinegar
2	cups water
2	cups catsup
1/2	cup chopped onion
3	tablespoons plus 2 teaspoons salt, divided
3	tablespoons plus 2 teaspoons pepper, divided
3	tablespoons sugar
3	tablespoons chili powder
1/4	cup paprika
2	teaspoons onion powder
2	teaspoons garlic powder
2	teaspoons white pepper
1	teaspoon ground red pepper
4	to 6 pounds pork loin back ribs or pork spareribs

For barbecue sauce, in a 3-quart saucepan, combine vinegar, water, catsup, onion, **3 tablespoons** of the salt, **3 tablespoons** of the pepper, sugar, and chili powder. Bring to boiling; reduce heat. Cook, uncovered, over medium-low heat for 1 1/2 hours, stirring every 10 minutes. Remove from heat. Cover and refrigerate for up to 4 weeks to blend flavors.

In a small mixing bowl, stir together paprika, remaining 2 teaspoons salt, remaining 2 teaspoons pepper, onion powder, garlic powder, white pepper, and ground red pepper. Sprinkle mixture evenly over ribs, then rub mixture into the surface of the ribs.

In a covered grill, arrange preheated coals in a circle or on sides, leaving a hole in the center. Test for medium-slow heat over the center. Place ribs in center of cooking grid or on rib rack. Grill, covered, for 5 to 6 hours or until tender, turning every 30 minutes. Add coals every 45 to 60 minutes to maintain grilling temperature.

Brush ribs with barbecue sauce and grill 20 minutes more, turning and brushing with barbecue sauce after 10 minutes. Makes 4 to 6 servings.

♦ ♦ ♦

PIGGIE PARTY

—

*As the "Memphis in May International Festival" came to be in the late '70s, there were those who felt strongly that a part of the celebration should be an event to highlight Memphis as "hands down, no questions asked, THE pork barbecue cooking capital of the world." As noted in the **Memphis in May International Cookbook**, "Pork barbecue—chopped or pulled, whole hog or shoulder, ribs wet or dry—and its mysterious sauces—tangy, sweet, hot, thick, or thin"— are dear to the hearts of Mid-Southerners and we soon found out that we had fellow barbecue lovers the world over.*

On May 5, 1978, 20 teams competed for a total prize of $1000 in a vacant lot downtown. In May of 1992, 180 contestants brought incredible equipment and theatrical settings to an expanded Tom Lee Park, vying for $10,000 in prize money. Competitors have come from 42 states and from other countries including Ireland, Estonia, Great Britain, Canada, and New Zealand. Today, the fun goes way beyond cooking. A crowd of over 100,000 roars its delight as competitions in hog-calling, showmanship, and Ms. Piggie look-alikes entertain in outrageous style. Exceeding its planners' wildest dreams for success, the Memphis in May Barbecue Contest is a carnival of food and fun, and it will be working its riverside magic for years to come.

♦ ♦ ♦

Chops Till You Drop

A great "friends in the backyard" recipe. Be sure the chops are at least an inch thick to ensure a moist, tender meat.

8	boneless center cut pork chops, cut 1 inch thick
1/4	cup cooking oil
2	tablespoons red wine vinegar
1	tablespoon snipped fresh sage or 1 teaspoon dried sage, crushed
1	teaspoon salt
1/2	teaspoon freshly ground pepper
2	cloves garlic, minced

Trim fat from chops, if necessary. Combine oil, red wine vinegar, sage, salt, pepper, and garlic. Place pork chops in a plastic bag set into a shallow dish. Pour marinade over meat. Close bag. Marinate in the refrigerator 4 to 24 hours, turning bag several times to distribute marinade.

Drain chops. Place chops on cooking grid. Grill, covered, directly over medium coals for 8 to 10 minutes per side or until no longer pink. Makes 8 servings.

Prime Time Pork Chops

These are definitely ready for prime time! They will please your family as well as dress up for company.

	Worcestershire sauce
4	pork loin chops, cut 3/4 to 1 inch thick
	Garlic powder
	Unseasoned meat tenderizer
	Lemon-pepper seasoning
	Desired barbecue sauce

Rub a generous amount of Worcestershire sauce over the surface of each chop. Lightly sprinkle with garlic powder, meat tenderizer, and lemon-pepper seasoning. Let stand at room temperature for 30 minutes or cover and refrigerate up to 4 hours.

Place chops on cooking grid. Grill, covered, directly over slow coals for 15 to 20 minutes per side or until no longer pink. Brush with barbecue sauce the last 10 minutes of grilling. Makes 4 servings.

Party Sausage

5	pounds kielbasa (Polish sausage)
1	1-ounce can ground cumin
3	tablespoons celery salt
2	tablespoons pepper
1	tablespoon salt
1	tablespoon ground red pepper

Score Polish sausage links 1/4 inch deep at 1-inch intervals; set aside. In a small bowl, stir together cumin, celery salt, pepper, salt, and red pepper. Rub about **1 tablespoon** of the mixture over the surface of **each** sausage link.

Place sausage on cooking grid. Grill, covered, directly over medium coals for 15 to 20 minutes or until the skins are lightly browned and begin to burst and juices run clear. Occasionally turn sausages during grilling. Makes 25-35 appetizer servings.

Wilder's Fabulous Barbecued Chicken

Tip #1: Do not leave the fire while grilling.
Tip #2: Serve with lots of big napkins!

- 4 cups hickory chips
- 3 tablespoons bourbon
- 1¹/₂ cups dry white wine or beer
- 3 tablespoons fresh lemon juice
  All-purpose Greek seasoning
  Lemon-pepper seasoning
  Worcestershire sauce
  Hot pepper sauce
- 1 2¹/₂- to 3-pound broiler-fryer chicken, split in half
  Desired barbecue sauce

Soak hickory chips in a mixture of bourbon and enough water to cover for 30 minutes. For basting sauce, combine wine or beer, lemon juice, and a dash each of Greek seasoning, lemon-pepper seasoning, Worcestershire sauce, and hot pepper sauce.

Drain hickory chips and place on preheated coals. Generously sprinkle chicken with Greek seasoning, lemon-pepper seasoning, Worcestershire sauce, and hot pepper sauce.

Place chicken, bone-side down, on cooking grid. Grill, covered, directly over medium-slow coals for 10 minutes; turn and baste with sauce. Grill breast-side down 5 minutes; turn and baste with sauce. Continue turning and basting 45 minutes more or until chicken is tender, cooking longer on bone side and less on meaty side to avoid drying out. Generously baste chicken with barbecue sauce the last 10 minutes of grilling. Makes 4 servings.

Mustard Barbecued Chicken

Try this recipe enjoyed by two law school classmates when long-awaited weekends finally arrived. They recommend a cold beer while it's cooking and a crisp Chardonnay at the table.

- 1 cup vinegar
- ¹/₂ cup lemon juice
- 5 tablespoons catsup
- 6 tablespoons prepared mustard, divided
- 5 teaspoons salt, divided
- ³/₄ teaspoon pepper, divided
- 8 medium chicken breast halves, skinned and boned
- 9 tablespoons butter or margarine
- 6 tablespoons sugar
- 3¹/₂ teaspoons Worcestershire sauce

For marinade, in a medium bowl, stir together vinegar, lemon juice, catsup, **2 tablespoons** of the mustard, **3¹/₂ teaspoons** of the salt, and ¹/₂ **teaspoon** of the pepper. Place chicken breasts in a large plastic bag set into a shallow dish. Pour marinade over chicken. Close bag. Marinate in the refrigerator for 1 hour, turning bag occasionally.

For sauce, in a 1-quart saucepan, combine butter or margarine, sugar, the remaining 4 tablespoons of the mustard, Worcestershire sauce, the remaining 1¹/₂ teaspoons salt, and remaining ¹/₄ teaspoon pepper. Cook and stir over medium heat until butter is melted.

In a covered grill, arrange preheated coals in a circle or on sides, leaving a hole in the center. Test for medium heat over the center.

Drain chicken, reserving marinade. Place chicken in center of cooking grid. Grill, covered, for 15 minutes. Brush with some of the reserved marinade; discard remaining marinade. Turn chicken. Grill 10 to 15 minutes more or until chicken is tender and no longer pink, brushing often with the sauce. Makes 8 servings.

♦ ♦ ♦

BARBECUED EGGS
—

"In the Mid-South, you have to put barbecue sauce on something in order for it to qualify as a barbecued dish (e.g. barbecued chicken, ribs, chops, etc.). Further north, the simple act of firing up the outdoor grill constitutes having a barbecue.

Just after college, I visited a friend in St. Louis. Imagine my surprise when her parents announced that for Sunday morning breakfast, we would be having barbecued eggs! (The thought was more than I could stand.)"

As you might imagine, there are as many barbecue sauces as there are cooks, and every outdoor chef considers his recipe the finest. The basic tomato base, vinegar, brown sugar, oil, and lemon are present in most versions, but seasonings vary and there is great care taken to protect the identity of certain "secret ingredients" which are a cook's pride.

♦ ♦ ♦

Nayla's Villa Montana Chicken

Turn this chicken into a perfect cold salad or sandwich the next day!

1	cup cooking oil
1/2	cup chopped onion
1/3	cup cider vinegar
1/4	cup chopped celery
2	tablespoons water
4	teaspoons sugar
1	tablespoon snipped parsley
1 1/2	teaspoons salt
3	cloves garlic
1	teaspoon poppy seed
1/4	teaspoon dry mustard
1/4	teaspoon paprika
1/8	teaspoon pepper
8	chicken breast halves, skinned and boned
1/2	lemon
	Salt and pepper

For marinade, in a blender container or food processor bowl, combine oil, onion, vinegar, celery, water, sugar, parsley, salt, garlic, poppy seed, dry mustard, paprika, and pepper. Cover and blend or process about 1 minute or until smooth.

Rub both sides of chicken pieces with lemon; season with salt and pepper. Place chicken in a plastic bag set into a shallow dish. Pour marinade over chicken. Close bag. Marinate overnight in the refrigerator, turning bag several times to distribute marinade.

Preheat the oven to 300°. Drain chicken, reserving marinade. Arrange chicken in a greased 13x9x2-inch baking pan. Bake for 10 to 12 minutes or until no longer pink on surface.

Immediately transfer chicken to cooking grid. Grill, covered, directly over slow coals for 20 to 30 minutes or until tender, turning and basting with reserved marinade halfway through grilling time. Makes 8 servings.

Grilled Chicken and Tortellini Salad

6	chicken breast halves, skinned and boned
1	8-ounce bottle clear Italian salad dressing
12	ounces fresh or frozen cheese tortellini
1/2	cup mayonnaise or salad dressing
3	hard-cooked eggs, chopped
1/2	cup chopped sweet red pepper
12	sun-dried tomatoes, slivered
	Salt and pepper to taste

Place chicken in a plastic bag set into a shallow dish. Pour Italian salad dressing over chicken. Close bag. Marinate in the refrigerator overnight, turning bag several times to distribute marinade.

Drain chicken. Place chicken on cooking grid. Grill, uncovered, directly over medium coals for 10 to 12 minutes or until tender, turning halfway through grilling time. Cut chicken into bite-size pieces.

Meanwhile, in a 6-quart Dutch oven or stockpot, cook fresh tortellini in 3 1/2 quarts boiling salted water for 8 to 10 minutes or until tender but still firm. (Or, cook frozen tortellini according to package directions.) Drain. Rinse with cold water; drain well.

In a medium bowl, combine mayonnaise, eggs, red pepper, tomatoes, salt, pepper, chicken, and tortellini; mix well. Add additional mayonnaise, if necessary, to reach desired consistency. Makes 6 servings.

Tudor Duck

1	cup cooking oil
1	cup pineapple-orange juice
1/2	cup dry white wine
1/2	cup white wine vinegar
2	teaspoons vinegar-based sweet marinade sauce
2	teaspoons liquid smoke
1/2	teaspoon salt
1/2	teaspoon unseasoned meat tenderizer
1/2	teaspoon all-purpose Greek seasoning
1/4	teaspoon dried thyme, crushed
1/4	teaspoon pepper
2	bay leaves
8	duck breast halves
8	slices bacon

For marinade, in a medium bowl, combine oil, pineapple-orange juice, wine, vinegar, marinade sauce, liquid smoke, salt, meat tenderizer, Greek seasoning, thyme, pepper, and bay leaves. Place duck breasts in a plastic bag set into a shallow dish. Pour marinade over duck breasts. Close bag. Marinate in the refrigerator overnight, turning bag occasionally.

Drain duck breasts; discard marinade. Wrap each duck breast with a bacon slice; secure with toothpicks. In a covered grill, arrange preheated coals in a circle or on sides, leaving a hole in the center. Test for medium heat over the center. Place duck breasts in center of cooking grid. Grill, covered, about 20 minutes or until bacon is cooked and duck is tender but not blackened, turning often. Makes 4 servings.

Grilled Duck Hollis

This easy treatment makes the duck taste almost like steak, as the wine cuts the "gamey" flavor. Great for the novice game bird chef. Amounts of herbs and seasonings can be varied to your taste.

1	cup dry white wine
2/3	cup cooking oil
1/3	cup white vinegar
2	tablespoons seasoned salt
2	tablespoons Worcestershire sauce
1	teaspoon salt
1	teaspoon lemon-pepper seasoning
1/2	teaspoon pepper
1/2	teaspoon dry mustard
1/2	teaspoon paprika
12	to 16 medium duck breast halves
12	to 16 slices bacon

For marinade, combine wine, oil, vinegar, seasoned salt, Worcestershire sauce, salt, lemon-pepper seasoning, pepper, dry mustard, and paprika. Place duck breasts in a large plastic bag set into a large bowl. Pour marinade over duck. Close bag. Marinate overnight in the refrigerator, turning bag occasionally to distribute marinade.

In a covered grill, arrange preheated coals in a circle or on sides, leaving a hole in the center. Test for very slow heat over the center. Wrap a slice of bacon around each duck breast half; secure with a toothpick. Place duck breasts in center of cooking grid. Grill, covered, for 1 hour or until tender, turning occasionally. Makes 6 to 8 servings.

Grilled Dove Breasts

Frequent fall hunts pack Mid-South freezers with dove. Then the hunt begins for the best ways to bring them to the table.

³/₄	cup olive oil
2	tablespoons balsamic vinegar or red wine vinegar
1	tablespoon snipped cilantro
1	tablespoon dried oregano, crushed
2	teaspoons minced garlic
1	teaspoon dried marjoram, crushed
1	teaspoon ground cumin
12	whole dove breasts, cleaned and boned
4	ounces Monterey Jack or cheddar cheese, cut into 24 small pieces
3	fresh jalapeño peppers, seeded and sliced into 24 strips
12	slices bacon

For marinade, combine olive oil, vinegar, cilantro, oregano, garlic, marjoram, and cumin. Place dove breasts in a plastic bag set into a shallow dish. Pour marinade over dove breasts. Close bag. Marinate in the refrigerator for 4 hours, turning bag occasionally to distribute marinade.

Drain dove breasts. With a sharp knife, cut a pocket in the meaty part of each breast half. Tuck a piece of cheese and a strip of jalapeño pepper into each pocket. Wrap a bacon slice around each breast; secure with a toothpick.

Place dove breasts on cooking grid. Grill, uncovered, directly over medium coals for 10 to 15 minutes or until dove is tender and bacon is well-cooked. Makes 6 servings.

Barbecued Dove

Game birds such as dove, duck, and quail should be frozen submerged in water so that it forms a solid block of ice around the meat. Pack birds loosely in milk cartons or coffee cans, making sure the water entirely surrounds the game. This method keeps the meat fresh longer and prevents freezer burn or dry-out.

1¹/₂	cups water
³/₄	cup butter or margarine
1	medium onion, grated
¹/₂	cup white vinegar
3	tablespoons fresh lemon juice
2	tablespoons brown sugar
1	tablespoon catsup
2	teaspoons salt
1	teaspoon pepper
1	teaspoon paprika
1	teaspoon prepared mustard
1	teaspoon chili sauce
1	teaspoon hot pepper sauce
¹/₂	teaspoon ground red pepper
¹/₂	teaspoon liquid smoke
18	to 20 whole dove breasts

In an 8-quart Dutch oven or stockpot, stir together all ingredients except dove. Add dove. Bring to boiling; reduce heat. Simmer for 10 to 20 minutes or until tender.

Transfer dove to cooking grid, reserving cooking sauce. Grill, uncovered, directly over medium coals for 8 to 10 minutes, basting occasionally with sauce. Makes 8 to 10 servings.

Great Balls of Fire Shrimp

Don't care to pull out the grill? You can broil the marinated shrimp in a shallow baking pan about 5 minutes.

1¹/₂	pounds fresh or frozen jumbo peeled and deveined shrimp
1	large lemon
¹/₂	cup butter or margarine
2	tablespoons pepper
2	tablespoons prepared mustard
3	cloves garlic, minced
2	bay leaves, crushed
1¹/₂	teaspoons ground ginger
¹/₂	teaspoon salt
¹/₂	teaspoon ground red pepper

Thaw shrimp, if frozen. Grate the rind of the lemon. Squeeze juice from lemon. For marinade, in a 1-quart saucepan, combine grated lemon rind, lemon juice, butter or margarine, pepper, mustard, garlic, bay leaves, ginger, salt, and red pepper. Cook over medium-low heat just until butter melts. Cool completely.

Place shrimp in a plastic bag set into a shallow dish. Pour marinade over shrimp. Close bag. Marinate in the refrigerator for 2 to 24 hours, turning bag several times to distribute marinade.

Lightly grease the cooking grill. Thread shrimp on six 12-inch skewers, leaving space between pieces. Place kebabs on cooking grid. Grill, covered, directly over medium coals for 8 to 10 minutes or until shrimp turn pink, turning halfway through grilling time. Makes 6 servings.

Blue Hawaii Shrimp

2¹/₄	pounds large or jumbo peeled and deveined shrimp
1	cup cooking oil
1	cup lemon juice
1	0.7-ounce package Italian dry salad dressing mix
2	teaspoons seasoned salt
1	teaspoon pepper
¹/₄	cup packed brown sugar
2	tablespoons soy sauce
1	cup chopped onion

Thaw shrimp, if frozen. Place shrimp in a plastic bag set into a shallow dish. For marinade, in a small bowl, stir together oil, lemon juice, salad dressing mix, seasoned salt, and pepper. Pour marinade over shrimp. Close bag. Marinate in the refrigerator for ¹/₂ to 1¹/₂ hours, turning bag occasionally to distribute marinade.

Drain shrimp, reserving marinade. On skewers, thread shrimp; set aside. For dipping sauce, in a 1-quart saucepan, stir together brown sugar and soy sauce. Stir in reserved marinade and onion. Bring to boiling; reduce heat. Cook over low heat about 5 minutes or until onion is tender. Keep warm while grilling shrimp.

Place shrimp on cooking grid. Grill, covered, directly over medium coals for 8 to 10 minutes or until no longer pink. Serve shrimp with dipping sauce. Makes 8 servings.

♦ ♦ ♦

GRILLING METHODS
—

There are two types of grilling methods: direct and indirect, and it is important to choose the correct method for the type of meat being cooked.

DIRECT GRILLING
—

•*Food is placed on the grid directly above the coals.*
•*The grill can be open or covered. Most foods cook more quickly when covered.*
•*This method is used most often for meats requiring short cooking times, such as steaks, burgers, and kebabs.*

To light the fire, follow these steps:
1. Open any vents in the bottom of the grill. Place charcoal briquets on an area equal to the space the food will occupy on the grill, leaving an additional 2 inches on all sides.
2. Mound the briquets into a pyramid shape or place in chimney starter and ignite.
3. When the coals are ash-covered and no longer flaming (about 30 to 45 minutes) spread them in a single layer again and check the cooking temperature.
4. To lower the temperature, spread the coals farther apart or raise the grid, if possible.
5. To make the fire hotter, move coals closer together and tap off ash.
6. Place the meat on the grid and cook to desired doneness.

♦ ♦ ♦

Grilled Salmon with Caper-Lemon Butter

¹/₂ cup butter
2 tablespoons capers, drained
1 tablespoon lemon juice
   Dash seasoned salt
   Dash Worcestershire sauce
¹/₃ cup mayonnaise
1 tablespoon snipped fresh dillweed or 1 teaspoon dried dillweed
2 pounds salmon fillets with skin (about 1 inch thick) or 4 salmon steaks,
   cut 1 inch thick

For caper-lemon butter, in a blender container or food processor bowl, combine butter, capers, lemon juice, seasoned salt, and Worcestershire sauce. Cover and blend or process until combined. Transfer to a 1-quart saucepan; set aside.

In a small bowl, stir together mayonnaise and dillweed. Spread mayonnaise mixture over both sides of each piece of salmon.

Place fillets (skin side down) or steaks on greased cooking grid. Grill, covered, directly over medium coals about 10 minutes or until salmon flakes easily with a fork. Do not turn.

Meanwhile, heat caper-lemon butter until melted. Carefully remove salmon to a serving platter. Pour some of the caper-lemon butter over salmon; pass remaining. Makes 8 servings.

Aycock Tuna Steaks

"We had spent a happy day at the Fayette County ranch of good friends hiking, shooting skeet, horseback-riding, and exploring. The invitation included 'something to eat' but didn't presage the delicious and beautiful surprise that awaited on the grill."

1 cup cooking oil
¹/₄ cup dry vermouth
2 tablespoons snipped cilantro
2 tablespoons lemon juice
1 teaspoon seasoned salt
¹/₂ teaspoon pepper
6 to 8 tuna or salmon steaks, cut 1 inch thick (6 to 8 ounces each)
1 or 2 sweet red peppers, seeded and sliced into rings
1 large head romaine lettuce

For marinade, combine oil, vermouth, cilantro, lemon juice, seasoned salt, and pepper. Place tuna or salmon steaks in a plastic bag set into a shallow dish. Pour marinade over tuna or salmon. Close bag. Marinate in the refrigerator for 1 to 2 hours.

Remove tuna or salmon from marinade. Top each fish steak with several red pepper rings. Wrap steaks in two or three lettuce leaves, then in heavy foil. Place on cooking grid. Grill, uncovered, directly over medium coals about 10 minutes or until tuna flakes easily with a fork. Makes 6 to 8 servings.

Marinated Grilled Tuna

    4   tuna or salmon steaks, cut 1 inch thick (6 to 8 ounces each)
  ¹/₂   cup olive oil
  ¹/₂   cup dry sherry
  ¹/₂   cup soy sauce
    2   tablespoons lemon juice
    2   cloves garlic, minced
    2   teaspoons grated gingerroot or ¹/₂ teaspoon ground ginger (optional)
         Dash pepper

In a 12x7¹/₂x2-inch baking dish, place tuna steaks in a single layer. For marinade, in a small bowl, stir together olive oil, sherry, soy sauce, lemon juice, garlic, gingerroot, and pepper. Pour marinade over tuna; cover and marinate in the refrigerator for 1 to 2 hours, turning tuna steaks occasionally.

Drain tuna; discard marinade. Place tuna on cooking grid. Grill, uncovered, directly over medium coals about 10 minutes or until tuna flakes easily with a fork. Makes 4 servings.

Catfish Capers

If you can't stand being inside while everyone else is grilling out, prepare the sauce on the grill.

    6   fresh or frozen catfish fillets (2 to 2¹/₂ pounds total)
  6¹/₂   teaspoons olive oil, divided
         Salt
         Lemon-pepper seasoning
         Dried dillweed
  ¹/₄   cup chopped onion
    1   cup mayonnaise
    1   2-ounce jar chopped pimiento, drained
    4   teaspoons capers
    1   tablespoon lemon juice
    1   tablespoon snipped parsley
  ¹/₄   teaspoon cracked black pepper
         Parsley sprigs
    2   lemons, thinly sliced
    2   limes, thinly sliced

Thaw catfish, if frozen. Lightly brush a 13x9-inch piece of heavy foil or a 13x9x2-inch foil pan with ¹/₂ **teaspoon** of the olive oil. Place fillets on foil or in pan; brush each with ¹/₂ **teaspoon** of the olive oil. Sprinkle fillets generously with salt, lemon-pepper seasoning, and dillweed. Do not turn.

Carefully transfer fish on foil to cooking grid. Grill, covered, directly over medium coals for 25 minutes for 6-ounce fillets and 30 to 35 minutes for 8-ounce fillets or until fish flakes easily.

For sauce, in a skillet, cook onion in remaining 1 tablespoon olive oil until tender. Remove from heat. Stir in mayonnaise, pimiento, capers, lemon juice, parsley, and pepper. Return to low heat to warm sauce.

Transfer fish to serving platter. Garnish with parsley, sliced lemons, and sliced limes. Serve with sauce. Makes 6 servings.

Fried Dill Pickles

Cool them slightly before popping them into your mouth—they are HOT! They taste great with horseradish cream.

²/₃	cup self-rising flour
1	teaspoon pepper
¹/₂	teaspoon salt
¹/₃	cup beer
1	32-ounce jar whole dill pickles, sliced into ¹/₂-inch slices
	Prepared mustard
	Cooking oil for deep-fat frying

For batter, in a medium bowl, stir together self-rising flour, pepper, and salt. Stir in beer until well combined.

Dip pickles in mustard to coat, then in batter. In a 12-inch skillet or deep-fat fryer, fry pickles in deep hot oil (375°) for 3 to 4 minutes or until golden brown. Remove from oil; drain on paper towels. Serve immediately. Makes about 10 dozen dill chips.

Note: For large crowds, double the recipe and use a large deep-fat fryer like a catfish cooker.

Richard's Rings

2	cups self-rising flour, divided
1	teaspoon pepper
¹/₂	teaspoon salt
	Ground red pepper to taste
1	cup beer
5	medium onions, sliced ¹/₄ inch thick
	Cooking oil for deep-fat frying

In a medium bowl, stir together **1 cup** of the flour, pepper, salt, and ground red pepper. Stir in beer until combined. Pour remaining 1 cup flour into a paper bag.

Separate onions into rings. Using a fork, dip onion rings into batter; drain excess batter. Shake coated onions in flour in bag; shake off excess flour. In a 12-inch skillet or deep-fat fryer, fry onions in deep hot oil (375°) for 2 to 3 minutes or until golden. Remove from oil. Drain on paper towels. Makes 6 servings.

PASTA

Rufus & Carla Thomas

Few performers are more recognized in the "Memphis music" scene than our famous father and daughter, Rufus and Carla Thomas.

Rufus has been stealing shows since the age of six with his flamboyant, jovial style. He's a master showman who has joked, danced, and sung his way through vaudeville, radio, recording, and countless rhythm and blues appearances. In 1953 he recorded "Bear Cat," the first hit for Sun Records, helping to launch that success story, and his Stax hits "Walkin' the Dog" and "Funky Chicken" are legendary.

Carla began her career at Satellite/Stax with the duet recording of "Cause I Love You" with Rufus and went on to wow the industry with her smash hit, "Gee Whiz," a '60's classic. Her performances take her far and wide but she fondly recalls a special homecoming concert with the Memphis Pops in the late '70s. Returning from a Paris engagement with the Stax Revue, she and her family, including brother Marvell, a talented keyboardist, shared a hometown tribute that she will always remember as "overwhelming." It's only fitting. Carla Thomas is Memphis' queen of soul. She loves this city and has even juggled her professional life to put in hours in our city schools promoting the arts.

Through it all they have been the best of city ambassadors. Rufus recently boasted to a New York R&B audience, "I'm from the home of the blues, MEMPHIS, Tennessee."

PASTA

◆ ◆ ◆

PICTURED OVERLEAF

—

Fettuccine with Asparagus and Smoked Salmon (page 207)

◆ ◆ ◆

*P*ASTA HAS BEEN ENJOYED FOR CENTURIES BUT ITS POPULARITY IS at an all-time high today. It is delicious, satisfying, and versatile. It can be served hot or cold, sauced elaborately or simply, combined with cheeses, vegetables, meat, poultry, or seafood. We are finding pasta to be a refreshing change from the standard starchy side dishes of potatoes and rice. In most of its forms, pasta can be a main dish or an accompaniment and it has found great favor as we look for lighter menu choices. It is even found on the menus of fast-food restaurants!

However it is presented, pasta is always welcomed by family members and guests alike. Children love it. (Everyone can visualize the picture of the happy tot sitting in front of a mountain of spaghetti!) Pasta makes adults smile, too. It is a wonderful choice for a party, for it is fun to eat, filling, and universally liked, and can often be made in advance.

Pasta lends itself to invention and can dress for any season. A chilled pasta salad provides a delightful lunch or supper for a Southern summer day, while a freshly baked lasagna layered with cheeses brings the comfort of a blanket on the coldest winter night. Enjoy! Enjoy! Pasta is perfect. You'll find *Heart & Soul's* selection a great excuse for a party. ♥

◆ ◆ ◆

PASTA POINTERS
—

Wondering how much pasta you should cook to wind up with the right amount? A single serving is generally considered to be 2 to 3 ounces (1 to 1½ cups) for a main dish and 1 ounce (about ½ cup) for a side dish.

To cook pasta, add pasta gradually to a pot of rapidly boiling water, allowing 3 quarts of water for 4 to 8 ounces of pasta and 4 quarts of water for each pound of pasta. Add salt to the boiling water, both for taste and to prevent sticking. Cook until any raw flour taste is gone, leaving the pasta still a bit firm to the bite (al dente).

◆ ◆ ◆

Lobster Pasta

½	cup sun-dried tomatoes packed in oil
3	cloves garlic, minced
¼	cup finely chopped shallots
5	teaspoons snipped fresh basil or 1½ teaspoons dried basil, crushed
¼	teaspoon white pepper
1	cup chicken broth
1	cup heavy cream
¾	cup dry vermouth
10	ounces angel hair pasta
3	cups sliced fresh mushrooms (8 ounces)
2	tablespoons butter or margarine
1	pound cooked lobster meat
½	cup chopped sweet red pepper
½	cup grated Parmesan cheese

Drain tomatoes, reserving **3 tablespoons** of the oil; cut tomatoes into slivers. In a 10-inch skillet, heat the reserved oil over medium-high heat. Add garlic and cook for 1 minute. Stir in shallots, basil, and white pepper. Add chicken broth, cream, and vermouth. Bring to boiling. Cook uncovered, stirring frequently, until sauce is reduced to 1½ cups. Remove from heat.

Meanwhile, in a 6-quart Dutch oven or stockpot, cook pasta in 3½ quarts boiling salted water for 2 to 4 minutes or until tender but still firm. Drain well.

In an 8-inch skillet, cook mushrooms in butter until tender. With a slotted spoon, remove mushrooms to cream mixture. Add lobster, red pepper, and Parmesan cheese to cream mixture. Cook for 2 minutes or until heated through.

To serve, spoon sauce over hot pasta and toss well. Serve immediately. Makes 4 main-dish or 8 side-dish servings.

Crawfish Fettuccine

1 pound fresh or frozen peeled crawfish tails or peeled and deveined shrimp
1/4 cup butter or margarine
2 tablespoons olive oil
1 14-ounce can artichoke hearts, drained
4 green onions, sliced
1/2 teaspoon salt
1/4 teaspoon white pepper
1/4 teaspoon ground red pepper
   Hot pepper sauce to taste
2 tablespoons all-purpose flour
1 tablespoon snipped parsley
5 cloves garlic, minced
1 1/2 to 2 cups light cream
10 ounces fettuccine
1/2 cup freshly grated Parmesan cheese

Thaw crawfish, if frozen. In a heavy 12-inch skillet, heat butter and olive oil over medium-high heat. Add artichoke hearts and onion and cook for 1 minute. Reduce heat to low. Add crawfish, salt, white pepper, red pepper, and hot pepper sauce; cook for 5 minutes. Stir in flour, parsley, and garlic. Add **1 1/2 cups** of the cream. Stir until well combined. Simmer over low heat for 20 minutes, stirring occasionally. Add additional cream to thin, if necessary.

Meanwhile, in a 6-quart Dutch oven or stockpot, cook fettuccine in 3 1/2 quarts boiling salted water for 8 to 10 minutes or until tender but still firm. Drain.

Stir Parmesan cheese into sauce. Pour sauce over pasta and toss. Serve immediately. Makes 4 main-dish servings.

Shrimp and Pasta with Tomato Cream Sauce

1 pound fresh or frozen medium shrimp, peeled and deveined
1/3 cup sun-dried tomatoes packed in oil
2 cloves garlic, minced
1 cup heavy cream
1 cup chicken broth
3/4 cup dry vermouth
2 tablespoons snipped fresh basil or 2 teaspoons dried basil, crushed
1 tablespoon snipped chives
3/4 teaspoon salt
1/2 teaspoon finely shredded lemon peel
1/4 teaspoon cracked black pepper
10 ounces linguine, fettuccine, or thin spaghetti
   Freshly grated Parmesan cheese

Thaw shrimp, if frozen. Drain tomatoes, reserving **3 tablespoons** of the oil. Sliver tomatoes and set aside. In a 2-quart saucepan, heat reserved oil over medium-high heat. Add garlic and shrimp. Cook for 2 to 4 minutes or until shrimp turn pink. Lift out with a slotted spoon and set aside.

Add cream, broth, vermouth, basil, chives, salt, lemon peel, pepper, and tomatoes to saucepan. Bring to a boil over high heat. Boil, stirring occasionally, for 12 to 15 minutes or until reduced to 1 1/2 cups. Return shrimp to saucepan and stir until heated through.

Meanwhile, in a 6-quart Dutch oven or stockpot, cook pasta in 3 1/2 quarts of boiling salted water for 8 to 10 minutes or until tender but still firm. Drain well. Toss pasta with sauce. Serve immediately, passing Parmesan cheese. Makes 4 main-dish servings.

Creole Shrimp Pasta

This is basically a shrimp remoulade tossed with pasta and ripe olives—a fabulous combination hot!

2	pounds fresh or frozen large shrimp in shells
2	tablespoons creole seasoning
1/4	cup concentrated crab and shrimp boil
3/4	cup cooking oil
1/2	cup brown creole mustard or spicy coarse-grained mustard
1/2	cup chopped onion
1/4	cup tarragon vinegar
2	teaspoons salt
2	teaspoons paprika
3/4	teaspoon ground red pepper
2	cloves garlic, crushed
1/2	cup sliced green onion
10	to 12 ounces vermicelli or capellini
1/2	cup sliced ripe olives

Thaw shrimp, if frozen. In a 6-quart Dutch oven or stockpot, combine 3 quarts water and the creole seasoning. Bring to boiling. Add shrimp. Cook, uncovered, for 1 to 3 minutes or until shrimp turn pink. Drain. In a large bowl, combine concentrated crab and shrimp boil with 2 cups ice cubes. Add shrimp and marinate for 20 minutes. Drain well. Peel, devein, and cut in half crosswise.

For sauce, in a blender container or food processor bowl, combine oil, mustard, onion, vinegar, salt, paprika, red pepper, and garlic. Cover and blend or process until smooth. Add green onion; cover and blend or process 2 seconds more.

In the same 6-quart Dutch oven or stockpot, cook pasta in 3 1/2 quarts boiling salted water for 4 to 7 minutes or until tender but still firm. Drain well and return to Dutch oven. Top with sauce. Add shrimp and ripe olives. Mix well. Cook over low heat just until heated through. Makes 4 to 6 main-dish servings.

Pasta Ala Elfo

8	fresh or frozen jumbo shrimp, peeled and deveined
8	ounces spaghetti
1	cup butter
10	cloves garlic, minced
1	cup sliced fresh mushrooms
	Salt and white pepper to taste
6	tablespoons grated Parmesan cheese

Thaw shrimp, if frozen. In a 6-quart Dutch oven or stockpot, cook spaghetti in 3 quarts boiling salted water for 10 to 12 minutes or until tender but still firm; drain well.

Meanwhile, in a 12-inch skillet, melt butter and add garlic. Cut each shrimp into thirds and add to skillet. Add mushrooms; cook and stir for 2 to 4 minutes or until shrimp turn pink. Add drained spaghetti, salt, and pepper. Cook until spaghetti is heated through. Do not let butter brown. Place in a serving dish and top with Parmesan cheese. Makes 4 main-dish or 8 side-dish servings.

Ronnie Grisanti & Sons
3rd Generation of Grisanti

Heavenly Shrimp Pasta

2   cups unsalted butter, softened
5   teaspoons minced garlic
5   teaspoons capers
5   teaspoons diced pimiento
1   tablespoon snipped parsley
1¹/₂   teaspoons snipped fresh thyme or ¹/₂ teaspoon dried thyme, crushed
1¹/₂   teaspoons snipped fresh oregano or ¹/₂ teaspoon dried oregano, crushed
1¹/₂   teaspoons snipped fresh basil or ¹/₂ teaspoon dried basil, crushed
1¹/₂   teaspoons Dijon-style mustard
¹/₄   teaspoon salt
     Ground red pepper to taste
2   pounds fresh or frozen large shrimp, peeled and deveined
1   cup heavy cream
3   tablespoons fresh lemon juice
     Salt and pepper to taste
¹/₄   cup butter
     Seafood seasoning
1   pound angel hair pasta, cooked and drained

For herb butter, in a large bowl, beat together butter, garlic, capers, pimiento, parsley, thyme, oregano, basil, mustard, salt, and ground red pepper with an electric mixer just until blended. **Do not whip.** Spoon herb butter along one edge of a piece of waxed paper. Roll up. Overwrap and chill for up to 2 weeks or freeze for longer storage.

Thaw shrimp, if frozen. Cut herb butter into small pieces; keep cold. In a 2-quart saucepan, heat cream over medium heat. Just as cream comes to a boil, start adding herb butter, 1 or 2 pieces at a time. Whisk constantly until all butter has been incorporated and the sauce has a creamy consistency. Remove from heat and add lemon juice, salt, and pepper. Keep sauce warm over double boiler over low heat.

In a 12-inch skillet, heat butter over medium heat. Add shrimp; season generously with seafood seasoning. Cook for 2 to 4 minutes or until shrimp turn pink. Place hot cooked pasta on individual serving plates. Place shrimp over pasta. Spoon sauce over each. Serve immediately. Makes 6 main-dish servings.

Tortellini with Gorgonzola Cream Sauce

¹/₃   cup fine dry breadcrumbs
1   tablespoon freshly grated Parmesan or Romano cheese
2   teaspoons butter, melted
¹/₂   teaspoon dried basil, crushed
¹/₄   teaspoon dried oregano, crushed
¹/₄   teaspoon dried marjoram, crushed
1¹/₃   cups heavy cream
3   ounces Gorgonzola cheese, crumbled
¹/₈   teaspoon ground nutmeg
1   9-ounce package fresh cheese tortellini

For topping, in a small bowl, combine breadcrumbs, Parmesan cheese, butter, basil, oregano, and marjoram; set aside. For sauce, in a heavy 1¹/₂-quart saucepan, combine cream, Gorgonzola cheese, and nutmeg. Bring just to boiling; reduce heat. Cook and stir until cheese melts. Simmer about 10 minutes more, stirring frequently, or until mixture is reduced to a thin sauce consistency.

Meanwhile, cook tortellini according to package directions. Drain well. Preheat the broiler. Add tortellini to sauce; cook and stir until heated through. Transfer tortellini mixture to a 12x7¹/₂x2-inch baking dish. Evenly sprinkle topping over pasta. Broil until top is lightly toasted. Makes 4 main-dish or 8 side-dish servings.

Yellow Pepper Pasta with Shrimp

2²/₃   pounds sweet yellow peppers, divided
2   cups all-purpose flour
1¹/₂   teaspoons salt, divided
3   beaten egg yolks
2   tablespoons plus 1 teaspoon Hungarian paprika paste, divided*
1¹/₂   pounds fresh or frozen peeled and deveined shrimp
¹/₄   cup olive oil
10   cloves garlic, minced
¹/₂   cup water
1   teaspoon Creole seasoning
1   teaspoon all-purpose Greek seasoning
¹/₂   teaspoon pepper
1   cup snipped fresh basil

Set aside ²/₃ **pound** of the yellow peppers for sauce. Remove and discard stems and seeds from remaining 2 pounds peppers; coarsely chop peppers. In a blender container or food processor bowl, place about **half** of the chopped peppers. Cover and blend or process until pureed. Transfer puree to a 1-quart saucepan. Repeat blending or processing the remaining chopped peppers until pureed and add to pureed peppers in saucepan. Bring pureed peppers to boiling; reduce heat. Simmer over medium heat until puree is reduced to 1¹/₃ cups. Set pepper puree aside to cool.

For noodles, in a large bowl, stir together flour and **1 teaspoon** of the salt. Make a well in the center of the mixture. In a medium bowl, combine ²/₃ cup of the pepper puree, beaten egg yolks, and **1 teaspoon** of the Hungarian paprika paste. Add to flour mixture; mix well.

Turn dough out onto a floured surface. Knead until dough is smooth and elastic (8 to 10 minutes total). Cover and let rest for 10 minutes. Divide dough into fourths. On a lightly floured surface, roll each fourth into a 12x12-inch square (about ¹/₁₆ inch thick). Cut as desired. Or, pass dough through a pasta machine according to manufacturer's directions until ¹/₁₆ inch thick and cut into noodles. Let dry overnight.

Thaw shrimp, if frozen. Remove and discard stems and seeds from the reserved ²/₃ pound yellow peppers; cut peppers into ¹/₄-inch strips. For sauce, in a 12-inch skillet, heat olive oil. Add garlic and cook over medium heat until tender. Add shrimp and pepper strips; cook for 1 minute. Stir in the remaining ²/₃ cup pepper puree, water, remaining 2 tablespoons Hungarian paprika paste, Creole seasoning, Greek seasoning, remaining ¹/₂ teaspoon salt, and pepper. Bring to boiling; reduce heat. Simmer for 1 to 2 minutes or until shrimp turn pink.

Meanwhile, in a 6-quart Dutch oven or stockpot, cook pasta in 4 quarts boiling salted water for 1 to 3 minutes or until pasta is tender but still firm. Drain pasta; return to Dutch oven. Pour sauce over hot pasta. Toss until coated. Add basil and toss again until combined. Transfer to a serving dish. Serve immediately. Makes 6 main-dish servings.

*For Hungarian paprika paste, in a custard cup, stir together **Hungarian paprika** and enough **water** to form a paste.

R&B
Servin' up

ESTELLE AXTON & JIM STEWART

THIS BROTHER AND SISTER TEAM FOUNDED STAX RECORDS, THE RHYTHM AND BLUES RECORDING COMPANY THAT BROUGHT US OTIS REDDING, ISAAC HAYES, CARLA THOMAS, BLUES STAR ALBERT KING, AND MANY OTHERS. THE SOUTHERN SOUL MOVEMENT OF THE '60S AND '70S WAS BORN AT STAX, WHICH MANY OF THE ORIGINAL STARS HAVE CALLED A "FAMILY." THE MEMPHIS SOUND CAME TOGETHER AT STAX AND MADE AN INDELIBLE IMPRESSION ON POPULAR MUSIC EVERYWHERE.

Pasta with Chicken, Red Peppers, and Black Beans

8	chicken breast halves, skinned and boned
¹/₂	cup all-purpose flour
1¹/₄	teaspoons salt, divided
1¹/₄	teaspoons freshly ground pepper, divided
²/₃	cup olive oil, divided
8	ounces fresh mushrooms, quartered
3	medium tomatoes, peeled, seeded, and cut into bite-size pieces
2	sweet red peppers, roasted, peeled, and cut into 1/2-inch slices
¹/₃	cup sliced green onion
2	cloves garlic, minced
1¹/₂	cups cooked black beans
2	tablespoons snipped fresh basil or 2 teaspoons dried basil, crushed
1	tablespoon snipped parsley
1	pound linguine
	Freshly grated Parmesan cheese

Cut chicken into bite-size pieces. In a plastic bag, combine flour, ¹/₄ **teaspoon** of the salt, and ¹/₄ **teaspoon** of the pepper. Add chicken pieces, a few at a time, shaking to coat. Shake off excess flour mixture.

In a heavy 12-inch skillet, heat ¹/₃ **cup** of the olive oil over medium heat. Add coated chicken pieces and cook until lightly browned. Add mushrooms, tomatoes, red peppers, green onion, garlic, remaining 1 teaspoon salt, and remaining 1 teaspoon pepper. Cook 5 to 7 minutes or until vegetables are crisp-tender. Add black beans, basil, parsley, and remaining ¹/₃ cup olive oil. Reduce heat to low and cook until heated through.

Meanwhile in a 6-quart Dutch oven or stockpot, cook linguine in 4 quarts boiling salted water for 8 to 10 minutes or until tender but still firm. Drain well and return to Dutch oven. Add chicken mixture and toss well. Sprinkle with Parmesan cheese. Makes 8 main-dish servings.

Chicken and Sun-Dried Tomatoes over Fettuccine

4	chicken breast halves, skinned and boned
1	7-ounce jar sun-dried tomatoes packed in oil
¹/₂	cup chopped onion
2	cloves garlic, minced
2	tablespoons snipped fresh basil or 2 teaspoons dried basil, crushed
¹/₄	cup sliced ripe olives
2	tablespoons capers (optional)
2	tablespoons olive oil
¹/₂	teaspoon salt
¹/₄	teaspoon pepper
¹/₄	teaspoon crushed red pepper
8	ounces fettuccine
	Freshly grated Parmesan cheese

Cut chicken into ¹/₂-inch strips; set aside. Drain sun-dried tomatoes, reserving oil. Coarsley chop tomatoes; set aside. In a 12-inch skillet, heat **1 tablespoon** of the reserved oil from tomatoes over medium heat. Add onion and garlic and cook until tender. Add chicken and cook about 8 minutes, stirring occasionally, or until chicken is tender.

Add basil and tomatoes; cook 1 minute more. Stir in ripe olives, capers, olive oil, salt, pepper, crushed red pepper, and **2 tablespoons** of the reserved oil from tomatoes; heat through.

Meanwhile, in a 6-quart Dutch oven or stockpot, cook fettuccine in 3 quarts boiling salted water for 8 to 10 minutes or until tender but still firm. Drain well; return pasta to Dutch oven. Add chicken mixture and toss well. Sprinkle with Parmesan cheese. Makes 4 main-dish servings.

Spaghetti Special

The flavor of this recipe improves if served a day or two after it's prepared. Hide it in the back of the fridge; once your family discovers it, there won't be leftovers!

5	slices bacon
1	cup chopped celery
1/2	cup chopped onion
1/2	cup chopped green pepper
3	pounds lean ground beef
1	28-ounce can whole tomatoes, cut up
1	10-ounce can diced tomatoes and green chilies
1	8-ounce can tomato sauce
3	tablespoons chili powder
2	tablespoons sugar
1	tablespoon lemon-pepper seasoning
1	teaspoon celery seed
1	teaspoon snipped parsley
1	teaspoon dried basil, crushed
1/2	teaspoon dried rosemary, crushed
1	clove garlic, minced, or 1/4 teaspoon garlic powder
2	or 3 bay leaves
41/2	cups sliced fresh mushrooms (12 ounces)
	Salt to taste
2	pounds vermicelli
3	tablespoons butter or margarine
	Freshly grated Parmesan cheese

In an 8-quart Dutch oven or stockpot, cook bacon until crisp. Drain, reserving **3 tablespoons** drippings. Crumble bacon and set aside. Add celery, onion, and green pepper to drippings in saucepan; cook until vegetables are almost tender. Add ground beef and cook until meat is browned. Drain.

Stir in **undrained** tomatoes, **undrained** tomatoes and green chilies, tomato sauce, chili powder, sugar, lemon-pepper seasoning, celery seed, parsley, basil, rosemary, garlic, and bay leaves. Cover and simmer for 1 hour. Add mushrooms and crumbled bacon. Cook 15 minutes more. Season to taste with salt.

Preheat the oven to 350°. In a 12-quart stockpot, cook vermicelli in 8 quarts boiling salted water for 5 to 7 minutes or until tender but still firm. Drain and add to sauce. Add butter or margarine and stir until melted. Divide mixture between two 3-quart casseroles. Bake about 30 minutes or until bubbly. Pass Parmesan cheese. Makes 16 main-dish servings.

Five Cheese Lasagna

1½   pounds ground beef
½   cup chopped onion
½   cup chopped green pepper
2   cloves garlic, minced
1½   cups water
1   8-ounce can tomato sauce
1   6-ounce can tomato paste
1½   teaspoons Italian seasoning, crushed
¾   teaspoon salt
½   teaspoon chili powder
½   teaspoon dried oregano, crushed
8   ounces lasagna noodles, cooked and drained
2   cups cream-style cottage cheese
6   cups shredded mozzarella cheese (1½ pounds)
3   cups shredded cheddar cheese (12 ounces)
2   cups ricotta cheese
1   cup grated Parmesan cheese

In a 4-quart Dutch oven, cook beef, onion, green pepper, and garlic until meat is brown. Drain. Add water, tomato sauce, tomato paste, Italian seasoning, salt, chili powder, and oregano. Simmer for 45 minutes or until sauce is desired consistency, stirring occasionally. Adjust seasonings if necessary.

Preheat the oven to 350°. In a 15x11½x2-inch baking dish, spread a thin layer of the meat sauce. Layer with **half** of the noodles, **half** of the cottage cheese, **half** of the remaining meat sauce, **half** of the mozzarella, **half** of the cheddar, **half** of the ricotta, and **half** of the Parmesan cheese. Repeat layering with remaining noodles, meat sauce, cottage cheese, mozzarella, cheddar, ricotta, and Parmesan. Tent foil over the baking dish. Bake for 45 minutes. Let stand for 15 minutes before serving. Makes 12 to 15 main-dish servings.

Excellent Eggplant Pasta

Try this for a wonderful meatless entrée.

12   ounces fettuccine
½   cup olive oil
1   small eggplant, sliced ¼ inch thick
6   cloves garlic, minced
1   green pepper, seeded and cut into julienne strips
6   large fresh mushrooms, sliced
2   tablespoons snipped fresh basil
½   teaspoon crushed red pepper
6   Italian plum tomatoes, peeled, seeded, and chopped
¼   cup pine nuts, toasted
     Freshly grated Parmesan cheese

In a 6-quart Dutch oven or stockpot, cook fettuccine in 3½ quarts boiling water for 8 to 10 minutes or until tender but still firm. Drain well.

In a 12-inch skillet, heat olive oil. Add eggplant and garlic. Cover and cook over medium heat about 5 minutes or until eggplant is just tender, stirring occasionally. Stir in pepper strips, mushrooms, basil, and crushed red pepper. Cook about 3 minutes or until mushrooms are tender. Stir in tomatoes and cook until mixture is heated through.

Transfer eggplant mixture to a large bowl. Add pasta and pine nuts and toss well. Serve with Parmesan cheese. Makes 4 main-dish or 8 side-dish servings.

Mainstreet Manicotti

When the clock is ticking away, substitute a 28-ounce jar of commercial spaghetti sauce for the homemade.

1	8-ounce package manicotti shells (14 shells)
1	pound bulk Italian sausage
1/4	cup chopped onion
2	cloves garlic, minced
2	tablespoons cooking oil
1	16-ounce can tomatoes, cut up
1	6-ounce can tomato paste
1	teaspoon dried oregano, crushed
1/2	teaspoon dried basil, crushed
1/2	teaspoon salt
3	cups shredded mozzarella cheese (12 ounces)
1 1/2	cups cream-style cottage cheese
1/2	teaspoon garlic powder
	Freshly grated Parmesan cheese

In a 6-quart Dutch oven or stockpot, cook manicotti shells in 4 quarts boiling salted water about 18 minutes. Drain well. In a 10-inch skillet, cook sausage; drain well. Transfer sausage to a large bowl and set aside.

For sauce, in the same skillet, cook onion and garlic in cooking oil until tender. Add **undrained** tomatoes, tomato paste, oregano, basil, and salt. Cover and simmer for 15 minutes, stirring occasionally.

Preheat the oven to 350°. Add mozzarella cheese, cottage cheese, and garlic powder to sausage in bowl. Stir until well combined. Fill manicotti with sausage mixture. Arrange in a greased 13x9x2-inch baking dish.

Pour sauce over manicotti and bake for 25 minutes. Sprinkle with Parmesan cheese. Makes 6 to 8 main-dish servings.

Creamy Vegetable Tortellini

1	9-ounce package fresh tortellini
1	medium carrot, bias-sliced 1/4 inch thick
1/2	cup fresh or frozen snow peas, trimmed and halved diagonally
6	tablespoons butter or margarine, divided
1	clove garlic, minced
2	cups sliced fresh mushrooms
1	medium zucchini, sliced 1/4 inch thick
1	cup freshly grated Parmesan cheese
1	cup heavy cream
1	14-ounce can quartered artichoke hearts, drained
2	tablespoons chopped pimiento

Cook tortellini in boiling salted water according to package directions. Drain. Meanwhile, in a 1-quart saucepan, cook carrot in 1/2 **cup water**, covered, for 4 minutes. Add snow peas and cook 2 to 3 minutes more. Drain.

In a 10-inch skillet, heat **3 tablespoons** of the butter. Add garlic and cook over medium-high heat for 30 seconds. Add mushrooms and cook about 3 minutes or until tender. Remove mushrooms with slotted spoon and set aside. Add zucchini to skillet and cook for 1 to 2 minutes or until crisp-tender. Remove with a slotted spoon.

In a 4-quart Dutch oven, combine tortellini, the remaining 3 tablespoons butter, and Parmesan cheese. Heat and toss until melted. Gently stir in cream, artichoke hearts, pimiento, carrot, snow peas, mushrooms, and zucchini. Heat through. Makes 4 main-dish servings.

♪ ♪ ♪

NICE TO NOTE
—

When shopping the refrigerated pasta section for this recipe, choose from the variety of fresh tortellini available: spinach pasta stuffed with cheese or plain pasta filled with cheese, meat, or chicken.

Tortellini Bundles in Tomato-Basil Cream

Piping hot pasta is a wonderful way to begin a meal. Almost any pasta will make a grand first course when served in small portions. It can also take the place of the starch in your meal.

1½   cups heavy cream
1   cup tomato sauce
2   tablespoons snipped fresh basil or 2 teaspoons dried basil, crushed
½   cup plus 1 teaspoon butter or margarine, divided
1   cup freshly grated Parmesan cheese, divided
1   9-ounce package fresh Italian sausage tortellini
8   ounces phyllo dough

For sauce, in a heavy 1-quart saucepan, simmer cream about 15 minutes or until reduced to 1 cup. Add tomato sauce and basil; bring to boiling. Remove from heat. Whisk in **1 teaspoon** of the butter and ½ **cup** of the Parmesan cheese.

Cook tortellini according to package directions. Rinse with cold water and drain thoroughly. Combine tortellini and **one-third** of the tomato-basil sauce. Set aside.

Melt remaining ½ cup butter. Cut phyllo dough into twelve 7-inch squares. Cover with waxed paper and overlay with a damp cloth to prevent drying. Working quickly, brush one phyllo square with some of the melted butter. Sprinkle with some of the remaining Parmesan cheese. Place another square of phyllo dough on top of the first, then brush with butter and sprinkle with cheese. Repeat with third square of phyllo, butter, and cheese to form a stack. Repeat layering to make 3 more stacks of phyllo squares.

Preheat the oven to 350°. Generously butter four 2-cup oven-safe bowls or gratin dishes. Place one stack of phyllo squares in each. Place 5 or 6 tortellini on top of each phyllo stack in bowl and top with **one tablespoon** of the tomato-basil sauce. Bring corners of pastry together and pinch to seal. Brush with melted butter. Bake for 20 to 25 minutes or until golden.

Heat remaining sauce and spoon onto 4 plates. Set phyllo bundle in center of each and serve immediately. Makes 4 main-dish or 8 side-dish servings.

Puffed Angel Hair

When potatoes or plain buttered pasta won't do....

4   ounces angel hair pasta
6   egg yolks
1   cup shredded Gruyère, or Havarti, or cheddar cheese
1   cup finely chopped prosciutto or Canadian bacon
3   tablespoons snipped chives
¾   teaspoon white pepper
⅛   to ½ teaspoon ground red pepper
8   egg whites

Preheat the oven to 375°. In a 6-quart Dutch oven, cook pasta in 3 quarts boiling salted water for 2 to 4 minutes or until tender but still firm. Drain. In a large bowl, beat egg yolks with an electric mixer about 5 minutes or until thick and lemon-colored. Stir in cheese, prosciutto, chives, white pepper, red pepper, and pasta.

Wash beaters well. Beat egg whites until soft peaks form (tips curl over). Stir a large spoonful of the egg whites into the yolk mixture, then gently fold in the rest of the beaten whites. Pour mixture into a buttered 2-quart soufflé dish, smoothing the top. With a knife, cut a circle about 2 inches deep around the top of the soufflé about 2 inches from edge of dish. Bake for 15 to 20 minutes or until puffed and golden. Makes 6 main-dish servings.

♪♪♪

NICE TO NOTE
—

If you cannot find Italian sausage tortellini, use meat tortellini and add your favorite Italian spices to the sauce. Here are some other tips for making this fabulous dish:

- *Make smaller bundles and you have a fabulous first course.*
- *Bundles can be prepared several hours in advance. Cover with a damp towel and refrigerate.*
- *The sauce can be prepared 1 day in advance.*

Four-Cheese Pesto Lasagna

2	cups ricotta cheese
1	cup shredded mozzarella cheese (4 ounces)
$^3/_4$	cup grated Parmesan cheese
$^3/_4$	cup grated Romano cheese
$^1/_2$	cup snipped parsley
$^1/_2$	cup finely sliced green onion
1	beaten egg yolk
1	teaspoon Italian seasoning, crushed
$^1/_2$	teaspoon dried marjoram, crushed
2	cloves garlic, minced
	Salt and freshly ground pepper to taste
12	ounces lasagna noodles, cooked and drained
	Pesto Sauce (see recipe below)

Preheat the oven to 350°. In a large bowl, combine ricotta cheese, mozzarella cheese, Parmesan cheese, Romano cheese, parsley, onion, egg yolk, Italian seasoning, marjoram, garlic, salt, and pepper.

To assemble, spread some of the cheese mixture on each lasagna noodle. Roll up, jelly-roll style, starting from one of the short sides. In a well-greased 15x11$^1/_2$x2-inch baking dish, arrange lasagna rolls, standing them vertically. Pour Pesto Sauce over lasagna rolls. Cover and bake for 30 to 40 minutes or until sauce is bubbly and lasagna rolls are heated through. Makes 6 main-dish servings.

Pesto Sauce

2	cups firmly packed fresh basil leaves
2	tablespoons grated Parmesan cheese
2	tablespoons grated Romano cheese
2	tablespoons pine nuts or blanched almonds, toasted
3	cloves garlic, minced
$^2/_3$	to 1 cup olive oil
	Salt and freshly ground pepper

In a blender container or food processor bowl, combine basil leaves, Parmesan cheese, Romano cheese, pine nuts, and garlic. Cover and blend or process with several on-off turns until a paste forms, stopping the machine several times and scraping the sides. With the machine running on low speed, add enough of the olive oil in a steady stream to make a thick, smooth sauce. Season to taste with salt and pepper. Makes about 1$^1/_2$ cups.

Servin' up JAZZ

HAROLD MABERN

HAROLD MABERN, WHO BEGAN HIS MAJOR JAZZ PIANO CAREER IN MEMPHIS, HAS PLAYED AND RECORDED WITH THE LATE MILES DAVIS, AS WELL AS LIONEL HAMPTON, AND SONNY RAWLINS. A WINNER OF THE *DOWNBEAT* MAGAZINE CRITICS AWARD, MABERN WAS ONLY 15 WHEN HE BEGAN HIS CAREER.

Sausage and Sweet Pepper Pasta

Try using sweet red peppers instead of the green, or maybe one of each.

1¼   pounds sweet Italian sausage
2   tablespoons cooking oil
½   cup finely chopped onion
2   green peppers, seeded and cut into julienne strips
1   16-ounce can Italian plum tomatoes
½   cup water
½   cup dry red wine
3   tablespoons snipped fresh basil or 1 tablespoon dried basil, crushed
2   tablespoons snipped fresh oregano or 2 teaspoons dried oregano, crushed
1½   teaspoon snipped fresh thyme or ½ teaspoon dried thyme, crushed
½   teaspoon fennel seed
⅛   teaspoon crushed red pepper
1   pound penne (diagonally-cut tube-shaped pasta) or rigatoni (tube-shaped pasta with ridges)
3   tablespoons snipped Italian parsley
3   or 4 cloves garlic, minced
    Salt and freshly ground pepper to taste
    Freshly grated Parmesan cheese

Prick sausage all over with the tip of a sharp knife. Put in a 3-quart saucepan with ½ inch of water. Simmer sausage, uncovered, about 20 minutes or until water evaporates. Continue to cook sausage about 10 minutes or until well browned, turning occasionally. Drain and set aside.

Add oil to saucepan. Add onion; cover and cook over low heat about 15 minutes or until tender. Add pepper strips and cook, uncovered, over medium heat for 5 minutes, stirring frequently. Add **undrained** tomatoes, water, wine, basil, oregano, thyme, fennel seed, and red pepper. Bring to boiling; reduce heat. Simmer, partially covered, for 30 minutes.

Slice sausage into ½-inch rounds. Add to sauce and simmer, uncovered, 30 minutes more. Meanwhile, in a 6-quart Dutch oven or stockpot, cook pasta in 4 quarts boiling salted water for 12 to 14 minutes or until tender but still firm. Drain well; return pasta to Dutch oven.

Stir parsley, garlic, salt, and pepper into sauce. Simmer 10 minutes more. Toss sauce with pasta and top with Parmesan cheese. Makes 6 main-dish servings.

NICE TO NOTE

With an incredibly wide variety of pasta on the market today, a true pasta lover could put together an entire menu from this Italian creation. The names themselves sound wonderful! Pasta can be a filling staple in soup (stellini or "little stars" and farfalle or "butterflies"), baked in a casserole (lasagna and macaroni), stuffed with meat, cheese, and vegetables (manicotti and cannelloni), or served deliciously alone. Spaghetti and its sisters linguine and fettuccine can be dressed simply with olive oil, butter and cheese, or enjoyed with the familiar marinara and Alfredo sauces.

∞

Zucchini Manicotti

Make this an even healthier, vegetarian delight by omitting the sausage in the sauce and using low-fat cheeses and part-skim ricotta.

1	8-ounce package manicotti shells (14 shells)
¹/₂	pound bulk Italian sausage
³/₄	cup finely chopped onion, divided
1	clove garlic, minced
3	cups sliced fresh mushrooms
1	16-ounce can whole tomatoes, cut up
1	6-ounce can tomato paste
¹/₂	cup dry red wine
1	tablespoon snipped fresh oregano or 1 teaspoon dried oregano, crushed
1¹/₂	teaspoons snipped fresh basil or ¹/₂ teaspoon dried basil, crushed
2	tablespoons olive oil
2	small zucchini, finely chopped
1	15-ounce container ricotta cheese
1	cup shredded mozzarella cheese
1	cup shredded Monterey Jack cheese
¹/₄	cup grated Parmesan cheese
2	beaten eggs
3	tablespoons snipped parsley or 1 tablespoon dried parsley flakes

In a 6-quart Dutch oven or stockpot, cook manicotti shells in 4 quarts boiling salted water about 18 minutes. Drain well.

For sauce, in a 3-quart saucepan, cook sausage, ¹/₄ cup of the chopped onion, and garlic until sausage is brown. Drain. Add mushrooms, **undrained** tomatoes, tomato paste, wine, oregano, and basil. Simmer for 45 minutes.

Meanwhile, in a 10-inch skillet, heat olive oil. Add zucchini and remaining ¹/₂ cup chopped onion; cook just until tender. In a large bowl, combine ricotta, mozzarella, Monterey Jack, Parmesan, eggs, and parsley. Stir in cooked zucchini and onion.

Preheat the oven to 375°. Fill manicotti shells with zucchini mixture. Arrange shells in a greased 13x9x2-inch baking dish. Pour sauce over shells. Bake for 45 minutes. If desired, sprinkle with additional grated Parmesan cheese. Makes 6 to 8 main-dish servings.

R & B
Servin' up

STEVE CROPPER & DUCK DUNN

STEVE CROPPER AND DUCK DUNN STARTED OUT IN THE '50S AS A BACK-UP BAND FOR STAX RECORDING WHEN STAX WAS STILL IN A GARAGE AND THEY WERE IN MESSICK HIGH SCHOOL IN MEMPHIS WITH STAX CO-FOUNDER ESTELLE AXTON'S SON, PACKY. THEIR BAND HAD A HIT IN 1961 ("LAST NIGHT") AND THEY WENT ON TO BE A BIG PART OF THE MEMPHIS SOUND. LATER, STEVE AND DUCK RECORDED WITH BOOKER T. AND THE M. G.S AND ON OTIS REDDING'S RECORDS. REVERED BY THE BEATLES, THEY SHARED A STAGE IN ENGLAND WITH OTIS AS PART OF THE STAX/VOLT REVUE IN 1966-67. MORE RECENTLY, STEVE CROPPER AND DUCK DUNN HAVE PERFORMED AS THE BACK-UP BAND FOR THE BLUES BROTHERS.

Father Dan's Favorite Pasta

1 28-ounce can stewed tomatoes
1 28-ounce can whole tomatoes, chopped and drained
3 tablespoons tomato paste
2 cloves garlic, minced
2 tablespoons snipped fresh oregano or 2 teaspoons dried oregano, crushed
2 tablespoons snipped fresh thyme or 2 teaspoons dried thyme, crushed
1 teaspoon salt
1 teaspoon freshly ground pepper
1¹/₂ cups light cream
1 cup dairy sour cream
¹/₄ cup dry white wine
1 cup freshly grated Parmesan cheese
6 ounces prosciutto, chopped
¹/₄ cup snipped fresh basil or 1 tablespoon dried basil, crushed
1¹/₂ pounds spinach fettuccine
Freshly grated Parmesan cheese or shredded mozzarella cheese

In a 4-quart Dutch oven, combine **undrained** stewed tomatoes, chopped tomatoes, tomato paste, garlic, oregano, thyme, salt, and pepper. Bring to boiling; reduce heat. Simmer, uncovered, over medium heat for 10 minutes. Stir in light cream, sour cream, and wine. Simmer, stirring occasionally, for 20 minutes. Stir in 1 cup Parmesan cheese, prosciutto, and basil; simmer 5 minutes more.

Meanwhile, in an 8-quart stockpot, cook fettuccine in 6 quarts boiling salted water for 8 to 10 minutes or until tender but still firm. Drain well and return to stockpot. Pour tomato mixture over hot pasta; toss until coated. Transfer pasta mixture to a serving dish and sprinkle with additional Parmesan cheese. Or, transfer to an oven-safe serving dish and sprinkle with mozzarella cheese; bake in a 350° oven about 3 minutes or until cheese is melted and begins to brown slightly. Makes 8 to 10 main-dish servings.

Memphis Macaroni

1¹/₂ cups elbow macaroni (6 ounces)
1¹/₂ cups milk, heated
1¹/₂ cups shredded American cheese (6 ounces)
2 beaten eggs
2 tablespoons chopped green pepper
2 tablespoons sliced green onion
2 tablespoon snipped parsley
2 tablespoons chopped pimiento (optional)
¹/₂ teaspoon salt
¹/₂ teaspoon pepper
¹/₄ teaspoon paprika
¹/₄ cup butter or margarine
1 cup soft bread crumbs

In a 4-quart Dutch oven, cook macaroni in 2¹/₂ quarts of boiling salted water about 10 minutes or until tender but still firm. Drain well.

Preheat the oven to 350°. In a large mixing bowl, stir together macaroni, milk, cheese, eggs, green pepper, green onion, parsley, pimiento, salt, pepper, and paprika until well mixed. Pour into a buttered 2-quart casserole. Place casserole in a 9-inch square baking pan on oven rack. Pour boiling water into the baking pan around casserole to a depth of 1 inch. Bake for 30 minutes.

Meanwhile, melt butter or margarine. Stir in soft bread crumbs. Sprinkle over macaroni; bake 20 minutes more or until crumbs are lightly browned. Makes 6 side-dish servings.

◆ ◆ ◆

WHEN IN ROME
—

"During a visit with a dear friend who was a priest in Rome, we were escorted to his favorite restaurant along the Appian Way in the ancient section of the city. This pasta was a premier 'starter' on the menu and we loved it. Dan asked for a hint at its ingredients and we scribbled them down. Upon his return to Memphis, we perfected the dish during several trial-and-error sessions and 'Father Dan' believes it's even better than the Roman original!"

◆ ◆ ◆

Linguine with Tomatoes and Basil

Easy and wonderful. Amounts of garlic and olives can be varied to suit your taste.

8	very ripe large tomatoes, peeled, seeded, and cut into bite-size pieces
1	cup extra virgin olive oil
1	cup fresh basil leaves, cut into strips
1	cup freshly grated Parmesan cheese
³/₄	cup sliced ripe olives
¹/₂	cup sliced green olives
3	to 6 cloves garlic, minced
1	tablespoon salt
1	teaspoon freshly ground pepper
1¹/₂	pounds linguine or spaghetti
	Freshly grated Parmesan cheese

In a large bowl, combine tomatoes, olive oil, basil, Parmesan cheese, ripe olives, green olives, garlic, salt, and pepper. Cover and let stand at room temperature 2 hours.

In an 8-quart stockpot, cook linguine in 6 quarts of boiling salted water for 8 to 10 minutes (10 to 12 minutes for spaghetti) or until tender but still firm. Drain well. Return pasta to stockpot. Add tomato mixture and toss. Serve with additional Parmesan cheese. Makes 12 to 15 side-dish servings.

Pasta with Pesto

2	cups firmly packed fresh basil leaves
¹/₂	cup olive oil
¹/₂	cup pine nuts or walnuts
¹/₄	cup freshly grated Parmesan cheese
2	cloves garlic, quartered
¹/₂	teaspoon salt
	Freshly ground pepper to taste
1	pound fusilli (twisted spaghetti), spaghetti, fettuccine, or farfalle (bow ties)
¹/₄	cup butter or margarine, softened
	Fresh basil leaves

For pesto, in a blender container or food processor bowl, combine basil leaves, olive oil, pine nuts, Parmesan cheese, garlic, and salt. Cover and blend or process until smooth, scraping sides of bowl once or twice. Season to taste with pepper.

In a 6-quart Dutch oven or stockpot, cook pasta in 4 quarts boiling salted water for 8 to 12 minutes or until tender but still firm. Drain well and return to Dutch oven. Toss with softened butter. Add pesto and toss until well combined. Transfer to a serving bowl and garnish with fresh basil leaves. Makes 8 to 10 side-dish servings.

Pasta with Summer Marinara Sauce

The marinara sauce is also superb over chicken, fish, or veal.

6   to 8 ounces rigatoni, rotini, or thin spaghetti
6   tablespoons butter or margarine, divided
1/4   cup finely chopped shallots
12   medium tomatoes, peeled, seeded and juiced over strainer, and chopped
2   cloves garlic, minced
    Salt, freshly ground pepper, and sugar to taste
2   tablespoons snipped parsley
2   tablespoons snipped fresh basil

In a 6-quart Dutch oven or stockpot, cook pasta in 3 quarts boiling salted water for 8 to 10 minutes (10 to 12 minutes for rigatoni) or until tender but still firm. Drain well.

In the same Dutch oven or stockpot, melt **4 tablespoons** of the butter over medium-low heat. Add shallots and cook about 3 minutes or until tender. Add tomatoes with their juice and garlic. Cover and cook over low heat, stirring occasionally, about 30 minutes or until tomatoes are soft enough to mash with a spoon.

Season with salt and pepper. Taste and add sugar, if necessary. Stir in parsley and basil. Whisk in remaining 2 tablespoons butter, a tablespoon at a time, until melted and well blended. Serve sauce over pasta. Makes 4 side-dish servings.

Four-Pepper Pasta

Great with steak, grilled chicken, or fish.

10   to 12 ounces angel hair pasta
3   tablespoons olive oil
2   sweet red peppers, seeded and cut into julienne strips
2   sweet yellow peppers, seeded and cut into julienne strips
2   cloves garlic, minced
1/4   to 1/2 teaspoon crushed red pepper
    Salt and freshly ground pepper to taste
1/4   cup freshly grated Parmesan cheese
2   tablespoons snipped fresh basil

In a 6-quart Dutch oven or stockpot, cook pasta in 3 1/2 quarts boiling salted water for 2 to 4 minutes or until tender but still firm. Drain well.

Meanwhile, in a 12-inch skillet, heat olive oil. Add pepper strips and garlic; cook over medium heat until peppers are crisp-tender. Remove from heat. Stir in the crushed red pepper, salt, and pepper.

Return the hot cooked pasta to the Dutch oven; add pepper mixture and toss. Add Parmesan cheese and basil; lightly toss again. Serve immediately. Makes 8 side-dish servings.

♪ ♪ ♪

NICE TO NOTE

Here's a tip on peeling and seeding tomatoes: Drop them into a pot of boiling water for 30 seconds. Scoop out with tongs or a slotted spoon and immerse in ice water. Core the tomatoes by cutting out the stem and slip off the skin. To seed, cut the tomatoes in half and squeeze gently. Most seeds should drop out easily and others can be removed with a teaspoon.

VEGETABLES

Elvis Presley

*E*lvis Presley took the world by surprise—and surprised even himself with the revolution that followed.

His new "rock and roll," and the daring, powerful style that went with it, astounded his audiences and set off a level of excitement and raw energy previously unknown. This was a musical nuclear reaction that continues decades after the original explosion.

From "That's All Right," his send-off single for Sam Phillips at "Sun" in 1956, through a chain of million-selling hits such as "Heartbreak Hotel," "Hound Dog," "Love Me Tender," and "It's Now or Never," the "King" has had the music world "All Shook Up" and even today the vibrations continue.

How did it happen? From his hard-times roots in rural Mississippi and Memphis came Elvis' feel for heart-soothing gospel, the lament of the black man's blues, and the white country music heritage passed down by generations of working men. He put them together with an unforgettable voice, dark good looks, a shy but mysteriously "come-on" charm, and that irrepressible body language— and the result was the legend of Elvis Aron Presley.

VEGETABLES

◆ ◆ ◆

PICTURED OVERLEAF

—

Clockwise from right:
Carrots with Horseradish
(page 220) and Venetian
Green Beans with Tomatoes
(page 217)

◆ ◆ ◆

*Y*ELLOW, GOLD, RED, GREEN, AND ORANGE; THE VEGETABLE HARVEST is lovely to behold. Year-round, Southern produce aisles present us with a gorgeous array and beckon us to buy. We can indulge without reserve, for there is nothing better for us.

For years, mothers have admonished little ones to eat their vegetables. Current wisdom confirms that this was very wise advice. Vegetables are low in fat and calories, high in fiber, and packed with vitamins, minerals, and a few preventive health magic tricks.

Let us not forget that vegetables are delicious as well, and can be prepared in a myriad of ways. For down-home good taste, it's hard to beat the Southern style: slow-cooked and liberally seasoned. But even miles below the Mason-Dixon line, we realize the pluses of fresh, snappy, barely-steamed vegetables. Summer squash, green beans, broccoli, corn, and carrots treated this way are crunchy-good and beautiful additions to the plate.

Vegetables also stand very nicely on their own as a meatless meal. Many Southern families look forward to all-veggie dinners, especially in the summer, and area restaurants serve "choose-your-own" vegetable plates, offering daily a dozen or more mouth-watering choices for an all-garden lunch or supper. So prepare yourself for something new, or rediscover an old favorite, but take your mother's advice and...Eat your vegetables! ♥

♦ ♦ ♦

AMEN

—

"As I was growing up we said a simple blessing before each dinner. This blessing was: 'God is great. God is good. Let us thank Him for our food.' One night my younger sister, who was about three, proudly announced that she wanted to say the blessing. We all bowed our heads to hear her say: 'God is apples, God is grapes. Amen.' When we began snickering and laughing, she indignantly exclaimed, 'Well! you call Him grapes!' I suppose that when our food is truly wonderful it is a compliment when our young ones praise Him with the names of food!"

♦ ♦ ♦

Artichokes au Gratin

5	tablespoons butter or margarine, divided
3	tablespoons all-purpose flour
1/2	teaspoon salt
1 3/4	cups milk
2	14-ounce cans artichoke hearts, rinsed, drained, and coarsely chopped
1	cup shredded cheddar cheese (4 ounces)
1/2	cup mayonnaise
	Cracked black pepper to taste
3/4	cup fine dry bread crumbs

Preheat the oven to 325°. In a 2-quart saucepan, melt **3 tablespoons** of the butter or margarine. Add flour and salt; stir until smooth. Cook and stir for 1 minute. Gradually add milk. Cook over medium heat, stirring constantly, until thickened and bubbly. Remove from heat. Stir in artichoke hearts, cheese, mayonnaise, and pepper. Spoon into a 1 1/2-quart casserole.

Melt the remaining 2 tablespoons butter or margarine. Stir in bread crumbs. Sprinkle over top. Bake about 45 minutes or until bubbly. Makes 6 servings.

Asparagus with Citrus Butter

 2   pounds fresh or frozen asparagus spears
 2   large oranges
 1/4 cup butter or margarine
 2   cloves garlic, minced
 1/4 teaspoon salt
 1/8 teaspoon pepper

If using fresh asparagus, snap off and discard tough ends from asparagus. With a sharp knife or vegetable peeler, scrape off scales. In a 3-quart saucepan, cook asparagus in a small amount of boiling salted water, covered, for 5 minutes. (Or, prepare frozen asparagus according to package directions.) Drain and set aside.

Grate the peel of **one** of the oranges to make **2 tablespoons** grated peel. Squeeze juice of the orange to make **1/4 cup** orange juice. Set aside.

In a 12-inch skillet, melt butter over medium heat. Add garlic and cook for 1 minute. Add orange peel and orange juice to butter in skillet. Add asparagus; cook for 3 to 5 minutes more or until tender. Remove asparagus to a serving platter. Spoon orange juice mixture over asparagus. Sprinkle with the salt and pepper.

Peel remaining orange, if desired. Cut orange into thin slices and arrange on platter with asparagus. Makes 6 servings.

Prosciutto-Wrapped Asparagus

12   large asparagus spears
 6   ounces prosciutto, thinly sliced
 5   ounces gouda cheese, cut into thin strips
 1/4 cup butter or margarine, divided
     Cracked black pepper

Snap off and discard tough ends from asparagus. If desired, scrape off scales. Steam spears for 5 to 8 minutes or until almost tender.

Preheat the oven to 400°. Divide prosciutto slices into 6 equal portions. Divide cheese slices into 6 equal portions. To assemble each bundle, place **three** asparagus spears on top of 1 slice of the prosciutto from each portion. Place **all but 2** of the cheese strips from each portion between the asparagus spears of each bundle. Top **each** bundle with 1 1/2 **teaspoons** of the butter or margarine. Sprinkle with cracked black pepper. Use remaining prosciutto slices from each portion to wrap around each bundle, keeping meat thickness as even as possible around asparagus.

In a lightly buttered 8-inch square baking dish, arrange bundles in a single layer. Place the two remaining strips of cheese from each portion in a crisscross pattern on top of the bundles. Dot with remaining 2 tablespoons butter or margarine. Bake about 20 minutes or until cheese is melted and lightly browned. Makes 4 servings.

Asparagus with Orange-Basil Hollandaise Sauce

 ¹/₂ cup unsalted butter
   1 pound medium asparagus spears
   3 beaten egg yolks
1¹/₂ teaspoons grated orange peel (set aside)
 ¹/₄ cup orange juice, divided
   1 teaspoon snipped fresh basil or ¹/₄ teaspoon dried basil, crushed
      Dash salt
      Dash freshly ground pepper

Cut butter into thirds and bring it to room temperature. Meanwhile, snap off and discard tough ends from asparagus. If desired, scrape off scales.

For sauce, in the top of a double boiler, combine egg yolks, **half** of the orange juice, basil, salt, and pepper. Add **one piece** of the butter. Place over boiling water (upper pan should not touch water). Cook, stirring rapidly with a wire whisk, until butter melts and sauce begins to thicken. Add the remaining butter, one piece at a time, stirring constantly. Cook and stir for 1 to 2 minutes or until sauce thickens. Immediately remove from heat. Stir in remaining orange juice and orange peel. (If sauce is too thick or curdles, immediately beat in 1 to 2 tablespoons **hot tap water**.)

Meanwhile, in a 10-inch skillet, bring a small amount of water to boiling. Add asparagus. Cover and cook over medium heat about 8 minutes (3 to 5 minutes for small spears) or until tender. Drain. Spoon sauce over asparagus. Serve immediately. Makes 4 servings.

Green Beans Y'all Won't Believe

Nothin' says "Southern" quite like "drippin's." No longer a diet mainstay in these health-conscious times, drippings have long been a flavor enhancer to Southern cooked vegetables. There are certain recipes in which nothing else will do. Forgive us!

1¹/₂ pounds fresh green beans or 2 16-ounce cans green beans
  10 strips bacon
   6 tablespoons sugar
   6 tablespoons vinegar
 ¹/₄ cup slivered almonds

If using fresh beans, wash the beans; remove ends and strings. Leave whole or cut into 1-inch pieces. In a 2-quart saucepan, cook beans in a small amount of boiling salted water, covered, for 20 to 25 minutes or until crisp-tender; drain. (Or, rinse and drain canned beans.) Set aside.

In a 10-inch skillet, cook bacon until crisp. Remove bacon and crumble, reserving drippings in skillet. Stir sugar and vinegar into drippings.

Preheat the oven to 350°. In a 1¹/₂-quart casserole, layer **half** of the beans, **half** of the crumbled bacon, and **half** of the almonds. Repeat layering. Pour prepared drippings over all. Bake about 45 minutes or until heated through. Makes 6 to 8 servings.

◆ ◆ ◆

THE PROPER USE OF Y'ALL — A SACRED TRUST

—

"Y'all" is not like "ain't"— it's proper English down here! Anyone raised in the South knows from an early age how the word is used, and nothing exposes a closet Yankee more quickly than the misuse of "y'all." A contraction of "you all," it is always plural, and it peppers everyday speech from Texas to Virginia. A few of us even say it with a smile and sprinkle our conversations with a few extra "y'alls" when talking to "Yankees" and "foreigners" from other areas of the country! After all, Mama always said that "You catch more flies with sugar than vinegar." Don't y'all agree?

◆ ◆ ◆

Venetian Green Beans with Tomatoes

Served chilled, this dish is a perfect accompaniment for cold ham and potato salad. Prepare it the night before the pre-game feast or symphony picnic. Photograph on page 210.

1 pound fresh green beans
1/4 cup olive oil
3 large tomatoes, peeled, seeded, and chopped, or 2 cups canned plum tomatoes, drained and chopped
2 cloves garlic, minced
1 tablespoon snipped fresh basil or 1 teaspoon dried basil, crushed
1 tablespoon snipped fresh oregano or 1 teaspoon dried oregano, crushed
1 tablespoon snipped parsley
Salt and freshly ground pepper
2 tablespoons freshly grated Parmesan cheese (optional)

Wash beans. In a 2-quart saucepan, cook beans in a small amount of boiling salted water, covered, for 7 to 9 minutes or until barely tender. Drain well.

In a 10-inch skillet, heat olive oil. Add drained beans and toss to coat. Add the tomatoes, garlic, basil, oregano, and parsley. Boil rapidly for 1 minute to evaporate any juice. Reduce heat to low. Cook 5 to 10 minutes more or until beans are tender. Season to taste with salt and pepper. Stir in cheese. Serve warm or chilled. Makes 4 servings.

Beale Street Baked Beans

Though always a hit at a backyard barbecue, this is not just fair-weather food. Try it as a dip for corn chips on a chilly night by the fireplace.

1 1/2 pounds ground beef or ground turkey
3/4 cup chopped onion
1 tablespoon lemon-pepper seasoning
1 teaspoon garlic powder
1 1/4 cups catsup
1/2 cup packed brown sugar
2 tablespoons Worcestershire sauce
1 tablespoon dry mustard
1 teaspoon freshly ground pepper
2 16-ounce cans pork and beans in tomato sauce

Preheat the oven to 350°. In a 10-inch skillet, cook ground beef and onion until meat is brown, sprinkling with lemon-pepper seasoning and garlic powder after meat has started to brown. Drain; transfer to a medium bowl. Add catsup, brown sugar, Worcestershire sauce, dry mustard, and pepper. Mix until well combined.

Carefully stir in beans until well mixed. Transfer to a 2 1/2-quart casserole. Bake, uncovered, about 30 minutes or until bubbly. Makes 10 to 12 servings.

Best Baked Beans

6   to 8 slices bacon
1   cup chopped onion
1   cup chopped green pepper
3   16-ounce cans pork and beans in tomato sauce
$^1/_2$ cup catsup
3   tablespoons brown sugar
$^1/_2$ teaspoon salt
$^1/_4$ teaspoon pepper

In a heavy 12-inch skillet, fry bacon until crisp. Remove bacon and set aside, reserving **2 tablespoons** of the drippings in the skillet.

Add onion and green pepper to drippings in the skillet. Cook until tender. Stir in beans, catsup, brown sugar, salt, and pepper. Cover and simmer over medium heat for 30 minutes.

To serve, transfer beans to a serving dish. Crumble bacon and sprinkle over beans. Makes 6 to 8 servings.

Soup Beans the Way Mama Does 'Em

This is the kind of recipe a Memphis mother might pass on to her newlywed daughter when she receives that harried first call for HELP!

16   ounces dry pinto beans
4   large slices sugar-cured country ham, chopped into bite-size pieces

Pick through the beans, removing rocks or beans with holes in them. Wash them 5 or 6 times until the water running over them runs clear. Soak beans overnight in water that levels about 1 inch over the beans.

The next day, bring the pot of beans to boiling in the same water. Drop in ham pieces and bring back to a boil, stirring occasionally. Reduce heat to low. Simmer, covered, for 2 to 3 hours or until beans are tender but not mushy, adding water occasionally, if necessary. The end result will be beans that are firm and whole in a thick broth known as "pot likker" that tastes even better after a day or two. Makes 6 to 8 servings.

Note: Sugar-cured country ham is very salty but ideal for soup beans. If unavailable, any leftover ham or meaty ham bone can be used if you salt the beans to taste.

♦ ♦ ♦

A TASTE OF HOME
—

"Soup Beans and Corn Bread has always been a favorite supper in our family. When we returned home from college for the weekend, Mama always had a big pot of soup beans waiting. She made hot corn bread in a black skillet and served a fresh green salad. One piece of corn bread goes in the bowl, and the beans and 'pot likker' are ladled over, and you need a second piece of corn bread slathered with butter on the side. Spicy tomato relish or chow-chow is also a must—our family spoons it over the beans. Even today, when my North Carolina brother-in-law visits Memphis, he eats soup beans every single day for lunch during his stay. My sister swears he married her for the soup beans!"

A NOTE ON "POT LIKKER"
—

"Pot likker," or pot liquor, is the broth that is thin at first, then thickens each day that the beans are in the refrigerator. Pot liquor is also a component of turnip greens and other dishes that are cooked in a long, slow, moist fashion. In Granddaddy's day, the pot liquor was a treat to be savored and occasionally used for medicinal purposes.

♦ ♦ ♦

Steamed Broccoli with Black Peppercorn Butter

- 3 pounds broccoli
- 1/2 cup butter
- 1 tablespoon soy sauce
- 1 tablespoon brandy
- 2 to 3 teaspoons freshly ground peppercorns
   Salt to taste

Wash and remove outer leaves and tough parts of stalks from broccoli. Cut broccoli into spears. Steam for 8 to 12 minutes or until crisp-tender. (Or, cook, covered, in a small amount of boiling salted water for 8 to 12 minutes).

Meanwhile, in a 1-quart saucepan, melt butter. Stir in soy sauce, brandy, pepper, and salt. Cook over low heat for 2 minutes. Pour butter mixture over hot broccoli. Toss until coated; serve immediately. Makes 8 servings.

Broccoli with Pine Nuts

- 1 large head broccoli (about 2 pounds)
- 1/2 cup butter or margarine
- 3 tablespoons pine nuts
- 1 tablespoon fresh lemon juice
   Salt and freshly ground pepper to taste

Cut broccoli into spears; peel ends of spears. Steam broccoli for 8 to 12 minutes or until crisp-tender.

Meanwhile, in a 12-inch skillet, melt butter or margarine over medium heat. Add pine nuts and cook for 3 minutes, stirring often. Add broccoli and cook 2 minutes more. Remove from heat. Drizzle with lemon juice and season to taste with salt and pepper. Makes 8 servings.

Crazy Cauliflower

- 1 cup water
- 1 tablespoon lemon juice
- 1 medium head cauliflower (about 2 pounds)
- 3/4 cup mayonnaise
- 1 tablespoon prepared mustard
- 1 teaspoon dry mustard
- 1/2 to 1 teaspoon curry powder
- 1 cup shredded sharp cheddar cheese (4 ounces)
   Fresh thyme sprigs

In a 3-quart saucepan, combine water and lemon juice. Bring to boiling. Add cauliflower head, flowerette side down. Return to boiling; reduce heat. Cover and cook about 15 minutes or until tender. Drain well.

Preheat the oven to 350°. In a small bowl, combine mayonnaise, prepared mustard, dry mustard, and curry powder. Place cauliflower, flowerette side up, in a deep 3-quart casserole. Spread cauliflower with mayonnaise mixture. Top with cheese. Bake for 10 to 15 minutes or until cheese is melted. Garnish with fresh thyme sprigs. Makes 6 servings.

NICE TO NOTE
—

For a very simple, very Southern meal, try white beans cooked slowly with a touch of pork until just right, served with skillet corn bread and a touch of sweet butter. Add a crisp green onion to munch alongside, or even better, well-seasoned turnip greens and you're in "hog heaven!"

∞

Carrots with Horseradish

This zesty side dish really perks up turkey, roast beef, or ham. Photograph on page 210.

    8   large carrots, cut into julienne strips
    1/2   cup mayonnaise or salad dressing
    2   tablespoons grated onion
    2   tablespoons prepared horseradish
    1   teaspoon lemon juice
    1/4   teaspoon salt
    1/4   teaspoon cracked black pepper
    1/2   cup fine dry bread crumbs
    1   tablespoon butter or margarine, melted

Preheat the oven to 350°. In a 3-quart saucepan, cook carrots in 1/2 cup boiling salted water, covered, for 5 to 7 minutes or until crisp-tender. Drain, reserving 1/4 **cup** of the cooking liquid. Arrange carrots in a 12x7 1/2x2-inch baking dish.

In a small bowl, combine mayonnaise, onion, horseradish, lemon juice, salt, pepper, and reserved cooking liquid. Pour mayonnaise mixture over carrots. Sprinkle with bread crumbs. Drizzle with melted butter.

Bake for 15 to 20 minutes or until heated through. Makes 6 servings.

Carrot Soufflé

    2   cups thinly sliced carrots or 1 15-ounce can carrots, drained
    1   cup sugar
    3   eggs
    1/2   cup butter or margarine, melted
    3   tablespoons all-purpose flour
    1   teaspoon baking powder
    1/2   teaspoon ground cinnamon
    1/4   teaspoon ground nutmeg
         Finely shredded orange peel curls

Preheat the oven to 350°. If using fresh carrots, cook carrots in a small amount of boiling salted water for 7 to 9 minutes or until tender; drain. In a food processor bowl or blender container, combine carrots, sugar, eggs, melted butter, flour, baking powder, cinnamon, and nutmeg. Cover and process or blend until smooth. Pour into a 1 1/2-quart casserole. Bake for 30 to 40 minutes or until a knife inserted near center comes out clean. Garnish with shredded orange peel curls. Makes 6 servings.

Corn Fritters

These fritters can be made ahead of time and frozen. Thaw on a baking sheet, uncovered, and then reheat in a 350° oven.

8	fresh ears of corn or 2 10-ounce packages frozen whole kernel corn
2	tablespoons butter or margarine
2	tablespoons sugar
1/4	cup all-purpose flour
1/4	cup matzo meal or finely crushed unsalted crackers
1	teaspoon baking powder
2	beaten eggs
2	tablespoons heavy cream
2	teaspoons snipped chives
	Dash ground red pepper
1/4	cup cooking oil

Using a sharp knife, cut kernels from cobs. (Or, cook frozen corn according to package directions; drain.) In a 10-inch skillet, melt butter over medium heat. Add corn and cook for 2 to 3 minutes. Stir in sugar. Transfer corn mixture to a large mixing bowl. Add flour, matzo meal or crushed crackers, baking powder, eggs, cream, chives, and red pepper. Stir until blended.

In another 10-inch skillet, heat cooking oil. Drop batter by heaping tablespoons, several at a time, into the hot oil. Cook about 3 minutes per side or until golden. Remove with a slotted spoon; drain on paper towels. Cool. Makes 8 to 10 servings.

Colmer Corn Stir-Fry

Heed a couple of tips to ensure outstanding results. Stir-fry the corn in a skillet or pan large enough that the level of the corn is 1/2 to 3/4 inch thick. Also, don't leave out the nutmeg, whatever you do. It lends a sweet flavor to the vegetables.

2	or 3 ripe medium tomatoes
6	fresh ears of corn or 3 cups frozen whole kernel corn, thawed
2	tablespoons butter or margarine
2	tablespoons cooking oil
1 1/2	teaspoons freshly ground pepper
1	tablespoon snipped fresh tarragon or 1 teaspoon dried tarragon, crushed
1	to 1 1/2 teaspoons ground nutmeg
3/4	cup freshly grated Parmesan cheese
	Salt to taste
	Fresh tarragon sprigs

Chop tomatoes, reserving the juice. Set aside. Using a sharp knife, cut kernels from cobs. Using the dull edge of the knife, scrape cobs, reserving juice from cobs. Place corn and juice from cobs in a 12-inch skillet or a large roasting pan set over 2 stovetop burners.

Add butter and oil to corn; cook over medium-high heat, tossing occasionally, until corn turns bright yellow. Add tomatoes and juice, the pepper, tarragon, and nutmeg. Simmer until tomatoes are tender. Remove from heat. Stir in Parmesan cheese until melted. Season with salt, if necessary. Garnish with fresh tarragon sprigs. Makes 6 servings.

♦ ♦ ♦

CORN-Y MEMORIES

—

"They say that the sense of smell is a powerful memory-evoker. I know this for certain whenever fresh corn fritters are in the skillet. Then I am taken back to our family vacation home in Michigan, and I swear I can also smell the pine trees and crisp night air that are part of the magic there. On the first night of our long-awaited getaway, the whole family gathered to revel in each other and savor Grandmother Bebe's feast, which always included these wonderful fritters. They are still my very favorite!"

♦ ♦ ♦

Grilled Corn

For a stronger herb flavor, add dried basil, thyme, or rosemary to the butter mixture.

- 1/2 cup butter or margarine, softened
- 2 tablespoons snipped chives
- 1 tablespoon lemon juice
- 4 fresh ears of corn, husks and silks removed

In a small bowl, combine butter, chives, and lemon juice. Place each ear on a piece of heavy foil. Spread butter mixture on each ear of corn. Wrap corn securely. Grill corn on an uncovered grill for 15 to 20 minutes, turning every 5 minutes. Makes 4 servings.

Chickasaw Corn Pudding

- 4 eggs
- 1/2 cup light cream
- 1 1/2 teaspoons baking powder
- 6 fresh medium ears of corn, cooked, or 3 cups frozen whole kernel corn, cooked according to package directions
- 6 tablespoons butter or margarine, divided
- 2 tablespoons sugar
- 2 tablespoons all-purpose flour
- 2 tablespoons brown sugar
- 1/4 teaspoon ground cinnamon

Preheat the oven to 350°. In a large bowl, beat eggs; add light cream and baking powder and stir well. Set aside.

If using fresh corn, cut kernels from cobs to make 3 cups corn; set aside. In a 1 1/2-quart saucepan, melt **4 tablespoons** of the butter. Stir in sugar and the flour until smooth. Remove from heat. Gradually add to egg mixture, stirring constantly until smooth. Add corn to egg mixture and stir well.

Pour corn mixture into a greased 1 1/2-quart shallow casserole. Bake for 30 to 40 minutes or until pudding is set. Melt the remaining 2 tablespoons butter; drizzle over pudding. Combine brown sugar and cinnamon; sprinkle over pudding. Bake 3 to 5 minutes more or until sugar melts. Makes 8 servings.

Sautéed Cucumbers

Pronounced delicious by those who couldn't imagine eating cucumbers in anything but salad.

2   large cucumbers
1   tablespoon salt
1   cup heavy cream
1   to 2 tablespoons snipped fresh dill or ¹/₂ to 1 teaspoon dried dillweed
    Freshly ground pepper
2   tablespoons butter or margarine

Peel cucumbers. Halve cucumbers lengthwise and seed with a spoon. Cut into thin slices. Place cucumber slices in a colander. Add salt and toss well. Let drain for 20 minutes. Rinse under cold water and drain thoroughly, patting dry with paper towels.

In a 1-quart saucepan, combine cream, dill, and pepper. Bring to boiling. Boil about 20 minutes or until reduced by half.

In a 10-inch skillet, melt butter over medium-high heat. Add cucumbers and cook for 3 to 5 minutes or until crisp-tender. Stir in cream mixture and cook for 2 to 3 minutes or until heated through. Makes 4 to 6 servings.

Extraordinary Eggplant Parmesan

A pound of cooked Italian sausage makes a nice addition to the sauce. Also, you can substitute a 32-ounce jar of meatless spaghetti sauce for the homemade sauce.

2   tablespoons olive oil (divided)
1   cup chopped onion
4   cloves garlic, minced (divided)
2   15-ounce cans tomato sauce
1¹/₂ teaspoons salt (divided)
1   teaspoon pepper (divided)
¹/₂ teaspoon dried oregano, crushed (divided)
2   tablespoons cooking oil
2   cups fine dry bread crumbs
1   tablespoon dried parsley flakes
1¹/₂ cups grated Parmesan cheese (divided)
    Cooking oil for deep-fat frying
1   large eggplant, peeled and sliced into 3x³/₄-inch strips
2   beaten eggs
1   pound sliced mozzarella cheese

For sauce, in a 3-quart saucepan, heat **1 tablespoon** of the olive oil. Add onion and **half** of the minced garlic; cook until tender. Add tomato sauce, ¹/₂ **teaspoon** of the salt, ¹/₂ **teaspoon** of the pepper, and ¹/₄ **teaspoon** of the oregano. Bring to boiling; reduce heat. Simmer for 30 minutes.

Meanwhile, in an 8-inch skillet, heat the 2 tablespoons cooking oil and remaining 1 tablespoon olive oil over medium heat; remove from heat. Stir in remaining garlic, then the bread crumbs, parsley flakes, remaining 1 teaspoon salt, ¹/₂ teaspoon pepper, and ¹/₄ teaspoon oregano. Transfer to a bowl; stir in ¹/₂ **cup** of the Parmesan cheese.

Preheat the oven to 350°. Heat 2 inches cooking oil in a wok or 12-inch skillet. Dip eggplant into beaten egg, then roll in bread crumb mixture. Cook in hot oil for 30 seconds per side or until golden; drain on paper towels. Place **half** of the eggplant in a 13x9x2-inch baking dish. Top with **half** of the mozzarella, ¹/₂ **cup** of the Parmesan cheese, and **half** of the sauce. Repeat layers. Bake for 30 minutes. Makes 8 to 10 servings.

Old-Fashioned Eggplant Soufflé

"This is the closest recipe I have found to the old-fashioned eggplant recipes I remember as a child. Sometimes people steer away from soufflés, but this is easy to make (there's nothing to chop!) and it turns out delicious every time."

1	medium eggplant
1/4	cup butter or margarine, melted
3	beaten eggs yolks
1	tablespoon Worcestershire sauce
1	cup finely crushed crackers (20 crackers)
1	cup shredded cheddar cheese (4 ounces)
1	cup milk
2	tablespoons snipped chives
1/2	teaspoon salt
1/2	teaspoon dry mustard
1/8	to 1/4 teaspoon ground red pepper
3	egg whites
1	clove garlic, halved

Preheat the oven to 300°. Wash eggplant; grease with shortening. Place in a shallow baking dish. Bake for 35 minutes or until tender. Peel eggplant. Place pulp in a large bowl. Mash with a potato masher or electric mixer. Stir in melted butter, the egg yolks, and Worcestershire sauce. Add cracker crumbs, cheese, milk, chives, salt, dry mustard, and red pepper; stir until well combined.

Increase the oven temperature to 350°. In a small bowl, beat egg whites with an electric mixer until stiff peaks form. Fold into eggplant mixture. Rub a greased 1 1/2-quart shallow casserole with the cut sides of the halved garlic clove. Transfer eggplant mixture to casserole. Bake about 40 minutes or until puffy and set. Makes 6 to 8 servings.

Okra and Tomatoes

2	tablespoons bacon drippings or cooking oil
1	pound fresh okra, cut into 1/4-inch slices
1	cup coarsely chopped onion
4	or 5 medium tomatoes, peeled and chopped, or 1 16-ounce can tomatoes, drained and chopped
1	clove garlic, minced
	Salt and pepper to taste
	Hot pepper sauce to taste

In a 12-inch skillet, heat bacon drippings or cooking oil. Add okra and onion; cook until lightly browned. Stir in tomatoes, garlic, salt, and pepper. Cover and cook over low heat for 20 minutes. Add water, if necessary, to prevent sticking. If too juicy, uncover and cook to desired consistency. Season with hot pepper sauce. Serve hot. Makes 4 to 6 servings.

♪ ♪ ♪

NICE TO NOTE

Okra, that small green pod with fuzzy skin and white seeds, is also known by the name "gumbo," which it gave to the famous thick soup of which it is a part. It has a mild taste, develops a slippery quality when cooked, and can be used as a thickener in soups and casseroles. Available year-round—fresh, frozen, or canned—it's a versatile vegetable that also makes a super solo side dish when pickled or sliced into rounds and fried.

Vidalia Onion Casserole

6   large Vidalia or mild sweet onions such as Walla Walla or Maui
$^1/_3$ cup butter or margarine
$^1/_2$ teaspoon salt
$^1/_2$ teaspoon sugar
$^1/_2$ teaspoon pepper
$^1/_2$ cup vermouth
1   teaspoon Worcestershire sauce
$^1/_2$ cup shredded Gruyère, Jarlsberg, or Swiss cheese
$^1/_4$ cup fine dry bread crumbs
1   teaspoon paprika
2   tablespoons butter or margarine, melted

Preheat the oven to 350°. Cut onions into $^3/_8$-inch slices. In a 12-inch skillet, cook onions in butter or margarine until tender. Sprinkle with salt, sugar, and pepper. Add vermouth and Worcestershire sauce; cook for 3 minutes.

Transfer onion mixture to a 13x9x2-inch baking dish. Sprinkle with shredded cheese. Combine bread crumbs, paprika, and melted butter; sprinkle over cheese. Bake for 20 minutes. Makes 6 servings.

Cry-A-River Onion Pie

$^1/_4$ cup plus 2 tablespoons butter or margarine, divided
1   cup finely crushed rich round crackers
2   medium sweet onions, thinly sliced and separated into rings
2   eggs
$^3/_4$ cup milk
$^3/_4$ teaspoon salt
$^1/_2$ teaspoon pepper
$^1/_2$ cup finely shredded sharp cheddar cheese (2 ounces)
  Paprika
  Snipped parsley

Preheat the oven to 350°. In a 1-quart saucepan, melt $^1/_4$ **cup** of the butter or margarine. Remove from heat and stir in crushed crackers. Press mixture evenly onto the bottom of an 8-inch pie plate.

In a 10-inch skillet, melt the remaining 2 tablespoons butter or margarine. Add onions and cook until tender but not brown. Spoon onions onto the crust.

In a medium bowl, beat together eggs, milk, salt, and pepper. Pour egg mixture over onions. Sprinkle with cheese and paprika. Bake about 30 minutes or until a knife inserted near the center comes out clean. Before serving, sprinkle with parsley. Makes 6 to 8 servings.

♪ ♪ ♪

NICE TO NOTE

—

Vidalia onions, the pride of Vidalia, Georgia, are quickly becoming one of the South's favorite summer treats. Sweet and mild, they can be eaten almost like an apple. Enjoy them roasted on the grill (brush them with melted butter, sprinkle with salt and pepper, and wrap them in foil) or use them in salads and cooked dishes. You'll love their unique flavor. But remember, you can only find them during the summer months.
Sigh.......

∾

Crab and Gouda Baked Potatoes

4	to 6 medium baking potatoes
1	cup cottage cheese
1	cup dairy sour cream
1/4	cup butter or margarine, melted
4	green onions, thinly sliced
	Salt and pepper to taste
8	ounces crabmeat, cartilage removed
1 1/2	cups shredded Gouda cheese (6 ounces)

Preheat the oven to 425°. Scrub potatoes thoroughly with a brush. Pat dry. Using the tines of a fork, prick potatoes. Wrap each potato in foil. Bake for 40 to 60 minutes or until tender.

Cut potatoes in half lengthwise. Using a spoon, gently scoop out pulp from each potato, leaving a thin shell. Set potato shells aside.

Transfer potato pulp to a large bowl. Using a potato masher, mash the potato pulp. Stir in cottage cheese, sour cream, melted butter or margarine, green onions, salt, and pepper until well combined. Stir in crabmeat.

Pile mashed potato mixture into potato shells. Place filled shells in a lightly greased 13x9x2-inch baking dish. Bake for 20 to 25 minutes or until lightly browned. Sprinkle with shredded cheese and bake for 2 to 3 minutes more or until cheese melts. Makes 8 to 12 servings.

Pyramid Potatoes

6	large all-purpose potatoes
2/3	cup milk
1/2	cup butter or margarine, softened
8	ounces cream cheese, softened
1	cup dairy sour cream
	Salt and pepper to taste
1	clove garlic, minced
1/4	cup thinly sliced green onion
1	cup shredded sharp cheddar cheese (4 ounces)

Peel and cube potatoes. In a 4-quart Dutch oven, cook potatoes in a small amount of boiling salted water, covered, for 20 to 25 minutes or until tender. Drain and cool. Place in a large bowl. Beat with an electric mixer on low speed. Add milk and butter; beat until fluffy.

Preheat the oven to 350°. Beat cream cheese, sour cream, salt, pepper, and garlic into potato mixture. Stir in onion. Transfer to a 2-quart round casserole. Top with cheese. Bake about 30 minutes or until bubbly. Makes 8 to 10 servings.

♦ ♦ ♦

MYSTERY ON THE MISSISSIPPI

—

Pyramids have always been surrounded by an aura of mystery. Memphis' own pyramid has posed more than a few unanswered questions since its opening in 1991 and an interesting discovery made in January 1992 in the riverside attraction inspired even more talk and intrigue. Construction workers found a crystal skull in the top of the pyramid, causing quite a buzz, and it was not until Hard Rock Café creator Isaac Tigrett admitted placing it there for fun that the mystery was solved. The truth is that the Pyramid is a stunning addition to the Memphis skyline, home of the Memphis State Tigers basketball team, scene of major Memphis musical events, and a reminder of the city's ties to Egyptian culture which began with the name we borrowed from Memphis on the Nile.

♦ ♦ ♦

226

Boursin Potato Gratin

This is so delicious that you'll be tempted to eat it cold out of the refrigerator the next day.

2 cups heavy cream
²/₃ cup Homemade Boursin Cheese With Black Pepper (see recipe below) or
　　 1 5-ounce package Boursin cheese with cracked black pepper
2 tablespoons minced shallots
1 clove garlic, minced
2¹/₂ pounds red new potatoes, scrubbed and sliced ¹/₄ inch thick
　　 Salt and freshly ground pepper
2 tablespoons snipped chives
2 tablespoons snipped parsley

Generously butter a 13x9x2-inch baking dish. In a heavy 1¹/₂-quart saucepan, heat cream, Boursin cheese, shallots, and garlic over medium heat, stirring until cheese melts.

Preheat the oven to 400°. Arrange **half** of the sliced potatoes in the baking dish in slightly overlapping rows. Generously season with salt and pepper. Pour **half** of the cheese mixture over potatoes. Sprinkle with the chives. Repeat layering with remaining potato slices, more salt and pepper, and cheese mixture.

Bake about 1 hour or until potatoes are tender and top is golden brown. Sprinkle with parsley. Makes 8 to 10 servings.

Homemade Boursin Cheese with Black Pepper

This can be made quickly with a mixer or food processor.

3 cloves garlic, minced
¹/₂ teaspoon salt
8 ounces cream cheese
¹/₄ cup butter
2 tablespoons finely snipped parsley
1 to 2 tablespoons coarsely ground black pepper

In a small bowl, make a paste with the garlic and the salt; set aside. In a food processor bowl or large mixer bowl, process or beat together cream cheese, butter, parsley, pepper, and garlic mixture until smooth. Cover and store for up to 2 weeks in the refrigerator. Serve at room temperature or transfer to a 2-cup oven-safe bowl or ramekin and bake in a 350° oven about 10 minutes or until warm. Serve with crackers, croustades, or as a filling for bite-size hors d'oeuvre puffs. Makes about 1¹/₃ cups.

♪♪♪

NICE TO NOTE

—

Boursin cheese is a creamy, spreadable cheese that is delectable as an appetizer spread for toasted baguettes or crisp crackers. It also melts beautifully, as you will discover during the preparation of the Boursin Potato Gratin. If you are lucky enough to find it in your local cheese shop, you may find a variety of boursin cheeses, such as herbed boursin or boursin with black pepper. But then, you don't have to shop for boursin at all if you make your own!

Sautéed New Potatoes with Garlic and Herbs

$^1/_3$ cup olive oil
$^1/_2$ cup chopped onion
4   small cloves garlic, minced
2   to 2$^1/_2$ pounds small new potatoes, scrubbed and sliced $^1/_4$ inch thick
1   tablespoon snipped fresh rosemary or 1 teaspoon dried rosemary, crushed
1   tablespoon snipped fresh marjoram or 1 teaspoon dried marjoram, crushed
1$^1/_2$ teaspoons snipped fresh thyme or $^1/_2$ teaspoon dried thyme, crushed
   Salt and freshly ground pepper

In a 12-inch skillet, heat olive oil. Add onion and garlic; cook for 5 minutes over medium heat. Add potatoes and toss to coat well. Cook, covered, over medium heat for 20 minutes, turning often. Add rosemary, marjoram, and thyme. Cook for 10 to 15 minutes more or until tender and brown, turning often. Season to taste with salt and pepper. Makes 6 servings.

Colcannon

A favorite vegetable dish in Ireland and Scotland, it has found a home in Memphis kitchens. It's an excellent winter partner for pork.

$^1/_2$ cup finely sliced green onion
3   tablespoons butter or margarine, divided
4   cups shredded cabbage (1 pound)
4   cups cooked mashed potatoes
   Salt and pepper to taste

In an 8-inch skillet, cook green onion in **1 tablespoon** of the butter or margarine until tender. Set aside. In a 2-quart saucepan, cook cabbage, uncovered, in a small amount of boiling salted water for 4 minutes. Cover and cook about 2 minutes more or until tender. Drain.

Preheat the oven to 350°. In a large mixing bowl, stir together mashed potatoes, cabbage, cooked green onion, salt, and pepper. Transfer to a buttered 2-quart casserole. Dot with the remaining 2 tablespoons butter or margarine. Bake for 20 to 25 minutes or until heated through. Makes 6 to 8 servings.

Black-Eyed Peas

Black-eyed peas, those harbingers of good luck, are a Southern staple on New Year's Day. As with most vegetables, fresh is best. Cook simply, season lightly, enjoy heartily. Keep hot pepper sauce on hand for those who like a little more bite.

1   pound fresh black-eyed peas
2   tablespoons cooking oil
   Salt to taste
$^1/_2$ cup chopped ham, bacon, or chopped onion (optional)
   Chopped onion

In a 3-quart saucepan, cover peas with water. Stir in oil and salt. Add ham, bacon, or chopped onion, if desired. Bring to boiling; reduce heat. Cover and simmer about 30 minutes or until tender. Pass chopped onion for topping. Makes 6 servings.

Note: For an eye-opening variation, add a sliced jalapeño pepper to the cooking water.

♦ ♦ ♦

**MORE THAN A
PENNY'S WORTH**

—

*"New Year's Day was always
Open House at my parents'.
There was food in the kitchen,
dining room, and living room;
every table had something on
it. Friends dropped by and
usually stayed most of the
afternoon, eating, drinking,
and watching one of the bowl
games playing on multiple
televisions scattered throughout
the house. It was a
comfortable, casual day, perfect
for starting the New Year,
surrounded by good friends.
Black-eyed peas were always
part of the buffet, and Mamma
put a bright copper penny in the
bottom of the bowl. Whoever
dished up the penny with their
peas was assured of
extraordinary good fortune in
the coming year. As a child, I
was thrilled that the penny
seemed to find me every year.
Of course, my mother always
had my plate ready for me and
it was not until I was grown
that I realized that love and
not just luck was responsible
for my extraordinary
good fortune."*

♦ ♦ ♦

Pommes Hasselback

    8   medium russet potatoes (about 3 pounds)
    6   tablespoons butter or margarine, melted
    1   teaspoon dried basil, crushed
 $1/4$ teaspoon salt
 $1/4$ teaspoon pepper
         Grated Parmesan cheese
         Snipped parsley

    Preheat the oven to 350°. Peel potatoes. Cut a thin lengthwise slice from the bottom of each potato so it will rest flat. With flat side down, make crosswise slits $1/4$ inch apart along the length of each potato, cutting to within $1/4$ inch of the bottom. Arrange potatoes in a greased 13x9x2-inch baking dish.
    In a small bowl, combine the melted butter, basil, salt, and pepper. Generously brush potatoes with butter mixture. Bake about 45 minutes or until barely tender, basting occasionally with butter mixture.
    Increase the oven temperature to 450°. Generously sprinkle potatoes with Parmesan cheese, making sure cheese fills slits. Bake about 15 minutes more or until potatoes are golden brown. Remove potatoes to a serving platter with a slotted spoon. Sprinkle with parsley. Makes 8 servings.

Thanksgiving Sweet Potatoes

To cut down on cooking time the day of the feast, bake them the day before for 1 hour. Cool, cover, and refrigerate for up to 24 hours. Bake 30 minutes before serving.

    4   beaten eggs
 $1^1/2$ cups milk
 $1^1/2$ cups sugar
    5   tablespoons butter or margarine, melted
    1   tablespoon vanilla
    1   teaspoon ground allspice
 $1/2$ teaspoon salt
 $1/2$ teaspoon ground cinnamon
 $1/4$ teaspoon ground cloves
    3   cups grated sweet potatoes

    Preheat the oven to 350°. In a large bowl, stir together eggs, milk, sugar, melted butter or margarine, vanilla, allspice, salt, cinnamon, and cloves. Add sweet potatoes and stir until well combined.
    Transfer potato mixture to a well-greased 2-quart casserole. Bake for $1^1/2$ hours. Makes 8 to 10 servings.

◆ ◆ ◆

TO GRANDMOTHER'S HOUSE
—

"When I was little, my family spent Thanksgiving at my grandmother's house in Helena, Arkansas, on the Mississippi River. I remember that it was always exciting to pay the toll to cross the bridge and know that we were almost there! I looked forward to great family times and a plate heaped with my grandmother's good cooking. These sweet potatoes were one of her specialities!"

◆ ◆ ◆

Sweet Potato Orange Cups

A tasty, pretty accompaniment for wild duck, quail, chicken, or turkey.

8	medium oranges
4	large sweet potatoes, peeled and cubed
1½	cups sugar
½	cup butter or margarine
1	teaspoon ground cinnamon
	Dash ground nutmeg
	Pinch salt
8	large marshmallows

Slice tops from the oranges. Grate ¼ **teaspoon** peel from orange tops; reserve peel. With a grapefruit spoon or knife, remove orange sections and save for another use. With a sharp knife, cut zigzag pattern around top of hollow orange cups. Set orange cups aside.

In a 3-quart saucepan, cook sweet potatoes in a small amount of boiling salted water, covered, for 10 to 12 minutes or until tender. Drain and cool. Place in a large bowl. Add sugar, butter or margarine, cinnamon, nutmeg, salt, and reserved orange peel. Beat until smooth and creamy.

Preheat the oven to 350°. Spoon sweet potato mixture into orange cups. Place in a greased 12x7½x2-inch baking dish. Bake for 20 to 30 minutes or until heated through. Top each orange with a marshmallow and bake 2 to 3 minutes more or until marshmallow is golden. Makes 8 servings.

Southern Sweet Potato Casserole

6	large sweet potatoes, peeled and cubed
½	cup milk
11	tablespoons butter or margarine, divided
1	cup sugar
2	eggs
1	tablespoon vanilla
1	teaspoon ground cinnamon
½	teaspoon salt
1	cup packed brown sugar
1	cup chopped pecans
1	cup flaked coconut
⅓	cup all-purpose flour

In a 4-quart Dutch oven, cook sweet potatoes in a small amount of boiling salted water, covered, for 20 to 25 minutes or until tender. Drain and cool. Place in a large bowl. Add milk and **3 tablespoons** of the butter. Beat with an electric mixer on low speed until fluffy. Add sugar, eggs, vanilla, cinnamon, and salt; beat until well mixed. Spread in a greased 3-quart casserole.

Preheat the oven to 350°. For topping, in a medium bowl stir together brown sugar, pecans, coconut, and flour. Melt remaining 8 tablespoons butter; stir into pecan mixture until well mixed. Sprinkle topping evenly over sweet potatoes. Bake for 30 minutes. Makes 10 to 12 servings.

♦ ♦ ♦

SHARING THE BOUNTY

—

"Our family reunion was in full swing. Shade trees gave us shelter from a mean August sun as dozens of cousins filed past heavily loaded tables and heaped Chinets to the breaking point. Children, too involved in having fun to be eager for food, ran circles around their parents, who were busy refilling trays and coolers. We feasted on black-eyed peas, turnip and collard greens, corn on the cob, string beans, macaroni and cheese, sliced tomatoes and Vidalia onions, spaghetti, ham, fried chicken, corn bread, and gallons of sweet tea. When we dispensed with these delights, we somehow managed to put away home-made ice cream and great slices of coconut cake, pound cake, and sweet potato pie. Afterward, there was nothing left to do but sit under the trees and tell stories that had been told before, with no more love or enjoyment."

♦ ♦ ♦

Currant Rice

Warm water
1 cup dried currants
1 14½-ounce can beef broth (about 2 cups)
1 10¾-ounce can condensed French onion soup
2 tablespoons butter or margarine
1 5-ounce package brown and wild rice mix
1 cup long grain rice
½ cup chopped green pepper
½ cup chopped sweet red pepper
½ cup sliced green onion
½ cup pine nuts, toasted

In a small bowl, pour enough warm water over currants to cover. Let stand while cooking rice.

Meanwhile, in a 3-quart saucepan, combine beef broth, French onion soup, and butter. Stir in brown and wild rice mix with seasoning packet and uncooked long grain rice. Bring to boiling; reduce heat. Cover and simmer about 20 minutes or until rice is tender and liquid is absorbed.

Drain currants; stir into rice mixture. Stir in green and red peppers, green onions, and toasted pine nuts. Makes 6 to 8 servings.

Wild Rice Pilaf

2 cups wild rice
4 cups water
2 teaspoons salt
1 cup butter or margarine
1½ cups finely chopped onion
1½ cups finely chopped green pepper
8 ounces sliced fresh mushrooms (3 cups) or 1 4-ounce can chopped mushrooms, drained
1 2-ounce jar chopped pimiento, drained
1 teaspoon dried thyme, crushed
½ cup golden raisins
Salt and pepper

Rinse the wild rice 2 or 3 times in cold water. In a 2-quart saucepan, combine the water and salt. Bring to boiling. Add rice. Return to boiling; reduce heat. Cover and simmer for 20 minutes. Drain well.

Preheat the oven to 325°. In a 12-inch skillet, melt the butter or margarine over medium-high heat. Add onion and green pepper; cook for 2 to 3 minutes or until almost tender. Stir in mushrooms, pimiento, and thyme; cook 3 to 4 minutes more or until vegetables are tender. Remove from heat. Add rice and raisins; toss until well combined. Season to taste with salt and pepper.

Transfer rice mixture to a 2-quart round casserole. Cover and bake for 1 hour. Makes 8 servings.

Stuttgart Rice

An easy drive across the bridge into Arkansas takes you to Stuttgart, home of the annual World Championship Duck-Calling Contest. Many Memphians are lured there by the abundant rice fields, lakes, and reservoirs, which make it a sportsman's dream.

4	cups water
1	teaspoon salt
2	cups brown rice
1/4	cup olive oil
1	cup chopped onion
1/2	cup chopped celery
4	to 6 cloves garlic, minced
1/2	cup shredded carrot
1/2	cup currants or raisins (optional)
2	teaspoons curry powder
	Salt and pepper

In a 2-quart saucepan, combine water and salt. Add rice. Return to boiling; reduce heat. Cover and simmer for 25 minutes. Remove from heat.

Meanwhile, in a 10-inch skillet, heat olive oil over medium-high heat. Add onion, celery, and garlic. Cook until vegetables are tender. Add onion mixture, shredded carrot, currants, if desired, and curry powder to rice. Cover and cook over low heat about 20 to 25 minutes more or until rice is tender. Makes 8 servings.

Spinach and Rice Ring

6	tablespoons butter or margarine, divided
1 1/2	cups long grain rice
1/4	cup finely chopped onion
3	cloves garlic, minced
3	cups chicken broth
1	pound fresh spinach
1	to 2 teaspoons pepper
1	teaspoon dried tarragon leaves, crushed
1/2	cup freshly grated Parmesan cheese
	Salt to taste

In a 12-inch skillet, melt **4 tablespoons** of the butter or margarine. Add uncooked rice, onion, and garlic. Cook over medium heat, stirring frequently, until rice is opaque. (Do not brown rice.) Stir in chicken broth. Bring to boiling; reduce heat. Cover and simmer for 18 to 20 minutes or until rice is **just** tender and all of the liquid is absorbed.

Meanwhile, wash and drain spinach; remove stems. Cook, covered, in a small amount of boiling salted water for 3 to 5 minutes or until tender. Drain spinach in a colander, pressing with a spoon to remove excess liquid. Chop spinach.

Preheat the oven to 300°. In a large bowl, stir together the remaining 2 tablespoons butter or margarine, rice, spinach, pepper, and tarragon. Stir in Parmesan cheese and salt. Press rice mixture into a well-greased 5-cup oven-safe ring mold.

Place ring mold in a 15x11 1/2x2-inch baking pan. Set pan on the oven rack. Pour **boiling** or **very hot tap water** into the pan around the mold to a depth of 1 1/2 inches. Loosely cover with foil. Bake for 10 minutes. Unmold and serve. Makes 8 servings.

◆ ◆ ◆

TABLE SUBTERFUGE

—

"When my two sisters and I were little, we always knew when Mother was serving an all-vegetable meal. She'd put out cloth napkins and candles and turn down the lights! She called it a 'Fancy Dinner' but we suspected that she dimmed the lighting so we couldn't see the dreaded vegetables. We used the cover of darkness to surreptitiously stuff the offending greens and yellows under the edges of our plates. Of course, we were always caught in the end. Oddly enough, today I am a fond devotee of vegetable plates in restaurants, even if they don't have candlelight!"

◆ ◆ ◆

Spinach Symphony

2   10-ounce packages frozen chopped spinach
2   tablespoons butter or margarine
8   ounces sliced fresh mushrooms (3 cups)
1   14-ounce can artichoke hearts, drained and chopped
1/2   cup mayonnaise
1/2   cup dairy sour cream
5   teaspoons fresh lemon juice
1/3   cup grated Parmesan cheese

Cook spinach according to package directions; drain well, squeezing out excess liquid. In a 10-inch skillet, melt the butter or margarine. Add mushrooms; cook and stir over medium heat until tender. Set aside.

Preheat the oven to 350°. In a 1 1/2-quart casserole, place artichoke hearts. Top with mushrooms. Place spinach on top. Combine mayonnaise, sour cream, and lemon juice; spread over spinach. Sprinkle with Parmesan cheese. Bake, uncovered, about 20 minutes or until bubbly and lightly browned. Makes 6 servings.

Spicy Spinach Pie

A wonderful luncheon dish with soup or salad.

1   cup sliced carrots
1   cup sliced leeks or green onions
2   10-ounce packages frozen chopped spinach
1 1/2   cups cream-style cottage cheese
1/2   cup grated Parmesan cheese
1   teaspoon celery salt
3/4   teaspoon ground cinnamon
3/4   teaspoon ground nutmeg
3/4   teaspoon pepper
12   sheets phyllo dough (8 to 10 ounces), thawed if frozen
1/4   cup butter or margarine, melted
1   cup sliced fresh mushrooms

Steam carrots and leeks for 8 to 10 minutes or until tender; set aside. Cook spinach according to package directions; drain, squeezing out excess liquid. In a medium bowl, combine spinach, cottage cheese, Parmesan cheese, celery salt, cinnamon, nutmeg, and pepper.

Preheat the oven to 375°. Generously butter a 9-inch pie plate with some of the melted butter. Place **six** of the phyllo sheets in the pie plate, overlapping edge of plate. Brush phyllo with more melted butter. Spoon in spinach mixture; top with carrots and leeks, then mushrooms. Top with remaining phyllo dough. Brush top with melted butter. Roll edges up to form a crust. Pinch to seal. Bake for 35 to 40 minutes or until golden. Makes 6 to 8 servings.

Squash, Sausage, and Soul

Sausage and spices give this squash "soul" and make it "in cognito" enough to tempt the youngsters.

$^1/_2$ to 1 pound bulk pork sausage
4 medium yellow summer squash, sliced $^1/_4$ inch thick
2 cups shredded sharp cheddar cheese (8 ounces)
1 cup dairy sour cream
3 tablespoons butter or margarine
1 teaspoon salt
1 teaspoon paprika
$^1/_2$ teaspoon pepper
4 egg yolks
1 teaspoon onion or garlic juice
   Fine dry bread crumbs

In a 10-inch skillet, cook sausage until no pink remains. Drain well on paper towel; set aside. In a 2-quart saucepan, cook squash in a small amount of boiling salted water, covered, about 3 minutes or until crisp-tender. Drain well and set aside.

Preheat the oven to 350°. In the same 2-quart saucepan, combine cheese, sour cream, butter or margarine, salt, paprika, and pepper. Cook over low heat until cheese melts. In a small bowl, beat egg yolks with a fork. Add onion or garlic juice; stir into cheese mixture. Stir in squash and sausage.

Transfer to a 2-quart casserole. Sprinkle with a thin layer of bread crumbs. Bake, uncovered, about 30 minutes or until bubbly. Makes 8 servings.

River Boat Squash

6 medium yellow summer squash
4 cups fresh spinach leaves or 1 10-ounce package frozen chopped spinach
3 ounces cream cheese, softened
2 beaten eggs
1 tablespoon butter, melted
1 teaspoon sugar
1 teaspoon cracked black pepper
$^1/_4$ teaspoon seasoned salt
$^1/_4$ teaspoon onion salt
   Salt
$^1/_2$ cup crushed rich round crackers (12 crackers)
4 slices bacon, cooked crisp and crumbled
2 tablespoons grated Parmesan cheese
   Paprika

Remove stems from squash. In a 4-quart Dutch oven or stockpot, cook whole squash in enough boiling water to cover about 15 minutes or until crisp-tender. Drain. Cut squash in half lengthwise. Scoop out pulp. Place pulp in a colander to drain.

If using fresh spinach, steam spinach for 3 to 5 minutes or until tender. (Or, prepare frozen spinach according to package directions.) Drain well, squeezing out excess liquid. Place spinach and squash pulp in a medium bowl. Stir in cream cheese, eggs, butter, sugar, pepper, seasoned salt, and onion salt until well combined.

Sprinkle squash boats with salt. Spoon in spinach mixture. Place in a well-greased 13x9x2-inch baking dish. Sprinkle with cracker crumbs, bacon, Parmesan cheese, and paprika. Bake, covered, in a 350° oven for 30 minutes. Makes 12 servings.

♦ ♦ ♦

VEGGIE ALLERGIES
—

"When I taught in a private girls' school long ago, I ate lunch at a table with my class every day. One year I had two little third-graders who absolutely despised vegetables. Whenever I encouraged them to taste any vegetable, their stock response was always 'Oh no! I am allergic to peas!' The next day these same two were allergic to corn, and so on. 'Allergic' became quite the code word at our family table. One Sunday I served this squash and my son announced, 'This is the only squash in the whole world that I'm not allergic to!' Needless to say, it's been on our menu list ever since."

♦ ♦ ♦

Zucchini and Yellow Squash

2 tablespoons butter or margarine
2 teaspoons instant chicken bouillon granules
2 cups sliced fresh mushrooms
4 medium yellow summer squash, sliced 1/4 inch thick
4 medium zucchini, sliced 1/4 inch thick
1/4 cup chopped onion
2 teaspoons fresh lemon juice
1/4 teaspoon seasoned salt
   Lemon-pepper seasoning to taste

In a 12-inch skillet, melt the butter or margarine. Stir in bouillon granules until dissolved. Add mushrooms, yellow squash, zucchini, and onion. Cook over medium heat for 10 minutes. Add lemon juice, seasoned salt, and lemon-pepper seasoning. Cook 5 minutes more or until tender. Makes 4 servings.

Skillet Green Tomatoes

If you can't get your hands on any green tomatoes, try swapping sliced okra for the tomatoes in this recipe.

3/4 cup white cornmeal
3/4 cup all-purpose flour
3/4 cup grated Parmesan cheese
3 or 4 firm unripe medium tomatoes, sliced 1/4 inch thick
3 tablespoons cooking oil
   Lemon-pepper seasoning
   Seasoned salt

In a medium bowl, combine cornmeal, flour, and Parmesan cheese. Dip tomato slices into cornmeal mixture, coating both sides. In a 12-inch skillet, heat oil over medium heat. Add tomatoes; cook about 4 minutes per side or until golden, sprinkling with lemon-pepper seasoning and seasoned salt before and after turning. Drain on paper towels. Serve immediately. Makes 4 servings.

Blue Baked Tomatoes

Easy, elegant, and delicious.

4 medium tomatoes
1 cup thick blue cheese salad dressing
1/4 cup sliced green onion
4 slices bacon, cooked crisp and crumbled
4 teaspoons snipped parsley

Plunge tomatoes into boiling water for 30 seconds. Dip immediately into cold water. Peel skin from tomatoes. Slice stem end from tomatoes. With a sharp knife, make 3 or 4 vertical cuts in top of tomato, cutting about halfway through tomato. Place, cut side up, in an 8-inch square baking dish. Pour 1/4 inch of water in bottom of dish.

Preheat the broiler. Combine blue cheese salad dressing and onion. Spoon a heaping tablespoon of mixture over each tomato. Broil about 4 minutes or until bubbly and lightly browned. Top with crumbled bacon and parsley. Makes 4 servings.

Tomato Pie with Basil

To make without the pie crust, simply grease the pie pan well and proceed.

1   9-inch frozen unbaked deep-dish pie crust
3   or 4 medium tomatoes, sliced, drained, and patted dry
    Salt and pepper to taste
8   slices bacon, cooked crisp and crumbled
3   tablespoons snipped fresh basil or 1 tablespoon dried basil, crushed
³/₄ cup grated Parmesan cheese
³/₄ cup mayonnaise
¹/₃ cup crushed rich round crackers

Preheat the oven to 350°. Thaw frozen pie crust for 10 minutes at room temperature. Arrange some of the tomato slices in pie crust to form a single layer. Lightly season tomatoes with salt and pepper. Sprinkle with some of the bacon and basil. Repeat layering, using remaining tomato slices, salt, pepper, bacon, and basil. Combine Parmesan cheese and mayonnaise; spread over tomatoes. Sprinkle with crushed crackers. Bake for 30 minutes or until crumbs begin to brown. Makes 6 to 8 servings.

Mary Joe's Turnip Greens

"Cook up," serve with fried chicken, pork chops, or country-fried steak, and enjoy a taste of the Deep South!

3   thick slices salt pork
6   cups water
3   pounds turnip greens

Rinse salt pork and place in a 3-quart saucepan. Add the water. Bring to boiling; reduce heat. Cook, uncovered, over medium heat for 45 to 60 minutes or until water is reduced to 1 cup.

Meanwhile, twist leaves from stems; discard stems. Wash greens thoroughly. Add greens to salt pork and water in saucepan. Bring to boiling; reduce heat to low. Cover and cook, stirring occasionally, about 1 hour or until tender. Makes 6 servings.

NICE TO NOTE

—

Talk about knowing their greens! Greens lovers in Memphis will tell you that if the greens are from Mississippi or Alabama where the soil is very sandy, you will need to wash them 7 or 8 times, changing the water each time. If they're from Cuba or Florida, you might get by with washing them only 5 times.

Eddie's Oyster Dressing

This makes a great appetizer, served with lots of French bread.

2	teaspoons cooking oil
1	cup chopped celery
$^1/_2$	cup chopped onion
$^1/_2$	cup chopped green pepper
4	cloves garlic, minced
1	tablespoon dried thyme, crushed
$1^1/_2$	teaspoons dried oregano, crushed
1	pound lean ground beef
$1^1/_2$	pounds shucked oysters, drained and chopped
1	teaspoon white pepper
1	teaspoon ground red pepper
$^1/_4$	teaspoon pepper
1	slightly beaten egg
$1^1/_2$	cups fine dry bread crumbs
2	tablespoons snipped parsley

In a 12-inch skillet, heat oil. Add celery, onion, green pepper, garlic, thyme, and oregano. Cook over low heat for 8 minutes, stirring occasionally.

Add ground beef to skillet. Cook and stir over medium-high heat until brown. Stir in chopped oysters. Cook over low heat for 3 minutes. Stir in white pepper, ground red pepper, and pepper.

Preheat the oven to 375°. In a large bowl, stir together beaten egg and bread crumbs until moistened. Stir in beef mixture and parsley. Transfer to a 2-quart casserole. Cover and bake for 20 to 25 minutes or until heated through. Serve warm. Makes 6 to 8 servings.

English Sage and Onion Dressing

$^1/_2$	of a 1-pound loaf white bread, cubed
2	cups chopped onion
$^1/_2$	cup water
1	to 2 tablespoons dried sage leaves, crushed
	Salt and pepper to taste

In a blender container or food processor bowl, blend or process bread cubes until fine. Transfer to a large bowl; set aside.

In a $1^1/_2$-quart saucepan, cook onion in water over medium heat until very tender. Drain onion, reserving liquid. Add cooked onion, sage, salt, and pepper to bread crumbs in bowl. Stir in enough of the reserved onion liquid (about $^1/_2$ cup) to bind mixture together. Mound mixture at one end of roasting pan alongside domestic duck, pork, or lamb. Bake at roasting temperature of meat for 20 to 30 minutes or until surface of dressing is crisp and golden, basting frequently with drippings. Or, bake in a $1^1/_2$-quart casserole in a 350° oven for 20 to 30 minutes. Makes 6 to 8 servings.

DESSERTS

Kallen Esperian

Soprano opera star Kallen Esperian is truly a "jewel in the crown" and Memphis is justly proud that she now calls it "home."

A stunning success since her 1986 debut in "La Boheme" with the Opera Company of Philadelphia, Kallen has gone on to appear on the world's finest opera stages. Whether in Paris, Genoa, Vienna, Chicago, or New York, she is acclaimed by audiences and critics alike.

Home in Memphis in March 1991 after a round of worldwide performances, Kallen Esperian appeared with the Memphis Symphony. She recalls, "I will never forget the support I felt from my many friends in the Symphony and, of course, from Maestro Alan Balter."

The best part of the evening for Kallen was yet to come. "The daughter of a security guard came up to me backstage after the performance, her first operatic concert. She looked at me with a sparkle in her young, sincere eyes and said, 'You sing so pretty!' This critique from a young child means more to me than any I have ever received. When my career life becomes difficult and I wonder 'Why am I doing this?', I have only to think of that little girl's heartfelt comment. It is something I'll remember forever."

KALLEN ESPERIAN

DESSERTS

◆ ◆ ◆

PICTURED OVERLEAF

—

*Clockwise from right:
Company Lemon Cheesecake
(page 246) and Pears
Marmalade (page 248)*

◆ ◆ ◆

241

*T*HE SWEET TASTE IS THE FIRST WE LEARN TO APPRECIATE AND
most of us never lose our enthusiasm for it! The Southern belief
and practice is that no meal, no matter how elaborate and satisfying, is
complete without dessert. Indeed, some families may expect a real meal
to end with two or more sweet offerings. Cakes, cookies, pies, ice
creams, and other frozen delights—these bring a gleam to the eye and are
worth abandoning all diets to enjoy. As Scarlett said, "Tomorrow is
another day!"

Desserts often stir up memories of childhood: a freshly-baked
apple pie at your grandmother's, a perfect pound cake heaped with
homemade ice cream, the chocolate confection you always tried to sneak
a sample of before supper was even on the table.

In Memphis and throughout the South, hostesses love to entertain
with teas and other gatherings where sweets are the primary fare. Many
families pass down well-guarded recipes for desserts that are coveted
and copied, but no self-respecting daughter or granddaughter would
dare to be careless with the family secrets! Any social gathering can
become a recipe swap and nothing causes more turned heads and
perked-up ears than a new dessert idea. Many a Southern family
tradition is built around that only-at-Christmas candy or special
homemade birthday cake. Start a family memory of your own with
some of *Heart & Soul's* sensational sweets. ♥

Quick Chocolate Pots de Crème

*One of the few desserts we know of that can literally be prepared in "just a few
minutes." If you have demitasse cups, they make pretty individual serving dishes.*

   1   6-ounce package (1 cup) semisweet chocolate pieces
   3   tablespoons very strong coffee
   2   tablespoons coffee liqueur or brandy
   2   eggs
  ²/₃ cup light cream, heated just to boiling
      Sweetened whipped cream
      Chocolate curls, chopped nuts, candied violets, or candied orange peel

In a blender container, combine chocolate pieces, coffee, coffee liqueur, eggs,
and heated cream. Cover and blend at high speed for 3 minutes. Pour into six 4-ounce
demitasse cups or 6-ounce custard cups. Chill at least 4 hours. Top with sweetened
whipped cream. Garnish with chocolate curls, nuts, candied violets, or candied orange
peel. Makes 6 servings.

Chocolate Almond Terrine with Raspberry Puree

3 egg yolks, slightly beaten
2 cups heavy cream, divided
16 squares (1 pound) semisweet chocolate
³/₄ cup light corn syrup, divided
¹/₂ cup butter or margarine
¹/₄ cup powdered sugar
1 teaspoon vanilla
¹/₄ teaspoon almond extract
1 10-ounce package frozen red raspberries, thawed
1 to 2 tablespoons raspberry liqueur or almond liqueur
Fresh red raspberries
Mint leaves

Line an 8x4x2-inch loaf pan with plastic wrap. In a small bowl, combine the egg yolks and ¹/₂ **cup** of the cream. In a 3-quart saucepan, combine chocolate, ¹/₂ **cup** of the corn syrup, and the butter. Cook and stir over medium heat until chocolate and butter are melted. Add egg yolk mixture. Cook for 3 minutes, stirring constantly. Cool to room temperature.

In a small bowl, beat remaining 1¹/₂ cups cream, powdered sugar, vanilla, and almond extract with an electric mixer until soft peaks form. Fold into chocolate mixture until no streaks remain. Pour into prepared loaf pan. Cover and chill overnight.

For puree, in a blender container or food processor bowl, puree raspberries; press through a sieve to remove seeds. Stir in remaining ¹/₄ cup corn syrup and the raspberry or almond liqueur. To serve, invert terrine and cut into ⁵/₈-inch slices. Pour some of the puree onto each dessert plate. Place slice of terrine over puree. Garnish with fresh raspberries and mint leaves. Makes 12 servings.

Fit and Fabulous Flan

¹/₂ cup sugar, divided
1 12-ounce can (1¹/₂ cups) evaporated skimmed milk
¹/₂ cup skim milk
³/₄ cup egg substitute or 6 egg whites
1 teaspoon vanilla
¹/₄ teaspoon almond extract
¹/₈ teaspoon salt
12 large fresh strawberries, halved
3 kiwi fruit, sliced
6 macaroons

In an 8-inch skillet, heat and stir ¹/₄ **cup** of the sugar over medium heat until sugar melts and becomes golden brown. Quickly pour melted sugar into six 6-ounce custard cups, tilting to coat bottom of cups. Cool.

In a 1¹/₂-quart saucepan, combine evaporated skimmed milk and skim milk. Heat until bubbles form around edge of pan.

Preheat the oven to 325°. In a small bowl, combine egg substitute, remaining ¹/₄ cup sugar, vanilla, almond extract, and salt; beat well with a wire whisk or fork. Gradually stir in ¹/₂ cup of the hot milk mixture. Stir this mixture into remaining hot milk mixture. Pour into sugar-coated custard cups.

Set cups in a 13x9x2-inch baking pan on oven rack. Pour very hot water around cups in pan to depth of 1 inch. Bake for 25 to 30 minutes or until a knife inserted halfway between center and edge comes out clean. Remove custard cups; cool. Chill for 4 to 24 hours.

Loosen custard from sides; invert onto dessert plates. Arrange strawberries, kiwi fruit slices, and macaroons around each flan. Makes 6 servings.

THE MEMPHIS HORNS

TRUMPETER WAYNE JACKSON AND SAXOPHONIST ANDREW LOVE HAVE BEEN IN BUSINESS TOGETHER AS THE MEMPHIS HORNS SINCE 1967. THEY HAVE PLAYED ON MORE THAN 300 GOLD ALBUMS FEATURING SUCH GREATS AS ELVIS PRESLEY, SAM AND DAVE, THE DOOBIE BROTHERS, AND ROD STEWART.

Chilled Orange Soufflé with Red Raspberry Sauce

It's gorgeous — a special occasion dessert.

1 envelope (1 tablespoon) unflavored gelatin
¼ cup cold water
3 egg yolks
¾ cup sugar
⅓ cup orange juice
1 to 2 tablespoons orange liqueur
2 teaspoons grated orange peel
2 cups heavy cream
3 egg whites
¼ teaspoon salt
   Red Raspberry Sauce (see recipe below)
   Mint leaves

In a 1-quart saucepan, sprinkle gelatin over cold water. Let stand for 1 minute. Cook and stir over low heat until gelatin is completely dissolved.

In a large bowl, beat egg yolks with an electric mixer until pale yellow. Gradually add sugar and beat until thick. Beat in orange juice, orange liqueur, orange peel, and a dash of salt. Add gelatin mixture. Allow mixture to cool until it starts to set but is not yet firm.

In a small bowl, beat cream with an electric mixer until stiff peaks form; fold into orange mixture. Wash bowl and beaters well. Beat egg whites and salt until stiff peaks form; fold into orange mixture. Pour into a 1½-quart soufflé dish. Chill for 6 to 8 hours or overnight.

To serve, spoon 3 or 4 tablespoons of the Red Raspberry Sauce onto each dessert plate. Spoon a portion of the soufflé into center of sauce. Garnish with mint leaves. Makes 6 to 8 servings.

Red Raspberry Sauce

2 cups fresh or frozen red raspberries
2 cups water
¼ cup sugar
2 tablespoons cornstarch
2 tablespoons cold water

In a 2-quart saucepan, combine raspberries and the 2 cups water. Bring to boiling; reduce heat and simmer for 30 minutes. Put raspberry mixture through a sieve, discarding seeds. Combine sugar and cornstarch. Stir in the 2 tablespoons cold water until smooth; add to berry mixture. Bring to boiling over medium heat, stirring constantly; reduce heat. Cook and stir for 1 to 2 minutes or until thickened. Remove from heat. Cool thoroughly. Makes about 3 cups.

ROCK
Servin' up

JOHN FRY

ARDENT RECORDING

IN 1966, JOHN FRY STARTED A RECORDING COMPANY IN HIS PARENTS' GARAGE. ONE OF THE OTHER FOUNDERS WAS FRED SMITH, NOW PRESIDENT AND CEO OF FEDERAL EXPRESS. ONE OF THE LARGEST AND MOST SUCCESSFUL STUDIOS IN THE REGION — SERVING UP A REAL MIXED BAG OF MUSIC FROM CHRISTIAN TO ROCK — ARDENT IS ALSO INVOLVED IN ARTIST DEVELOPMENT AND PRODUCTION, AS WELL AS VIDEO AND FILM PRODUCTION. SOME OF THE HEAVY-HITTERS WHO'VE RECORDED THERE INCLUDE STEVIE RAY VAUGHAN, THE ALLMAN BROTHERS BAND, LYNYRD SKYNYRD, AND THE FABULOUS THUNDERBIRDS.

Marilyn's Crème Brûlée

3 eggs
1 cup sugar
³/₄ cup heavy cream
2 teaspoons vanilla
½ cup caramel topping
8 tablespoons brown sugar

Preheat the oven to 350°. In a medium bowl, combine eggs and sugar; mix well. In a heavy 1-quart saucepan, heat cream until almost boiling. Stir in vanilla. Slowly pour cream mixture into egg mixture, stirring constantly.

Place **1 tablespoon** of the caramel topping in each of 8 ramekins or 6-ounce custard cups. Pour egg and cream mixture over caramel topping. Set ramekins or custard cups in a 13x9x2-inch baking pan on oven rack. Pour very hot water around ramekins in pan to depth of 1 inch. Bake for 1 hour or until a knife inserted halfway between center and edge comes out clean. Remove ramekins. Immediately chill in the refrigerator for at least 3 hours.

Preheat the broiler. Sprinkle **1 tablespoon** of the brown sugar over each ramekin. Broil 3 inches from heat for 15 seconds or until sugar begins to bubble. Chill until serving time. Makes 8 servings.

Amaretto Cheesecake

For a chocolate crust, substitute 2 cups very finely crushed chocolate sandwich cookies with white filling for the vanilla wafers and omit the ¼ cup sugar in the crust.

1 cup lightly salted butter or margarine
2 cups very finely crushed vanilla wafers
1³/₄ cups sugar, divided
2 pounds cream cheese, softened
3 ounces German sweet baking chocolate, melted
4 tablespoons Amaretto, divided
1 tablespoon light rum
  Dash salt
4 eggs, room temperature
¼ cup miniature semisweet chocolate pieces
2 cups dairy sour cream

For crust, in a 1-quart saucepan, melt butter or margarine. Remove from heat and stir in crushed vanilla wafers and ¼ **cup** of the sugar. Press mixture onto the bottom and about 2 inches up the sides of a 10-inch springform pan; set aside.

Preheat the oven to 350°. For filling, in a large bowl, beat cream cheese, 1¼ **cups** of the remaining sugar, melted chocolate, **2 tablespoons** of the Amaretto, light rum, and salt with an electric mixer until smooth. Add eggs. Beat on low speed just until combined. Stir in chocolate pieces. Pour filling into the crust-lined springform pan. Bake cheesecake on a shallow baking pan for 40 minutes. Remove from oven and let stand for 10 minutes.

Meanwhile, for topping, in a medium bowl stir together sour cream, the remaining ¼ cup sugar, and the remaining 2 tablespoons amaretto. Carefully spread topping over cheesecake. Return cheesecake to the oven and bake for 15 minutes. Cool in pan for 15 minutes. Loosen crust from sides of pan. Cool for 30 minutes more. Remove sides of pan and cool for 4 hours. Cover and chill until serving time. Makes 12 to 16 servings.

♪ ♪ ♪

NICE TO NOTE

*Cut back considerably
on the fat, cholesterol, and
guilt you get from eating
cheesecake by using
Neufchâtel cheese instead of
regular cream cheese. Also
known as "light cream
cheese," Neufchâtel has the
creaminess, consistency, and
flavor of cream cheese with
about one-third less fat,
cholesterol, and calories.
Neufchâtel won't turn
cheesecake into diet food, but
it will help cut overspending
on the calorie budget.*

∽

Company Lemon Cheesecake

*When grating the rind from a lemon or other citrus fruit, avoid grating the white layer
which can be bitter. The photograph for this three-layered cheesecake is on page 239.*

2	cups cinnamon graham cracker crumbs
1/2	cup finely chopped walnuts
6	tablespoons butter or margarine, melted
1	cup sugar, divided
24	ounces cream cheese, softened
3	eggs
2	teaspoons grated lemon peel
1/4	cup lemon juice
1	tablespoon vanilla, divided
2	cups dairy sour cream
	Lemon Glaze (see recipe below)
	White rose petals, orange peel curls, edible violet blossoms, mint leaves, and lemon leaves

Preheat the oven to 350°. Lightly butter a 9-inch springform pan. In a medium
bowl, stir together cracker crumbs, walnuts, melted butter, and **2 tablespoons** of the
sugar. Press mixture evenly onto bottom and sides of prepared pan. Bake for 5 minutes.
Cool.

In a large bowl, beat together cream cheese and ³/₄ **cup** of the sugar with an
electric mixer. Add eggs one at a time, beating well after each addition. Mix in lemon
peel, lemon juice, and **1 teaspoon** of the vanilla until well blended. Pour into cooled
crust. Bake at 350° for 35 minutes.

Meanwhile, for topping, in a small bowl stir together sour cream, remaining
2 tablespoons sugar, and remaining 2 teaspoons vanilla. Remove cheesecake from oven.
Gently spread topping over cheesecake. Bake 12 minutes more. Cool on rack for
30 minutes.

Spread Lemon Glaze on cheesecake. Chill several hours before removing sides of
pan. Garnish with white rose petals, orange peel, violets, mint leaves, and lemon leaves.
Makes 12 to 16 servings.

Lemon Glaze

1/2	cup sugar
4	teaspoons cornstarch
1/4	teaspoon salt
3/4	cup water
1	teaspoon grated lemon peel (set aside)
1/3	cup lemon juice
1	slightly beaten egg yolk
1	tablespoon butter or margarine

In a heavy 1-quart saucepan, combine sugar, cornstarch, and salt. In a small bowl,
combine water, lemon juice, and egg yolk. Add to sugar mixture. Cook over low heat,
stirring constantly, until mixture is thickened and bubbly. Sir in butter or margarine
and grated lemon peel. Cool slightly, but do not allow glaze to become set. Makes
about 1¹/₃ cups.

Irish Whiskey Cheesecake

This spirited dessert tastes best 1 or 2 days after preparation, giving the flavors time to blend and mellow. Serve it in fairly small portions—it's wonderfully rich!

1½	cups finely crushed vanilla wafers
¼	cup finely chopped walnuts or pecans
1¼	cups packed dark brown sugar, divided
½	teaspoon ground cinnamon
¼	cup butter or margarine, melted .
24	ounces cream cheese, softened
4	eggs, room temperature
2	tablespoons coffee liqueur
½	teaspoon vanilla
5¾	teaspoons instant espresso powder, divided
½	cup Irish whiskey
1½	cups plus 1 tablespoon heavy cream, divided
2	tablespoons sugar

Preheat the oven to 325°. Lightly butter a 9-inch springform pan. For crust, in a small bowl, combine finely crushed wafers, nuts, **1 tablespoon** of the brown sugar, and the cinnamon. Stir in butter. Press crumbs onto bottom and 1½ inches up sides of prepared pan. Bake about 8 minutes or until lightly browned. Cool thoroughly.

For filling, in a food processor bowl or in a large bowl using an electric mixer, combine cream cheese and remaining 1 cup plus 3 tablespoons brown sugar. Process or beat until smooth, stopping to scrape sides of bowl occasionally. Mix in **one** egg, the coffee liqueur, and vanilla.

In a small bowl, dissolve **5 teaspoons** of the instant espresso powder in the whiskey. Stir into cheese mixture. Whisk in remaining eggs, one at a time. Pour filling into cooled crust. Bake at 325° about 45 minutes or until outer 2 inches of cake are firm and slightly puffed. (Center will appear moist and edges may crack slightly.) Cool to room temperature on rack. Cover and chill at least 4 hours.

For topping, dissolve the remaining ¾ teaspoon espresso powder in **1 tablespoon** of the heavy cream. In a small bowl, beat the remaining 1½ cups heavy cream and the sugar with an electric mixer until soft peaks form. Fold in espresso-cream mixture.

To serve, spoon topping over chilled cheesecake. Makes 12 to 16 servings.

Country Fresh Apple Bake

³/₄	cup sugar, divided
1¹/₂	teaspoons ground cinnamon
1	package (8) refrigerated crescent rolls
1	large apple, cored, peeled, and cut into 8 slices
¹/₂	cup heavy cream
1	egg
1	tablespoon Amaretto or ¹/₂ teaspoon almond extract plus 2 teaspoons water
¹/₂	cup sliced almonds

Preheat the oven to 375°. In a small bowl, combine ¹/₄ **cup** of the sugar and the cinnamon. Separate dough into 8 triangles. Using only **half** of the sugar-cinnamon mixture, sprinkle the mixture evenly over each triangle, gently pressing with fingertips to slightly flatten triangles. Place an apple slice on the wide end of each triangle; tuck in edges around apple slice. Roll up, starting at wide end. Seal seams.

Arrange, seam side down, in an ungreased 9-inch round baking dish or pie plate, placing long side of 7 filled crescent rolls around outside edge of dish and 1 in center. Bake for 15 to 20 minutes or until golden brown.

For sauce, in a small bowl, use a wire whisk to beat together the remaining ¹/₂ cup sugar, cream, egg, and Amaretto. Spoon sauce evenly over rolls. Sprinkle with almonds and the remaining sugar-cinnamon mixture. Bake 13 to 18 minutes more or until deep golden brown. Cover baking dish with foil during the last 5 minutes of baking, if necessary, to prevent excessive browning. Serve warm. Makes 8 servings.

Pears Marmalade

This can be made in the morning and reheated when you're ready to serve dessert. Be careful not to overcook the pears. Photograph on page 238.

2	cups water
2	cups orange juice
2	tablespoons orange liqueur
6	medium pears
1	cup orange marmalade
2	tablespoons brown sugar
1	tablespoon butter or margarine
	Dash ground cloves
	Dash ground cinnamon
	Decorative orange wedges

In a 3-quart saucepan, combine water, orange juice, and orange liqueur. Bring to boiling. Meanwhile, carefully core whole pears, leaving stem attached. Lower pears into boiling liquid. Return to boiling; reduce heat. Cover and simmer about 15 minutes or until pears are just tender. With a slotted spoon, remove pears from saucepan. Reserve ¹/₄ **cup** of the cooking liquid.

For sauce, in a 1-quart saucepan, combine marmalade, brown sugar, butter, cloves, cinnamon, and reserved cooking liquid. Bring to boiling; gently boil for 1 to 2 minutes or until sauce is of desired consistency.

To serve, arrange pears on individual dessert plates. Garnish with decorative orange wedges. Serve with sauce. Makes 6 servings.

Sarah's Summer Torte

"We first served this gorgeous dessert at a luncheon following the christening of our daughter, Sarah. It has been a favorite for special occasions at our house ever since that lovely day." Photograph on the cover.

6	egg whites, room temperature
1/2	teaspoon cream of tartar
1 1/4	teaspoons vanilla, divided
1 3/4	cups sugar, divided
1/3	cup whole blanched almonds, divided
4	cups fresh strawberries, hulled, divided
1	cup powdered sugar
4	teaspoons milk, heated
2	teaspoons instant coffee crystals
1	cup heavy cream
1	medium peach or 2 medium apricots, cut into thin slices
1/4	cup fresh blueberries
1/4	cup fresh golden or red raspberries

Line 2 baking sheets with parchment paper. Trace a 10-inch circle onto each sheet. Preheat the oven to 300°. For meringue, in a large bowl, combine egg whites, cream of tartar, and 1/2 **teaspoon** of the vanilla. Beat with an electric mixer until stiff peaks form. Add 1 1/2 **cups** of the sugar, a tablespoon at a time, beating on high speed until very stiff peaks form and sugar is almost dissolved. Spread meringue onto circles on parchment paper, building sides up slightly. Bake for 1 hour. Carefully lift baked meringues onto wire racks. Remove paper and cool.

Increase oven temperature to 350°. Spread almonds on baking sheet. Toast in the oven for 7 to 8 minutes or until light brown. Cool. Grind in food processor bowl or blender container.

Slice strawberries into thirds. Place **2 cups** of the strawberries in a bowl. Sprinkle with **2 tablespoons** of the remaining sugar and toss lightly.

For icing, in a small bowl, combine powdered sugar, heated milk, coffee crystals, and 1/4 **teaspoon** of the remaining vanilla. Spread icing on **one** of the meringues, coating it completely. Top with the strawberry-sugar mixture, arranging strawberries to cover icing. Top strawberry layer with second meringue layer.

In a chilled small bowl, combine cream, remaining 2 tablespoons sugar, and remaining 1/2 teaspoon vanilla. Beat with chilled beaters on medium speed until stiff peaks form. Spread whipped cream on top of second meringue. Generously sprinkle toasted almonds over whipped cream. Arrange remaining strawberries, peach slices, blueberries, and raspberries on top of whipped cream. Chill torte until serving time. Makes 10 servings.

♦ ♦ ♦

ALTAR ANXIETY
—

A new baby's baptism, often called a christening, is a time of great joy and excitement, and in the South, it is generally celebrated with a brunch or luncheon following the church service. Family and friends gather to embrace the newest member of God's family and to offer their affection and support to the parents, grandparents, and godparents, who are always, literally, aglow. (Much pride is involved here, but it must be admitted that some of the glow results from anxiety over hoped-for socially-appropriate behavior of the baby and its young siblings in church, particularly while directly in front of the congregation!) Afterward, champagne may put a little more pink in the adults' cheeks, but it is most welcome. A handsomely-decorated cake is generally at the center of the celebration and gets much attention from the small set.

♦ ♦ ♦

Poached Peaches with Mixed Fruit and Sauce Sabayon

"Sabayon" is the French version for the Italian "Zabaglione"—the same heavenly sauce! Prepare the fruit in advance, if you like, but hold off on making the sauce until right before serving.

1	cup water
1	cup dry white wine
1	cup sugar
2	teaspoons shredded lemon peel
3	tablespoons fresh lemon juice
1	vanilla bean or $^1/_2$ teaspoon vanilla
4	large peaches, peeled, halved, and pitted
3	to 4 cups assorted fresh fruit: strawberries, raspberries, blueberries, or pitted dark sweet cherries
	Sauce Sabayon (see recipe below)
8	amaretto cookies, broken into crumbs (optional)

In a 3-quart saucepan, combine water, wine, sugar, lemon peel, lemon juice, and vanilla. Bring to boiling. Add peach halves. Simmer for 5 to 6 minutes or until just tender. Remove peaches and chill. Remove poaching liquid from heat; add mixed fresh fruit and let stand for 10 minutes. Remove fruit and chill.

Place peach halves, cut side up, on individual dessert plates. Fill centers with mixed fruit. Pour Sabayon Sauce over all. Sprinkle with cookie crumbs, if desired. Makes 8 servings.

Sauce Sabayon

6	egg yolks
1	cup sugar
1	teaspoon finely shredded lemon peel
$^1/_2$	teaspoon vanilla
$^1/_4$	cup dry white wine
$^1/_4$	cup light rum or sherry

In a small bowl, beat egg yolks, sugar, lemon peel, and vanilla with an electric mixer until well combined. Add wine and rum or sherry. Transfer to a double boiler. Cook over low heat, beating vigorously, about 8 minutes or until frothy, thick, and light in color. Remove from heat. Place double boiler over ice water. With a whisk, beat mixture until chilled. Serve immediately. Makes about 2 cups.

Maple Apple Pie

You can't get more American than this!

- ³/₄ cup finely crushed gingersnaps
- ¹/₂ cup sugar
- ¹/₂ cup chopped walnuts or pecans
- ¹/₂ cup butter or margarine, melted
- 1 tablespoon all-purpose flour
- ¹/₂ teaspoon ground cinnamon
- ¹/₈ teaspoon salt
- 6 to 8 cooking apples, cored, peeled, and thinly sliced
- 1 9-inch unbaked pie shell
- ¹/₃ cup maple syrup or maple-flavored syrup

Preheat the oven to 350°. Combine crushed gingersnaps, sugar, pecans, melted butter, flour, cinnamon, and salt; set aside. Spread **half** of the apples in the pie shell. Spread **half** of the gingersnap mixture over apple layer. Repeat layers. Bake for 50 minutes. Heat maple syrup to boiling and pour over pie. Bake 15 minutes more. Makes 8 servings.

Almond Peach Pie

- ¹/₃ cup finely crushed vanilla wafers (about 10 wafers)
- ¹/₄ cup chopped almonds
- 10 tablespoons butter or margarine, divided
- 1 cup sugar
- 2 tablespoons all-purpose flour
- 2 beaten eggs
- ¹/₄ teaspoon almond extract
- 6 to 8 medium peaches, pitted, peeled, and sliced
- 1 9-inch unbaked pie shell
   Vanilla ice cream or whipped cream

In a small bowl, combine crushed wafers, almonds, and **2 tablespoons** of the butter. Set aside.

Preheat the oven to 400°. In a 1-quart saucepan, combine sugar, flour, and eggs. Add the remaining ¹/₂ cup butter and cook over low heat for 3 to 5 minutes. Stir in almond extract.

Arrange peaches in pie shell. Pour egg mixture over peaches. Sprinkle with wafer mixture. Bake for 8 minutes. Reduce oven to 350°. Bake 45 minutes more. Serve warm with vanilla ice cream or whipped cream. Cover and chill to store. Makes 8 servings.

Key Lime Tart

Key lime juice is made from the juice of the small key lime, which is sweeter than the more common lime. Look for key lime juice or fresh key limes in your supermarket or specialty food shop.

$1/2$	cup finely crushed gingersnaps
$1/2$	cup finely crushed graham crackers
$1/2$	cup flaked coconut
$1/4$	cup finely chopped pecans
5	tablespoons butter or margarine, melted
4	egg yolks
1	14-ounce can sweetened condensed milk
$1^{1}/_2$	teaspoons finely shredded lime peel
$1/3$	cup key lime juice or lime juice
1	cup heavy cream
2	tablespoons sugar
$1/2$	teaspoon vanilla
	Lime slices (optional)

Preheat the oven to 350°. For crust, in a small bowl, combine crushed gingersnaps, crushed graham crackers, coconut, and pecans. Add melted butter; mix well. Press firmly and evenly over the bottom and $3/4$ inch up the sides of a 9-inch springform pan. Bake in a 350° oven for 5 minutes. Chill.

In a large bowl, beat egg yolks with a wire whisk until lemon colored. Add sweetened condensed milk, lime peel, and lime juice, mixing well. Spoon lime mixture into chilled crust. Chill about 4 hours or until firm.

For topping, in a chilled small bowl, combine heavy cream, sugar, and vanilla. Beat with an electric mixer on medium speed until soft peaks form. Spread whipped cream over tart. If desired, garnish with lime slices that have been slit halfway through and twisted. Cover and chill to store. Makes 8 servings.

Chewy Coconut Chess Pie

5	beaten eggs
$1^{1}/_2$	cups sugar
$1/2$	cup butter or margarine, melted
1	tablespoon vinegar
2	teaspoons vanilla
$1/2$	teaspoon salt
$1^{1}/_2$	cups flaked coconut
1	9-inch unbaked pie shell

Preheat the oven to 325°. In a medium bowl, beat together eggs, sugar, melted butter, vinegar, vanilla, and salt until well-blended. Stir in coconut. Pour into pie shell. Bake for 45 to 50 minutes or until a knife inserted near center comes out clean. Cool on a rack. If desired, serve with vanilla ice cream. Makes 8 servings.

◆ ◆ ◆

SWEET DREAMS

—

"There are dozens of dishes that come to my mind when I think of my mother's kitchen—fantastic caramels, divinity fudge, a luscious coconut cake with meringue and fresh coconut topping, the best, richest pecan pie in the world..."

A Feast Made for Laughter
Craig Claiborne

◆ ◆ ◆

Fabulous Pecan Pie

Interesting new ingredients give this old favorite a little "kick."

- 2   cups all-purpose flour
- 1   cup plus 2 teaspoons sugar, divided
- 1   teaspoon ground cinnamon
- 1/4 teaspoon ground allspice
- 3/4 cup shortening
- 6   tablespoons cold water
- 1 1/2 cups pecan halves
- 1   cup semisweet chocolate pieces (optional)
- 2   tablespoons butter or margarine, melted
- 3   beaten eggs
- 1   cup dark corn syrup
- 1   tablespoon vanilla
- 1   teaspoon grated lemon peel
- 1/8 teaspoon ground nutmeg

In a medium bowl, combine flour, **2 teaspoons** sugar, the cinnamon, and allspice. Cut in shortening until mixture resembles coarse crumbs. Gradually sprinkle in cold water while kneading by hand. Roll dough into a ball. Wrap in waxed paper and chill at least 1 hour.

Preheat the oven to 375°. Roll dough to 1/8-inch thickness. Ease pastry into a lightly greased 9-inch pie plate. Trim and flute edges. Spread pecans and, if desired, chocolate pieces over pastry. In a small mixing bowl, combine melted butter, remaining 1 cup sugar, the eggs, corn syrup, vanilla, lemon peel, and nutmeg. Pour into pastry-lined pie plate. Bake for 15 minutes. Reduce oven temperature to 350° and bake 30 minutes more or until a knife inserted near the center comes out clean. Cool. Cover and chill to store. Makes 8 servings.

Peanut Butter Fudge

- 2   cups sugar
- 2/3 cup milk
- 1/2 cup peanut butter
- 1   teaspoon light corn syrup
- 1   teaspoon butter or margarine

Butter an 8-inch square baking dish. Butter the sides of a heavy 2-quart saucepan. In the saucepan, stir together sugar, milk, peanut butter, and corn syrup. Cook and stir over medium-high heat to boiling. Carefully clip a candy thermometer to side of saucepan. Cook and stir over medium heat to 250° (hard-ball stage). Remove from heat; stir in butter.

Place saucepan in a container filled with 2 inches of cold water. Beat vigorously with a wooden spoon until mixture becomes very thick. Pour into prepared baking dish. Score into squares while warm. Cool about 30 minutes or until firm. Cut into squares. Makes 36 squares.

Ginger Pumpkin Pie

1	9-ounce package chocolate wafers, crushed (about 38 wafers)
1/2	cup melted butter or margarine, divided
2	16-ounce cans pumpkin
1 1/2	cups sugar
4	beaten eggs
1/4	cup molasses
2	tablespoons all-purpose flour
2	teaspoons ground ginger
2	teaspoons ground cinnamon
1	teaspoon salt
1	teaspoon freshly grated nutmeg
1/2	teaspoon freshly ground pepper
3	cups light cream
	Brandied Whipped Cream (see recipe below)
1/4	cup finely chopped crystallized ginger

Preheat the oven to 375°. For crust, combine crushed chocolate wafers and 1/4 **cup** of the melted butter. Press mixture onto bottom and sides of **two** 9-inch pie plates.

In a large bowl, combine remaining 1/4 cup melted butter, pumpkin, sugar, eggs, molasses, flour, ground ginger, cinnamon, salt, nutmeg, and pepper. Stir in light cream. Pour into prepared crusts. Bake for 1 hour and 10 minutes or until a knife inserted near the center comes out clean. Cool on wire racks. Spoon Brandied Whipped Cream onto pies. Top with crystallized ginger. Cover and chill to store. Makes 16 servings.

Brandied Whipped Cream

1 1/2	cups heavy cream
1/4	cup dairy sour cream
3	tablespoons sugar
3	tablespoons brandy
2	teaspoons vanilla

In a small bowl, combine heavy cream, sour cream, and sugar. Beat with an electric mixer until soft peaks form. Beat in brandy and vanilla. Cover and chill to store. Makes about 3 1/2 cups.

♪ ♪ ♪

NICE TO NOTE
—

Ginger has been called "the spice lover's spice" and presents itself in two different forms in this pie. The ground ginger found in the filling is actually the root of a lily-like plant that has been dried and bleached in the sun, and then ground. The crystallized ginger garnishing the top of the pie is made from the same root, but instead of being dried, it is boiled and preserved in a sugar solution. Although you will find both forms of ginger in the spice display at the supermarket, crystallized ginger is not really considered a spice, but a confection.

Bread Pudding with Winter or Summer Sauce

Take one bite of this New Orleans classic and you'll be transported!

- ¼ cup butter or margarine
- ½ of a 1-pound loaf unsliced French bread, torn into 1-inch pieces (about 6 cups)
- 4 cups milk
- 4 beaten eggs
- 2 cups sugar
- 2 tablespoons vanilla
  Winter or Summer Sauce (see recipes below)

Preheat the oven to 350°. Place butter or margarine in a 12x7½x2-inch baking dish. Place baking dish in the preheating oven just until butter melts.

Add bread to melted butter or margarine in the baking dish. Pour milk over bread. In a medium bowl, stir together beaten eggs, sugar, and vanilla. Pour egg mixture over bread-milk mixture in baking dish. Bake for 40 to 45 minutes or until a knife inserted near the center comes out clean. Serve warm with Winter Sauce or Summer Sauce. Makes 8 servings.

Winter Sauce

- ¾ cup sugar
- ½ cup butter or margarine
- ½ cup bourbon

In a 1-quart saucepan, combine sugar, butter or margarine, and bourbon. Cook and stir over medium heat until butter melts and sugar dissolves. Serve warm over bread pudding. Makes about 1½ cups.

Summer Sauce

- 3 cups sliced, peeled peaches
- 2 tablespoons sugar
- 1 teaspoon lemon juice
  Whipped cream (optional)

In a medium bowl, combine peaches, sugar, and lemon juice. Let stand for 2 hours before serving. Serve over warm bread pudding topped with whipped cream. Makes about 2½ cups.

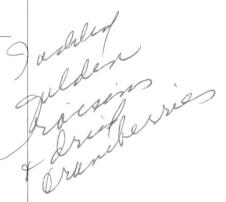

Old English Sherry Trifle

If you don't have a true trifle bowl, use any straight-sided round glass bowl—the layers look beautiful from the side.

1	10³/₄-ounce frozen loaf pound cake
1	12-ounce jar seedless red raspberry jam
¹/₂	cup dry sherry
6	tablespoons sugar
1	teaspoon cornstarch
2	cups milk
5	beaten egg yolks
2	teaspoons vanilla
3	cups fresh fruit such as cut-up, peeled peaches, kiwi fruit, or tangerines; raspberries; or sliced strawberries
1¹/₂	cups heavy cream
3	tablespoons powdered sugar
	Additional fresh fruit

Cut cake into 1-inch cubes. Split cubes in half. Spread jam on one side of **half** of the split cubes; reassemble each cube by replacing the top half of the cube.

Arrange **one-third** of the cubes on the bottom of a 2-quart, straight-sided, clear glass serving bowl. Sprinkle cake cubes with the sherry. Let stand at room temperature for 1 hour.

Meanwhile, for custard, in a heavy 1-quart saucepan stir together sugar and cornstarch. Stir in milk. Cook and stir over medium heat until thickened and bubbly. Cook and stir for 2 minutes more. Remove from heat. Gradually stir about **1 cup** of the hot mixture into the egg yolks. Return all of the egg yolk mixture to the mixture in the saucepan. Bring to a gentle boil; reduce heat. Cook and stir for 2 minutes more. Remove from heat and stir in vanilla. Cool.

To assemble, arrange **1 cup** of the fruit on top of the cake in serving bowl. Pour about **one-third** of the custard mixture over the fruit. Repeat layering cake, fruit, and custard 2 more times.

In a medium bowl, combine heavy cream and powdered sugar. Beat with an electric mixer on medium speed until soft peaks form. Spread over trifle. If desired, garnish with additional fresh fruit. Makes 8 to 10 servings.

Mrs. Thomas' Frosting

"My good friend, Mrs. Thomas, makes this unusual frosting for many cake flavors. It has fans in three states!"

1	cup milk, divided
¹/₄	cup all-purpose flour
¹/₂	cup butter or margarine
¹/₂	cup butter-flavored shortening
1	cup sugar
2	teaspoons vanilla

In a screw-top jar combine ¹/₂ **cup** of the milk and flour. Cover and shake until well combined. Add remaining ¹/₂ cup milk and shake again. Pour milk mixture into a 1-quart saucepan. Cook and stir over medium heat until thickened and bubbly. Cook and stir for 1 minute more. Refrigerate mixture until cool.

In a large bowl, beat butter or margarine and shortening with an electric mixer on medium speed about 30 seconds or until combined. Beat in sugar and vanilla. Then add the cooled, thickened milk mixture and beat for 4 to 5 minutes or until smooth and creamy. Makes about 2¹/₂ cups frosting, enough to frost tops and sides of two 8- or 9-inch cake layers.

Chocolate Pound Cake

Photograph on page 7.

3 cups all-purpose flour
1¹/₂ teaspoons baking powder
4 squares (4 ounces) unsweetened chocolate
²/₃ cup heavy cream
2 tablespoons instant coffee crystals
¹/₄ cup hot water
1¹/₂ cups butter, softened
2 cups sugar
5 eggs, room temperature
2 tablespoons brandy or cognac
1¹/₂ teaspoons vanilla
　Sifted powdered sugar
　Lemon leaves, candied lemon slices, and edible yellow flower petals

　Grease and flour a 10-inch fluted tube pan. In a medium bowl, combine flour and baking powder; set aside. Place chocolate squares in the top of a double boiler over gently boiling water. Cook, stirring constantly, until chocolate melts. Gradually stir in cream. Cool. Dissolve coffee crystals in hot water; stir into chocolate mixture.
　Preheat the oven to 300°. In a large bowl, beat butter and sugar with an electric mixer until well combined. Add eggs, one at a time, beating thoroughly after each addition. Batter should be satiny smooth and fall in ribbons from a spoon. Add flour mixture alternately with cooled chocolate mixture and cream until well combined. Beat in brandy and vanilla.
　Pour batter into prepared tube pan. Bake for 1¹/₄ to 1¹/₂ hours or until a toothpick inserted near center comes out clean. If necessary, cover with foil during the last 15 minutes to prevent overbrowning. Cool in pan for 20 minutes. Remove from pan; cool thoroughly. Sprinkle with powdered sugar. Garnish with lemon leaves, candied lemon slices, and edible yellow flowers. Makes 16 servings.

♪ ♪ ♪
NICE TO NOTE
—

Pound cakes were originally named for the pound each of butter, sugar, eggs, and flour that went into them. They are known for their rich taste, moist texture, and dense crumb. The secret to making a moist pound cake that is not too heavy is letting the eggs come to room temperature before adding them to the batter. This results in a greater volume of batter and thus, a higher, lighter cake.

∞

Georgia Peach Pound Cake

3 cups all-purpose flour
¹/₂ teaspoon salt
¹/₄ teaspoon baking soda
1¹/₄ cups butter or margarine, softened
2¹/₂ cups sugar
6 eggs, room temperature
1 teaspoon vanilla
¹/₂ teaspoon almond extract
¹/₂ cup plain yogurt
2 cups peeled and chopped ripe peaches
　Sweetened whipped cream
　Freshly grated nutmeg

　Preheat the oven to 350°. Grease and flour a 10-inch tube pan. Stir together flour, salt, and baking soda; set aside. In a large bowl, beat together butter and sugar with an electric mixter until well combined. Add eggs, one at a time, beating 1 minute after each addition. Stir in vanilla and almond extract. Add flour mixture alternately with yogurt, beating until well combined. Fold in peaches.
　Pour batter into prepared tube pan. Bake for 1 to 1¹/₄ hours. Cool in pan for 20 minutes. Remove from pan; cool thoroughly. To serve, dollop with sweetened whipped cream and sprinkle with nutmeg. Makes 16 servings.

Cream Cheese Pound Cake with Fresh Strawberry Sauce

1½   cups butter or margarine, softened
8   ounces cream cheese, softened
3   cups sugar
2   teaspoons grated lemon peel
6   eggs, room temperature
1   teaspoon vanilla
3   cups all-purpose flour
      Fresh Strawberry Sauce (see recipe below)

Preheat the oven to 325°. Grease and flour a 10-inch fluted tube pan. In a large bowl, beat together butter and cream cheese. Add sugar and lemon peel; beat with an electric mixer until well combined. Add eggs, one at a time, beating 1 minute after each addition. Beat in vanilla. Gradually add flour, beating until combined.

Pour batter into prepared pan. Bake about 1¼ hours or until a toothpick inserted near center comes out clean. Cool in pan for 20 minutes. Remove from pan; cool thoroughly. Serve with Fresh Strawberry Sauce. Makes 16 servings.

Fresh Strawberry Sauce

6   tablespoons water
¼   cup sugar
2   tablespoons cornstarch
1   teaspoon finely shredded lemon peel
2   tablespoons lemon juice
2   cups sliced fresh strawberries

In a 2-quart saucepan, combine water, sugar, cornstarch, lemon peel, and lemon juice. Stir in strawberries. Cook and stir until bubbly. Cook and stir 2 minutes more. Cool. Makes about 2½ cups.

Lemon Nut Cake

3   cups all-purpose flour
1   tablespoon baking powder
2½   cups chopped nuts
2   cups golden raisins
2   cups butter or margarine
2   cups sugar
2   tablespoons fresh lemon juice
1   to 2 tablespoons lemon extract
6   eggs

Preheat the oven to 350°. Grease and flour a 10-inch fluted tube pan. In a large bowl, stir together flour and baking powder. Add nuts and raisins; toss until well coated. Set aside.

In another large bowl, beat butter with an electric mixer until softened. Add sugar and lemon extract and juice; beat until well combined. Add eggs, one at a time, beating one minute after each. Gradually beat in flour mixture. Transfer batter to prepared pan. Bake for 1 hour or until a toothpick inserted near the center comes out clean. Cool in pan 10 minutes. Remove; cool thoroughly. Makes 12 servings.

Coconut Carrot Cake

Keep any unused coconut in an airtight container in the freezer.

- 2 cups all-purpose flour
- 2 teaspoons ground cinnamon
- 1¹/₂ teaspoons baking soda
- 1 teaspoon salt
- 2 cups sugar
- 1¹/₂ cups cooking oil
- 4 eggs
- 2 cups grated carrots
- 1 cup flaked coconut
- 8 ounces cream cheese, softened
- 4¹/₂ cups sifted powdered sugar

Preheat the oven to 350°. Grease and flour three 9-inch round baking pans. In a small bowl, stir together flour, cinnamon, baking soda, and salt. In a large bowl, stir together sugar and oil. Beat in eggs, one at a time, mixing well after each addition. Stir in flour mixture until combined. Fold in carrots and coconut.

Pour batter into prepared pans. Bake about 30 minutes or until a toothpick inserted near center comes out clean. Cool in pans 10 minutes on racks. Remove cakes; cool thoroughly.

For frosting, beat together cream cheese and powdered sugar until smooth. Assemble cake layers, spreading frosting between layers, on sides, and on top. Makes 12 servings.

♪ ♪ ♪

NICE TO NOTE
—

Many Memphis brides choose a carrot or spice recipe for their wedding cake. A beautiful buttercream lattice or spun sugar frosting and fresh flowers on top make this the crowning glory of any bride's table and guests are pleasantly surprised to find this deliciously different cake within.

∞

Quadruple Chocolate Cupcakes   *yes!*

Choose these for a picnic sweet or serve them at home with the best vanilla ice cream on the side.

- 1 cup all-purpose flour
- 3 tablespoons unsweetened cocoa powder
  Pinch salt
- 1 cup butter or margarine
- 2 squares (2 ounces) unsweetened chocolate
- 2 squares (2 ounces) semisweet chocolate
- 1¹/₂ cups sugar
- 4 beaten eggs
- 1 teaspoon vanilla
- ¹/₄ teaspoon almond extract
- 1 12-ounce package (2 cups) semisweet chocolate pieces

Preheat the oven to 350°. Line muffin pans with foil-lined paper bake cups. In a large bowl, stir together flour, cocoa powder, and salt. In a 2-quart saucepan, melt butter, unsweetened chocolate, and semisweet chocolate. Stir sugar, eggs, vanilla, and almond extract into chocolate mixture. Add chocolate mixture to flour mixture, mixing until combined. Stir in chocolate pieces.

Fill muffin cups half full. Bake for 12 to 14 minutes or until done. Makes about 20 cupcakes.

Spice Cake with Caramel Icing

2$^{1}/_{4}$ cups sifted cake flour
1$^{2}/_{3}$ cups sugar
2 teaspoons ground cinnamon
1 teaspoon baking powder
1 teaspoon ground nutmeg
$^{3}/_{4}$ teaspoon baking soda
$^{3}/_{4}$ teaspoon ground cloves
$^{1}/_{4}$ teaspoon salt
Pinch pepper
1 cup butter or margarine, melted
1 cup buttermilk
3 eggs
1 teaspoon vanilla
1 cup chopped walnuts
Caramel Icing (see recipe below)

Preheat the oven to 350°. Grease and flour two 9-inch round baking pans. In a large bowl, stir together cake flour, sugar, cinnamon, baking powder, nutmeg, baking soda, cloves, salt, and pepper. Add melted butter, buttermilk, eggs, and vanilla; beat with a wooden spoon until thoroughly blended. Stir in walnuts.

Pour batter into prepared pans. Bake for 25 to 30 minutes or until a toothpick inserted near center comes out clean. Cool in pans on racks for 10 minutes. Remove cakes; cool thoroughly. Frost with Caramel Icing. Makes 12 servings.

Caramel Icing

1$^{1}/_{3}$ cups packed brown sugar
$^{1}/_{2}$ cup milk
$^{1}/_{4}$ teaspoon salt
3 tablespoons butter or margarine
1 teaspoon vanilla
3 cups sifted powdered sugar

In a 2-quart saucepan, combine brown sugar, milk, and salt. Bring to boiling; reduce heat. Cook about 5 minutes or until slightly thickened. Remove from heat; add butter or margarine and vanilla. Cool slightly. Add powdered sugar and beat until smooth. Frosts tops and sides of two 8- or 9-inch cake layers.

Chocolate Raspberry Cake

2	cups sifted cake flour
2	teaspoons baking soda
1/2	teaspoon salt
1/2	cup butter or margarine
3	squares (3 ounces total) unsweetened chocolate, melted and cooled
2	cups packed brown sugar
1 1/2	teaspoons vanilla
3	eggs
3/4	cup dairy sour cream
1	cup strong coffee
1/4	cup coffee liqueur
1/2	cup red raspberry preserves
	Chocolate Butter Frosting (see recipe below)

Preheat the oven to 350°. Grease and lightly flour two 9-inch round baking pans. In a small bowl, stir together cake flour, baking soda, and salt. Set flour mixture aside.

In a large bowl, beat together butter or margarine and melted chocolate with an electric mixer on medium speed about 30 seconds or until combined. Add brown sugar and vanilla and beat until fluffy. Add eggs, one at a time, beating until combined. Beat in sour cream. Alternately add flour mixture with strong coffee and coffee liqueur, beating on low to medium speed after each addition just until combined.

Pour batter into prepared pans. Bake about 35 minutes or until a toothpick inserted near the center comes out clean. Cool cakes in pans on wire racks for 10 minutes. Remove from pans; cool thoroughly.

To assemble, spread raspberry preserves between cake layers. Spread sides and top with Chocolate Butter Frosting. Makes 12 servings.

Chocolate Butter Frosting

1/2	cup butter or margarine
4	squares (4 ounces total) unsweetened chocolate, melted and cooled
4 1/2	cups sifted powdered sugar
1/3	cup evaporated milk
2	teaspoons vanilla

In a large bowl, beat together butter or margarine and melted chocolate with an electric mixer on medium speed until smooth. Gradually add **2 cups** of the sifted powdered sugar, beating on low to medium speed. Slowly beat in evaporated milk and vanilla. Gradually beat in the remaining 2 1/2 cups sifted powdered sugar. If necessary, beat in additional evaporated milk to make frosting of spreading consistency. Makes about 2 1/2 cups.

Caramel-Frosted Butter Cake

This cake improves with age. The caramel frosting flavors the cake the longer it is on. It can be made a week ahead and stored, well-covered, in the refrigerator.

   3   cups sugar, divided
   1   cup heavy cream
       Dash salt
 1/3   cup butter or margarine
   1   package 2-layer-size regular butter cake mix
   1   cup dairy sour cream
 3/4   cup cooking oil
   4   eggs

For caramel frosting, in a double boiler, place **2 cups** of the sugar, heavy cream, and salt. Place over gently boiling water (upper pan should not touch water). Bring mixture to boiling. Do not stir.

Meanwhile, in a heavy 8-inch skillet, cook 1/2 **cup** of the remaining sugar over medium-high heat until sugar begins to melt, shaking the skillet occasionally to heat sugar evenly. Do not stir. Reduce heat to low and cook about 5 minutes more or until the sugar is melted and golden brown, stirring frequently.

Pour the melted sugar over the boiling cream mixture in the double boiler. Clip a candy thermometer to the side of the double boiler. Cook to 236° (soft-ball stage). Remove upper pan from water. Stir in butter or margarine. Let stand for 5 to 10 minutes or until slightly cool. Replace upper pan over gently boiling water and cook again to 236° (soft-ball stage). Remove upper pan and let stand to cool while baking cake.

Preheat the oven to 350°. Grease and flour a 10-inch fluted tube pan. For cake, in a large bowl, combine cake mix, sour cream, oil, and the remaining 1/2 cup sugar. Beat on low speed until moistened. Add eggs, one at a time, beating on medium speed until combined. Beat for 2 minutes more. Pour batter into prepared tube pan. Bake about 45 minutes or until a toothpick inserted near the center of the cake comes out clean. Cool on a wire rack for 10 minutes. Remove from pan; cool thoroughly.

While cake is still warm, frost cake with the caramel frosting. (If frosting slides off the warm cake, spread it back onto the cake. The frosting will eventually begin to harden.) Makes 12 servings.

Mint Ice Cream

Even Memphians with "brown thumbs" keep a patch of fragrant mint growing at the back door for fruit salad garnish, iced tea, mint juleps, and this luscious ice cream.

   2   cups firmly packed fresh mint leaves
 1 1/2 cups sugar
 1 1/2 cups water
   1   cup fresh pineapple chunks
   1   cup light corn syrup
   1   cup unsweetened pineapple juice
   2   cups milk
   2   cups heavy cream
 1/2   cup crème de menthe
       Fresh mint leaves

In a blender container or food processor bowl, combine mint leaves, sugar, water, pineapple chunks, corn syrup, and pineapple juice. Cover and blend or process until smooth. Pour into freezing can of an ice cream freezer. Stir in milk, cream, and crème de menthe. Freeze according to manufacturer's directions. To serve, scoop into bowls. Garnish with fresh mint leaves. Makes 3 1/2 quarts.

R&B
Servin' up

WILSON PICKETT

WILSON PICKETT WAS BORN IN ALABAMA AND GREW UP IN DETROIT, BUT MEMPHIS CLAIMS HIM AS A FAMOUS SON BECAUSE OF HIS HITS RECORDED AT STAX WHILE HE WAS SIGNED TO ATLANTIC RECORDS. THIS WRITER/SINGER WORKED WITH STEVE CROPPER TO PRODUCE THE MEGA-HIT "IN THE MIDNIGHT HOUR," GUARANTEED TO GET ANY PARTY MOVING! OTHER WELL-KNOWN PICKETT TITLES ARE "MUSTANG SALLY," "FUNKY BROADWAY," AND "6-3-4-5-7-8-9."

Lemon Cream Sherbet

More like ice cream than sherbet, this light and creamy dessert is a perfect conclusion to an outdoor barbecue.

2   cups milk
1   cup plus 2 tablespoons sugar, divided
2   teaspoons grated lemon peel
6   tablespoons fresh lemon juice
2   egg whites
2   cups heavy cream

In a large bowl, stir together milk and **1 cup** of the sugar until sugar dissolves. Stir in lemon peel and lemon juice.

In a small bowl, beat egg whites and remaining 2 tablespoons sugar with electric mixer until stiff peaks form. In another bowl, beat heavy cream with electric mixer until slightly thickened. Add beaten egg whites to beaten cream. Fold cream mixture into lemon mixture. Pour into freezing can of an ice cream freezer. Freeze according to manufacturer's directions. Makes 2 quarts.

Pat's Fresh Peach Ice Cream

The best peach ice cream is made with fresh peaches at the peak of ripeness. Be sure they are soft to the touch.

12 to 15 ripe medium peaches (3 pounds)
1   cup sugar
3   tablespoons fresh lemon juice
1   tablespoon peach liqueur (optional)
1   teaspoon almond extract
2   cups light cream
1   package 6-serving-size instant vanilla pudding mix
    Milk

Pit, peel, and cut up peaches. Place in a large bowl and mash. Add sugar, lemon juice, peach liqueur, if desired, and almond extract. (If peaches are tart, add more sugar.) Stir in light cream and pudding mix. Pour mixture into freezing can of ice cream freezer and add milk to reach fill line. Stir well. Freeze according to manufacturer's directions. Makes 3 quarts.

Homemade Peppermint Ice Cream

This is even better topped with good chocolate sauce.

- 4   7½-ounce bags striped round peppermint candies
- 2   cups light cream, divided
- 2   cups heavy cream

In a blender container or food processor bowl, place unwrapped candies and **1 cup** of the light cream. Cover and blend or process until candies are crushed.

Pour peppermint mixture into freezing can of an ice cream freezer. Stir in the remaining 1 cup light cream and heavy cream. Freeze according to manufacturer's directions. Makes about 1½ quarts.

Germantown Chocolate Pie

- 1   4-ounce package German sweet chocolate, coarsely chopped
- ⅓   cup milk, divided
- 1½   teaspoons instant coffee crystals
- 3   ounces cream cheese, softened
- 3   tablespoons sugar
- ½   teaspoon vanilla
- 1   cup heavy cream, whipped, or 2 cups whipped dessert topping
- 1   9-inch baked pie shell or graham cracker pie shell
         Chocolate curls

In a 1-quart saucepan, combine chocolate, **2 tablespoons** of the milk, and the instant coffee crystals. Cook and stir over low heat until chocolate melts. Cool to room temperature.

In a small bowl, beat together cream cheese, sugar, vanilla, remaining milk, and cooled chocolate mixture with an electric mixer until smooth. Fold in whipped cream. Spoon into pie shell. Freeze about 4 hours or until firm. Let stand at room temperature for 5 minutes. Garnish with chocolate curls before serving. Makes 8 servings.

Minetry's Magic

After Sunday lunch, send everyone outside to the porch for more conversation — and belt-loosening! Then, serve this scrumptious treat.

- ½   gallon vanilla ice cream
- 24   almond macaroons
- ¼   cup bourbon
- 6   to 8 chocolate covered toffee bars, coarsely chopped

Soften vanilla ice cream. Dip macaroons, one at a time, into bourbon just until moistened. Place **half** of the dipped macaroons in the bottom of a 3-quart bowl. Layer with **half** of the softened ice cream and **half** of the chopped toffee bars. Repeat layers. Cover and freeze until firm. Makes 12 servings.

Frozen Chocolate Hazelnut Mousse

^{1}/$_3$ cup sugar
^{1}/$_3$ cup water
1 cup semisweet chocolate pieces
2 tablespoons hazelnut liqueur
3 egg yolks
1^1/$_2$ cups heavy cream
^{2}/$_3$ cup chopped toasted hazelnuts (filberts)

In a 1-quart saucepan, stir together sugar and water. Bring to boiling; reduce heat to medium and gently boil for 1 minute. Remove from heat.

In a blender container or food processor bowl, place chocolate pieces. With blender or food processor running on medium speed, add hot sugar syrup in a steady stream. Continue blending or processing until smooth. Add liqueur and egg yolks, one at a time, blending or processing until well combined. Set mixture aside.

In a large bowl, beat cream until soft peaks form. Fold in the chocolate mixture. Fold in hazelnuts. Pour mixture into 6 freezer-safe serving dishes or a 6-cup bombe pan. Freeze until firm. Before serving, let stand at room temperature for 5 minutes. If using bombe pan, invert mousse onto a serving plate. Remove pan. Makes 6 servings.

Mississippi Mocha Mud

2 cups finely chopped pecans
^{2}/$_3$ cup packed brown sugar
^{1}/$_2$ teaspoon ground cinnamon
^{1}/$_2$ teaspoon instant coffee crystals
^{1}/$_4$ cup butter or margarine, melted
4 squares (4 ounces) unsweetened chocolate
^{2}/$_3$ cup strong coffee
1 cup sugar
1 quart coffee ice cream

Preheat the oven to 350°. For crust, in a small bowl, combine pecans, brown sugar, cinnamon, and coffee crystals. Add melted butter; mix well. Press mixture into the bottom of a 10x6x2-inch or an 8-inch square baking dish. Bake 12 to 15 minutes or until lightly browned. Cool.

For chocolate sauce, in a 1-quart saucepan, combine chocolate and strong coffee. Cook over low heat, stirring constantly, until chocolate melts and mixture is smooth. Stir in sugar and cook, stirring constantly, until sugar dissolves. Cool and chill.

Let ice cream stand at room temperature to soften slightly. Spread softened ice cream into cooled crust, smoothing top. Cover and freeze until ice cream is firm. Top with chocolate sauce and freeze at least 8 hours. Makes 8 servings.

BLUES *Servin' up*

HOWLIN' WOLF

BORN CHESTER ARTHUR BURNETT IN RURAL MISSISSIPPI, HOWLIN' WOLF WAS A HUGE MAN, BOTH PHYSICALLY AND AS A BLUES SINGER AND HARMONICA PLAYER. DISCOVERED BY IKE TURNER, WHO WAS THEN A TALENT SCOUT, WOLF RECORDED FIRST FOR SAM PHILLIPS, THEN WENT ON TO HISTORICALLY ALTER THE CHICAGO BLUES SCENE.

Mocha Macadamia Chocolate Chunk Cookies

Rich, delicious, and addictive!

¹/₂	cup unsalted butter
6	tablespoons sugar
6	tablespoons dark brown sugar
1	egg
1	teaspoon vanilla
¹/₄	teaspoon salt
1¹/₂	teaspoons instant espresso powder
1	teaspoon boiling water
1	cup plus 2 tablespoons all-purpose flour
2	tablespoons unsweetened cocoa powder
¹/₂	teaspoon baking soda
12	ounces semisweet chocolate candy bars, chopped
1	cup chopped macadamia nuts

Preheat the oven to 325°. In a large bowl, beat butter with an electric mixer until softened. Add sugar and brown sugar and beat until well combined. Beat in egg, vanilla, and salt. Dissolve espresso powder in the boiling water; add to butter mixture and beat well.

In a small bowl, combine flour, cocoa powder, and baking soda. Add to butter mixture and beat until combined. Stir in chopped chocolate and nuts. Drop by heaping teaspoons onto a lightly greased cookie sheet. Bake for 12 to 15 minutes or until edges are firm. Cool on wire racks. Makes about 36.

High Tea Lemon Cookies

You'll find cornstarch in a lot of old-fashioned cookie recipes. It lends tenderness and a certain charm that have made these cookies a favorite of generations.

2¹/₃	cups butter or margarine, divided
4²/₃	cups powdered sugar, divided
2	teaspoons finely shredded lemon peel, divided
¹/₂	teaspoon vanilla
2	cups all-purpose flour
1¹/₃	cups cornstarch
¹/₃	cup lemon juice

Preheat the oven to 350°. In a large bowl, beat **2 cups** of the butter until softened. Add **²/₃ cup** of the powdered sugar; beat until well combined. Add **1 teaspoon** of the lemon peel and the vanilla; beat well. In a medium bowl, stir together flour and cornstarch; add to butter mixture and beat well.

Roll dough into 1-inch balls. Place on ungreased cookie sheets. Bake about 15 minutes or until bottoms are lightly browned. Cool on wire racks.

For icing, in a medium bowl beat together the remaining ¹/₃ cup butter or margarine and the remaining 1 teaspoon lemon peel until butter is softened. Add remaining 4 cups powdered sugar and beat until well combined. Add lemon juice and beat well. Spread icing on cookies. Makes about 72.

NICE TO NOTE

Teatime in Memphis can be as simple as a dessert tea to introduce a new bride or as grand as High Tea at the Peabody. Elegantly arrayed on an antique silver tray or nestled in a basket on the porch, these lemon cookies and other sweet tidbits are always at tea to tempt the Southern sweet tooth.

Raisin Honey Chews

Your children will make a bee-line to the cookie jar for these.

³/₄ cup shortening
³/₄ cup sugar
¹/₂ cup honey
1 egg
¹/₂ teaspoon grated orange peel
1¹/₄ cups all-purpose flour
1 teaspoon baking soda
¹/₂ teaspoon salt
2 cups quick-cooking rolled oats
1 cup raisins

 Preheat the oven to 375°. In a large bowl, beat together shortening, sugar, honey, egg, and orange peel with an electric mixer. Add flour, baking soda, and salt; beat well. Stir in oats and raisins.
 Drop by tablespoons onto greased baking sheets. Bake for 8 to 10 minutes or until evenly browned. Cool on cookie sheets for 2 or 3 minutes. Remove to wire racks; cool thoroughly. Makes about 36.

Your Heart's Desire

Remember when baking cut-out cookies at your mom's side was "your heart's desire?"

4 cups all-purpose flour
2 cups sugar
1 teaspoon baking powder
¹/₄ teaspoon baking soda
1 cup plus 2 tablespoons butter or margarine, divided
2 eggs
¹/₄ cup milk
1 teaspoon vanilla
³/₄ teaspoon almond extract, divided
2 cups sifted powdered sugar
 Milk
 Food coloring (optional)

 In a large bowl, stir together flour, sugar, baking powder, and baking soda. Cut in **1 cup** of the butter or margarine until mixture resembles coarse crumbs. Add eggs and mix well. Beat in milk, vanilla, and ¹/₂ **teaspoon** of the almond extract until well combined. Cover and chill at least 2 hours or until easy to handle.
 Preheat the oven to 350°. Working with one-third of the dough at a time, on a well-floured surface, roll dough ¹/₈ inch thick. Cut into desired shapes with cookie cutters. Place on a lightly greased cookie sheet. Bake for 8 to 10 minutes or until edges are firm and bottoms are very lightly browned. Cool on wire racks.
 For icing, in a small bowl, beat together powdered sugar, the remaining 2 tablespoons butter or margarine, and the remaining ¹/₄ teaspoon almond extract with an electric mixer until well combined. Beat in 4 to 5 teaspoons of milk until icing is of piping consistency. For a spreadable icing, beat in more milk. If desired, stir in a few drops food coloring. Pipe or spread icing on cookies. Makes 72 to 96.

Chapel Cookies

Memphis wedding receptions are often large cocktail-party affairs and the bride rarely has a chance to eat. The newlyweds may take a goodie basket as they leave the celebration and these old-fashioned wedding cookies would be a sweet start to the honeymoon.

1	cup butter or margarine
1/4	cup honey
2	teaspoons vanilla
1/2	teaspoon salt
2	cups all-purpose flour
1	cup chopped nuts (optional)
1	cup sifted powdered sugar

Preheat the oven to 325°. In a large bowl, beat butter with an electric mixer until softened. Add honey, vanilla, and salt; beat until well combined. Add flour and beat until well mixed. Stir in chopped nuts, if desired.

Shape into 1-inch balls. Place on a lightly greased cookie sheet. Bake for 20 minutes or until bottoms are lightly browned. While still hot, roll in powdered sugar. Cool. Roll in powdered sugar again. Makes about 36.

Cinnamon Apple Squares

1/3	cup butter or margarine
1	cup packed brown sugar
2/3	cup applesauce
1	beaten egg
1	teaspoon vanilla
1 1/4	cups all-purpose flour
1	teaspoon baking powder
1/2	teaspoon salt
1/2	teaspoon ground cinnamon
1/4	teaspoon baking soda
1/2	cup chopped pecans or walnuts
1/2	cup golden raisins
	Powdered sugar

Preheat the oven to 350°. In a 1 1/2-quart saucepan, melt butter or margarine. Stir in brown sugar, applesauce, beaten egg, and vanilla. Set apple mixture aside.

In a small bowl, stir together flour, baking powder, salt, cinnamon, and baking soda. Stir flour mixture into apple mixture. Stir in nuts and raisins. Spread into a greased 9x9-inch baking pan. Bake about 25 minutes or until a toothpick inserted near center comes out clean. Cool in the pan on a wire rack. Before serving, lightly sift powdered sugar over the top. Cut into bars. Makes 36.

White Chocolate Brownies

Serve with homemade chocolate sauce and vanilla ice cream and your spouse will forget the wrecked car, bounced checks, bad report cards, income taxes.......

1	cup butter or margarine, melted
1	cup sugar
2	beaten eggs
2	teaspoons vanilla
1/4	teaspoon salt
1	cup all-purpose flour
2	3½-ounce white chocolate candy bars, chopped
1	cup roasted and salted macadamia nuts, chopped

Preheat the oven to 350°. In a medium bowl, combine melted butter, sugar, eggs, vanilla, and salt. Stir in flour until combined. Stir in chopped candy bars and macadamia nuts. Spread mixture in an 8-inch square baking dish. Bake for 20 to 25 minutes or until edges are firm. Cool on a wire rack. Cut into bars. Makes 24.

Death-to-the-Diet Brownies

Cut into tiny squares—they're very gooey and rich. For a treat that will make you swoon, pop one in the microwave for 30 seconds and top with vanilla ice cream.

4	squares (4 ounces) unsweetened chocolate
1	cup butter or margarine
2	cups sugar
1	cup all-purpose flour
4	beaten eggs
2	teaspoons coffee liqueur, brandy, or vanilla
1	cup semisweet chocolate pieces
1	cup chopped nuts

Preheat the oven to 325°. In a heavy 1-quart saucepan, melt chocolate and butter, stirring constantly. Remove from heat. In a large bowl, stir together sugar and flour. Add melted chocolate mixture, eggs, and coffee liqueur. Mix well. Stir in chocolate pieces and nuts.

Spread batter in a greased 13x9x2-inch baking pan. Bake for 35 minutes or until edges are firm. (Center will be soft.) Cool 30 to 60 minutes on a wire rack before cutting. Chill at least 2 hours before serving. Makes 48.

◆ ◆ ◆

HOMECOMING BROWNIES

—

"Every fall our group of old college friends hires a driver and piles into a large motor home for the six-hour ride to our alma mater's homecoming. The women plan ahead for snacks and a hearty lunch. We have a wonderful time catching up on news and solving world problems while the men play poker in the back.

I took these brownies along the first year and now they have become an integral part of the trip. One year I left them behind and the ribbing from the men was intense! Now, before we take off, the last question is not, 'Did you lock the house?' but 'Did you get the brownies?'"

◆ ◆ ◆

*H*eart and Soul is grateful to the following individuals and businesses who have helped in the creation of our book. They are numerous and include recipe and prop contributors, testing committees, food sources, and graphic and editorial consultants. For monetary support, loans of personal possessions, and the gift of uncounted hours of volunteer time, we give them our heartfelt thanks. ♥

CONTRIBUTORS

Buff Adams
Eileen Adams
Karla Adams
Kathy and Ben Adams
Lisa Adams
Sue Adams
Diane Adler
Laine Agee
Tricia Aiken
Ann Albertine
Ingrid Aldridge
Diana Allen
Jill Allen
Mrs. Richard Allen
Sally Alston
Roberta Anderson
Dolly Angel
Merrill Angelo
Wendy Ansbro
Lee Ansley
Susan Arney
Anne Dillard Arnold
Jennifer Atkins
Lisa Ayerst
Jeanne Ayres
Ruthie Baddour
Emily Bader
Debbie Bailey
Molly Bailey
Sharon Bailey
Margaret Barr
Gwynne Barton
Julie Barton
Steve Barzizza
Amy Baskin
Neely Battle
Ann Baxter
Perry Pidgeon Beasley
Terry and Jim Beaty
Betsy and Bill Bell
Lelia Bell
Jayne Berube
Kathy Black
Kimberly and Earl Blankenship
Karen Blockman

Dudley Boren
Mrs. Kimbrough Boren
Anne-Clifton Bowling
Martha Bradon
Martha Brahm
Sarah Brandon
Suzanne Brandon
Margaret Ann Brickey
Dr. and Mrs. Louis G. Britt
Billy Britton
Wanda Brooks
Carolyn Brown
Lisa Brown
Rosalyn Brown
Debbie Campbell
Mary Campbell
Mrs. John W. Campbell
Pam Campbell
Steve Campbell
Sherry Cannon
Colleen and Larry Capstick
Diane Cardwell
June Carlson
Beth Carson
Leslie Carter
Linda and Scott Carter
Shain C. Carter
Shari Carter
Cat's Compact Discs & Cassettes
Cellular One
Ann Chaney
Nancy Chase
Antoinette Cheney
Arden Cheney
Christ United Methodist Church
Lee Ann Clark
Sue Clark
Jennifer Cleary
Baxter Lee Clement
Janet and Duke Clement
Eleanor Cobb
Leigh Cobb
Lu Lee Cobb
Nancy Coe
Lisa and John Colcolough
Ann Cole
Kathryn Coleman
Christina Collier
Meg Collier
John Colmer
Nancy Cook
Renee Cooley
Mrs. Bailey Cowan
Alison Cox
Lucia Crenshaw
Marion Crenshaw
Stacy Crenshaw
Elise Crockett
Nancy Crosby
Cynthia and Mike Cross
Georgia Cross
Kathleen Cruzen
Suzanne Cunningham
Virginia and Ed Curry
Anne Curtis
Betsy Daniels
Mary Helen Darden
Ann Davis
Cindy Davis
Leslie Davis

Leona DeMere-Dwyer
Laura Dickinson
Patty Dietrich
Terry Dillard
Leslie and John Dillon
Mrs. John Dobbs
Sue Don
Michael Donahue
Mr. and Mrs. Frank Donelson Jr.
Judy Douglass
Suzanne Douglass
Jack Dowell
Amy Drennon
Peggy Drinkard
Susan Driscoll
Camille Duke
Leslie Dunavant
Lee Duncan
Tammy Duncan
Laura Echols
Laila Eckels
Judy Edmundson
Mary Edwards
Robin Edwards
Wendy Edwards
Missy Elder
Margaret Eldridge
Katie Eleazer
Beth Elzemeyer
Barbara Evangelisti
Dianne Dupree Evans
Ann Everett
Janet Everett
Claire Farmer
Dot Fisher
Jan Flanagan
Cindy and Andy Flanzer
Jill Flournoy
Mr. and Mrs. Robert E. Flowers
Sarah Flowers
Carey Folk
Debbie Folk
Fascinating Foods
Magaret Fox
Martha Culvahouse Fox
Lysbeth Frances
Elise Frick
Kate Friedman
Lynn Fulton
Catherine Swann Funk
Rachel Gabrielleschi
Christine Gaiennie
Rebecca E. Galyon
Sara Bess Galyon
Allen Garner
Nanette Garrett
Virginia Gaston
Susan Gates
Kathy Gatlin
Sloan Germann
Jennifer Ghess
Kim Gibson
Elizabeth Gillespie
Elisabeth Glassell
Jennifer Goblirsch
Patti Gonzales
Patti Gooch
Debbie Gould
Elenia Gray
Betty Green

Virginia Watson Griffee
Lisa Grunkemeyer
Mary Harvey Gurley
Ann Gusmus
Catherine Gwaltney
Marietta and Fletcher Haaga
Julia Halford
Gina Hall
Llewellyn Hall
Sally Halle
Bonnie Hallsmen
Melinda Hamilton
Becky Harkins
Penny Harmon
Sallie Harris
Tama Harris
Bonnie Hartzman
Peggy Harwell
Lynn Hays
Margaret Headrick
Susan Hedgepeth
Mary Ben Heflin
Mrs. John Heflin, Jr.
Theresa and Bill Heidrich
Edith Heller
Gaye and Haywood Henderson
Janie and Jim Henderson
Marilyn Hergenrader
Sidney Herman
Dan Herwood
Martha and Bob Hester
Dot Hicks
Jan Hicky
Mrs. L. D. Hill
Jane Hobson
Karen Hoff
Stephanie Hoffman
Jeanne and Richard Hollis
Sarah Holner
Janie Hopkins
Pat Horn
Susan and Bill Huffman
Lily Humphreys
Tricia Hunt
Catherine Hutchison
Katie Hutton
Cathy Hynes
Betty Ingram
Macon Ivy
J. L. Jalenak, Jr.
Robert Jamison
Lori Jobe
Rosalie Johnson
Jeannie Jones
Lexie Jones
Louise Jones
Rosie Jones
Sharon Jones
Stephanie Jones
Valerie Jones
Beth Kakales
Ann Keesee
Lisa Kellett
Emily Kennedy
Mary Kenner
Eliza Kirk
Mary Joy Knowlton
Lynn and Brad Koeneman
Mrs. Leslie Koinberg
M'Leigh Koziol

Meta Laabs
Ann and Dudley Langston
Frances Larkin
Karie Leatherman
Shannon Lenoir
Judy Lindy
Carolyn Loftin
Gail Loftin
Cindy Lone
Diane Long
Teresa Long
Judy Looney
Cindy Love
Mary Loveless
Katherine Lucas
Nita Lux
Carol MacGregor
Becky Maddux
Lisa Mallory
Margaret Mallory
Julie Maroda
Jessie Marshall
Lou and Jerry Martin
Carol and Paul Mathis
Sue and Paul Matthews
Anne Maury
Becky Maury
Susan Mays
Mamel McCain
Mrs. James McCann
Tracy McCalmont
Alice McCarthy
Kirk McClintock
Chris McClure
Caroline McCool
Leslie McCraw
Elizabeth McCuddy
Catherine McCuistion
Tonya Lauck McDonald
Harriet McGeorge
Mrs. Harold L. McGeorge, Jr.
Dr. Tom McInish
Martha McIntosh
Emily McKinney
Gretchen Perkins McLallen
Kathy McLallen
Beth McLaren
Tina McWhorter
Meat Board Test Kitchens
Amy Meyers
Ann Miller
Cindy Miller
Julie Mills
Janie Mims
Emily Minor
Lisa and Bo Mitchum
Didi Montgomery
Frances Montgomery
Betty Moore
Bond Moore
Brandon Morrison
Cindy and John Morrison
Gray Morrison
Nancy Morrow
Jamie Moskovitz
Ann Mueller
Camille and Bill Mueller
Linda Mundinger
Thomas Murray
Micki Muse
Tootie Muse
Larry Nagar
Nayla and George Nassar
Dorothy Neale

Lynn Nelson
Carroll Nenon
Marilyn Newton
Nancy R. Newton
Melissa Neyland
Lissa Noel
Joyce Turner Nussbaum
Mrs. Joseph O'Brien
Sharon O'Brien
Sara O'Dell
Herbie O'Mell
Opera Memphis
The Orpheum
Sarah O'Ryan
Blythe Patton Orr
Caroline Orr
Dolores Ostrowski
Carita and Alston Palmer
Laine Park
Jill Parker
Toni Parker
Gwen Parrish
Helen and Keith Parsons
Debbie and Sam Patterson
Helen and Richard Patterson
Jan Patterson
Jean Patterson
Kathy Daniel Patterson
Scott Patterson
Mrs. Hal Patton
Dorothy Pennypacker
Joan and Tommy Peters
Amanda Phillips
Jennifer Phillips
Paige Phillips
Sandy Phillips
Sisty Phillips
Weetie Phillips
Missie Pidgeon
Pier 1 imports
Pam and Will Pierce
Piggly Wiggly Eastgate
Kathy and John Pitts
Kim and Johnny Pitts
Beth and Tom Ploch
Mr. and Mrs. Herbert Ploch
Mary Ellen Plyler
Molly Polatty
Pat and Jack Pope
Poplar Tunes Records
Lisa Popwell
Dixie Power
Anne Pringle
Jean Price
Meredith Pritchartt
Prop Room, Chicago
Eileen Prose
Jennifer Pthoes
Anna-Grace Quinn
Julie Raines
Dr. Richard Ranta
Ellen Rardin
Dr. Robert Reeder
Meg Reid
Alice Reilly
Dr. and Mrs. Richard J. Reynolds
Mike Richards
Peggy Riggins
Janice Robbins
Jessica Robinson
Jan Miller Rochelle
Peg and Ron Ross
Melinda Angel Rothenberg
Debbie Rouse

Royal Worcester Porcelain
Ginger Rucks
Liz Rudolph
Ruetenik Gardens
Mary Ruleman
Gwen Rush
Ann Rutherford
Rita Rutherford
Jodie Sain
Chris Sanders
Patty Satterfield
Stephanie Satterfield
Nancy Sawyer
Susan Schaefer
Kristy Schaeffer
Linda Schmitz
Andrea Schoppet
Katie Schumacher
Peter Schutt
Lacy Scott
Joyce Sellers
Kathy Sellers
Scott and Grey Sellers
Amelia Shannon
Kathy Shannon
Laura Shappley
Juli Sharp
Ruthann Shelton
Sandy Sherman
Catherine Shirley
Jane Slatery
Sally Smart
Bernie Smith
Mary and Dan Smith
Jennifer Smith
Margaret Ivy Smith
Mary Smith
Miriam Smith
Mrs. Louise Smith
Rhoda Smith
Julia & Ham Smythe
Mr. and Mrs. Ham Smythe, III
Jack Soden
Center for Southern Folklore
Beatrice Spiegel
Kathy St. John
Linda St. John
Milner Stanton
Margaret Steffner
Peggy Stephens
Prudy Stevenson
Kitty Stimson
Andrea Stratton
Margery Stratton
Kathy Stubblefield
Sharon Tagg
Catherine Talbot
Cindy Taylor
Linda Taylor
Ruthie Taylor
Deborah Terry
Jennifer & Steve Thomas
Joan Thomas
Libby Thomas
Mr. and Mrs. Clint Thomas
Verena Thomas
Anne Thompson
Anne Tinker
Julie Tipton
Mr. and Mrs. George Carroll Todd
Ginny Towner
Kathleen Towner
Nancy Utkov
Marilee Varner

Paula Slack Verbois
Kate Vergos
Beverly Wade
Gigi Wade
Ginger Wade
Beth Waldrup
Jana Walker
Margaret Walker
Stephanie Wall
Jill and Jon Wallace
Rivers Rhodes Wallace
Sarah Walne
Marianne Walter
Danette Watkins
Beverly Weels
Katie & Peter Weien
Adele Wellford
Beverly Wells
Kelly & Geordy Wells
Lynn Wells
Anne Wesberry
Paul Wesphal
Carole West
Cheryl West
Mrs. William West
Gina White
Lesley Whitehead
Russell Whitehead
Sandie Whittington
Lisa and Bob Wilder
Courtney Williams
Barbara and Lewis Williamson
Carolyn Brown Wills
Laura Wininger
Caroline Winters
Mary Ruth Witt
Ann Witt
Craig Witt
Karen Witt
Randolf Witt
Randy Witt
Samantha Witt
Stacey Witt
Stephanie Witt
Mary and Malcolm Wood
Denise Wright
Eddie Wright
WSMS
Beth Yerger
Carol Yochem
Irwin Zanone
Toni Zanone
Paul Zilch
Wurzburg, Inc.

PLEASE SEND ME:

_____copies of HEART AND SOUL @ $19.95 each. (TN residents + $1.65 tax = $21.60) $ _____

_____copies of MEMPHIS COOKBOOK @ $10.95 each. (TN residents + $ .84 tax = $11.79) $ _____

_____copies of PARTY POTPOURRI @ $14.95 each. (TN residents + $1.16 tax = $16.11) $ _____

_____copies of GOOD ABODE @ $26.95 each. (TN residents + $2.09 tax = $29.04) $ _____

Postage and handling @ $ 3.50 each $ _____

Total enclosed $ _____

Mail cookbook(s) to:

Name _____   Address _____

City_____   State _____   Zip _____

Make checks payable to: Memphis Junior League Publications

Charge to: ☐ VISA **VISA**   ☐ MasterCard **MasterCard**   Valid thru _____

Account number _____   Signature _____

All profits from cookbook sales will be returned to the community through Junior League of Memphis, Inc. projects.

Junior League of Memphis Publications
HEART & SOUL
3475 Central Avenue
Memphis, TN 38111-4401

PLEASE SEND ME:

_____copies of HEART AND SOUL @ $19.95 each. (TN residents + $1.65 tax = $21.60) $ _____

_____copies of MEMPHIS COOKBOOK @ $10.95 each. (TN residents + $ .84 tax = $11.79) $ _____

_____copies of PARTY POTPOURRI @ $14.95 each. (TN residents + $1.16 tax = $16.11) $ _____

_____copies of GOOD ABODE @ $26.95 each. (TN residents + $2.09 tax = $29.04) $ _____

Postage and handling @ $ 3.50 each $ _____

Total enclosed $ _____

Mail cookbook(s) to:

Name _____   Address _____

City_____   State _____   Zip _____

Make checks payable to: Memphis Junior League Publications

Charge to: ☐ VISA **VISA**   ☐ MasterCard **MasterCard**   Valid thru _____

Account number _____   Signature _____

All profits from cookbook sales will be returned to the community through Junior League of Memphis, Inc. projects.

Junior League of Memphis Publications
HEART & SOUL
3475 Central Avenue
Memphis, TN 38111-4401